Europe 2020

Towards a More Social EU?

P.I.E. Peter Lang

Bruxelles · Bern · Berlin · Frankfurt am Main · New York · Oxford · Wien

Eric MARLIER and David NATALI (eds.),
with Rudi VAN DAM

Europe 2020

Towards a More Social EU?

"Work & Society"
No.69

This book was written at the request of the Belgian Presidency of the Council of the European Union as an independent academic contribution to developing the operational basis for the Europe 2020 Strategy. It builds on the background document prepared for the international conference on "EU Coordination in the Social Field in the Context of Europe 2020: Looking Back and Building the Future" (September 2010, La Hulpe, Belgium). The conference was organised by the EU Belgian Presidency and the European Commission, with the support of the RECWOWE (Reconciling Work and Welfare in Europe) Research Network. Special thanks go to the Belgian Federal Public Service Social Security for their support throughout the project. It should be stressed that the book does not represent in any way the views of the European Commission, the European Union, the EU Belgian Presidency or the Belgian Federal Public Service Social Security. All the authors have written in a strictly personal capacity, not as representatives of any Government or official body. Thus they have been free to express their own views and to take full responsibility for the judgments made about past and current policy and for the recommendations for future policy.

Cover picture: © Hugh Frazer, "Tour Madou, Brussels", 2008.

© P.I.E. PETER LANG S.A.
Éditions scientifiques internationales
Brussels, 2010
1 avenue Maurice, B-1050 Brussels, Belgium
info@peterlang.com; www.peterlang.com

ISSN 1376-0955
ISBN 978-90-5201-688-7
D/2010/5678/74

Printed in Germany

CIP available from the Library of Congress, USA and the British Library, GB

Bibliographic information published by "Die Deutsche Nationalbibliothek".

"Die Deutsche Nationalbibliothek" lists this publication in the "Deutsche National-bibliografie"; detailed bibliographic data is available on the Internet at <http://dnb.d-nb.de>.

Contents

Foreword

Reinforcing the European Union (EU) coordination and cooperation in the social field was a major priority for the 2010 Belgian Presidency of the Council of the EU. As Maurizio Ferrera reminds us in this book, there are at least three fundamental reasons why a strong social EU dimension is required. First and foremost, it is a matter of social justice. Secondly, social protection is a productive factor. And thirdly, the EU needs a social face to retain the support of its citizens. Still, there are important threats to the European Social Model(s) of which the aftermath of the financial crisis of 2008 is the most recent and probably the most acute one.

In this context the Belgian Presidency was very pleased to be able to take up the challenge of contributing to the collective endeavour of the Union and its Member States to develop the "Europe 2020" Strategy. This Strategy for smart, sustainable and inclusive growth, which was endorsed by the 27 EU Heads of State and Government at their June 2010 European Council, sets the EU five integrated and mutually reinforcing targets to be reached by 2020. One of them is to lift at least 20 million people out of the risk of poverty and exclusion. EU leaders also adopted economic and employment Guidelines. These should guide the policies which EU and Member States will deploy in pursuit of the new Strategy's objectives and targets.

Moreover, the Lisbon Treaty, which came into force on 1 December 2009, gives an increased status to social issues and contains a number of important provisions to enhance an integrated policy approach for economic, employment, social and environmental issues. One of the Treaty's fundamental innovations is the so-called "Horizontal Social Clause" which offers an important stepping stone for mainstreaming social objectives in all relevant policies at EU, national and sub-national levels.

With the Europe 2020 framework, the European Council clearly opted for a different, more integrated and stringent approach to ensure progress on our common objectives. Important tools are now available. Whether the Europe 2020 Strategy will lead to a more Social EU will depend on its rigorous implementation by Member States and the European Commission. The European Parliament as well as the national and sub-national Parliaments will also have an important role to play in this respect.

11

To elucidate some of the key issues at stake, the Belgian Presidency organised with the support of the European Commission an international Conference on "EU Coordination in the Social Field in the Context of Europe 2020: Looking Back and Building the Future" (14-15 September 2010, La Hulpe, Belgium). Bringing together a large number of policy-makers, key experts and stakeholders, the conference was intended to serve as ideas' box on how to strengthen the EU's social dimension and how to address the current patchwork of social policies.

This book builds on the background document that was prepared for the Conference. It also builds on the conference's very rich presentations and discussions. I hope that the thorough analysis and concrete proposals it contains will support and inform the implementation of the Europe 2020 Strategy in the coming years.

Laurette ONKELINX
Belgian Vice-Prime Minister and Minister of Social Affairs and Public Health, in charge for Social Integration

List of Main Abbreviations
and Acronyms Used

BEPG	Broad Economic Policy Guideline
CJEU	Court of Justice of the European Union
COFACE	Confederation of Family Organisations in the EU
CPAG	Child Poverty Action Group
DG	Directorate-General
DG ECFIN	DG for Economic and Financial Affairs of the European Commission
DG EMPL	DG for Employment, Social Affairs and Equal Opportunities of the European Commission
EAPN	European Anti-Poverty Network
EES	European Employment Strategy
EIoP	European Integration online Papers
EMCO	Employment Committee
EMU	European Monetary Union
EPAP	European Platform against Poverty
EPC	Economic Policy Committee
EPSCO	EU "Employment, Social Policy, Health and Consumer Affairs" Council of Ministers
ESF	European Social Fund
ESN	European Social Network
EU	European Union
EU-15	The 15 "old" EU Member States, before the May 2004 and January 2007 Enlargements (Austria, Belgium, Germany, Denmark, Spain, Finland, France, Greece, Ireland, Italy, Luxembourg, Netherlands, Portugal, Sweden, United Kingdom)
EU-27	All 27 EU Member States (EU-15 plus Bulgaria, Cyprus, Czech Republic, Estonia, Hungary, Lithuania, Latvia, Malta, Poland, Romania, Slovenia, Slovakia)
EU-SILC	EU Statistics on Income and Living Conditions
FEANTSA	European Federation of National Organisations Working with the Homeless
FP	Framework Programme

HCSACP	Haut-Commissaire aux Solidarités Actives Contre la Pauvreté
IA	Impact assessment
IG	Integrated Guideline
IORP	Institutions for occupational retirement provision
JRSPSI	Joint Report on Social Protection and Social Inclusion
NAP	National Action Plan
NAP/inclusion	National Action Plan for social inclusion
NAP/employment	National Action Plan for employment
NARB	National Report on Poverty and Wealth
NGO	Non-Governmental Organisation
NHS	National Health Service
NRP	National Reform Programme (for growth and jobs)
NSR	National Strategy Report
NSRF	National Strategic Reference Framework
NSRSPSI	National Strategy Report on Social Protection and Social Inclusion
NUTS	Nomenclature d'Unités Territoriales Statistiques (Nomenclature of Territorial Units for Statistics)
OECD	Organisation for Economic Cooperation and Development
OMC	Open Method of Coordination
PROGRESS	Community Programme for Employment and Social Solidarity
PSA	Public Sector Agreement
SEA	Single European Act
SCP	Stability and Convergence Programme
SGP	Stability and Growth Pact
SME	Small and medium size enterprise
Social OMC	OMC for social protection and social inclusion
SPC	EU Social Protection Committee
TEEC	Treaty establishing the European Community
TFEU	Treaty on the Functioning of the European Union

1. Europe 2020:

Towards a More Social EU?

Hugh FRAZER and Eric MARLIER,
with David NATALI, Rudi VAN DAM and Bart VANHERCKE

1.1 Policy Context and Objectives of the Book

2010 was a critical juncture for the European Union (EU) in at least two major respects. First, the Lisbon Treaty, which came into force on 1 December 2009 and gives an increased status to social issues, started to be implemented. One of the Treaty's fundamental innovations is the so-called "Horizontal Social Clause" (Article 9 of the Treaty on the Functioning of the European Union (TFEU)) which states that "In defining and implementing its policies and activities, the Union shall take into account requirements linked to the promotion of a high level of employment, the guarantee of adequate social protection, the fight against social exclusion, and a high level of education, training and protection of human health" (European Union, 2009).[1] Another important innovation in the new Treaty is that it guarantees the freedoms and principles set out in the Charter of Fundamental Rights (which the Treaty introduces into EU primary law) and gives its provisions a binding legal force; this concerns civil, political and economic as well as social rights.

A second reason why 2010 was a turning point for the EU is that the Lisbon Strategy, launched by the European Council[2] in March 2000 as a framework for EU socio-economic policy coordination, ended in June 2010 with the adoption by EU leaders of the new Europe 2020 Strategy. During 2010, discussions took place at EU and country levels on how

---

[1] It is important to highlight that "the Union" refers here to both the EU as a whole and its individual Member States.

[2] The European Council, which brings together the EU Heads of State and Government and the President of the European Commission, defines the general political direction and priorities of the EU. Every spring, it holds a meeting that is more particularly devoted to economic and social questions – the *Spring European Council*. With the entry into force of the Treaty of Lisbon on 1 December 2009, it has become an official institution and has a President. The Conclusions of the June 2010 European Council are available at: http://ec.europa.eu/eu2020/pdf/council_conclusion _17_june_en.pdf.

best to implement the new Strategy so as to achieve its objectives of "smart, sustainable and inclusive growth" (European Commission, 2010; European Council, 2010).

These institutional and policy developments happened in a difficult social, employment, economic and budgetary context marked by slow recovery from the global economic and financial crisis. This was a very different situation from that of March 2000 when EU leaders set the EU "strategic goal" of becoming by 2010 "the most competitive and dynamic knowledge-based economy in the world capable of sustainable economic growth with more and better jobs and greater social cohesion" (European Council, 2000).

The Spanish and Belgian Presidencies of the EU Council of Ministers (hereafter: "Council"), in the first and second half of 2010 respectively, had the challenging task of contributing to shaping and implementing the EU's post-2010 socio-economic governance during this difficult period. The subsequent Presidencies, and in particular the Hungarian Presidency in the first half of 2011, will have to fine-tune the actual implementation of the new Strategy.

This book was prepared at the request of the EU Belgian Presidency as an independent academic contribution to developing the operational basis for the Europe 2020 Strategy. It builds on the background document that was prepared for the international conference on "EU coordination in the social field in the context of Europe 2020: Looking back and building the future", organised by the Belgian Presidency and the European Commission in La Hulpe (Belgium) in September 2010. It also builds on the conference's very rich presentations and discussions. The main focus of the book is on the role that EU coordination and cooperation in the social field[3] should or at least could potentially play in the new EU governance framework. In doing this, one of its key tasks is to draw lessons from the past decade to inform the development of this future cooperation and coordination.

The three main objectives of the book are:

1. to assess both the procedural and substantive aspects of EU coordination and cooperation in the social field to date (in the broad "Lisbon Strategy" context) – its main strengths and weaknesses;

---

[3] It is on purpose that the expression "EU coordination and cooperation in the social field" rather than "Social Open Method of Coordination (OMC)" has been used as the book wishes to adopt a broad approach to the future Social EU.

2. to put forward some first ideas on the format and role of EU coordination and cooperation in the social field in the new Europe 2020 Strategy – the opportunities and risks; and

3. to make proposals for the further reinforcement of EU coordination and cooperation in the social field in the socio-economic context marked by the crisis, and for the improvement of the different instruments available at EU, national and sub-national levels (including proposals on how to address the current patchwork of social policies).

We hope that the analysis presented in the book and the concrete proposals on how to use the new opportunities provided by the Europe 2020 agenda can be used by policy-makers, researchers and other stakeholders to contribute to building a more Social EU. We also hope that it will help to encourage new ideas and innovative approaches.

In the remainder of this introductory chapter, we introduce (in Section 1.2) the overall architecture of the new EU socio-economic governance and explain the complex interplay between its different parts: the three priorities, the five EU headline targets which need to be translated into national targets, the seven flagship initiatives, the ten Integrated Guidelines for employment and economic policies, and the newly introduced concept of a "European semester" that should contribute to mobilising the different instruments in support of the new Strategy and to aligning it with the Stability and Growth Pact. We also discuss the (potentially) key role of the EU Social Protection Committee (SPC)[4] in implementing and monitoring the social dimension of Europe 2020. In Section 1.3, we then briefly outline the contents of the individual chapters and their main messages. The chapters assess the logic of the new Strategy and of the instruments to be mobilised for improving social policy coordination and cooperation at EU level. In doing so many contributions reflect on and draw lessons from the Social Open Method of Coordination (OMC) over the past decade while others consider the broader aspects of EU governance in the social field (e.g. cohesion policy, EU and national targets, social impact assessment, etc.). Finally, Section 1.4 concludes and makes concrete recommendations in relation to nine interrelated areas in which we consider that the Europe 2020 Strategy's institutional arrangements can be developed so as to maximise the possibility of building a more Social EU.

---

[4] The SPC consists of officials from mainly Employment and Social Affairs Ministries in each Member State as well as representatives of the European Commission. The SPC reports to the EU "Employment, Social Policy, Health and Consumer Affairs" (EPSCO) Council of Ministers.

1.2 Overall Architecture of Europe 2020

In the words of the European Commission (2010), Europe 2020 is a Strategy "to turn the EU into a smart, sustainable and inclusive economy delivering high levels of employment, productivity and social cohesion. (…) This is an agenda for all Member States, taking into account different needs, different starting points and national specificities so as to promote growth for all."

Efficient socio-economic governance at EU, national and sub-national levels is a necessary condition for a successful implementation of this agenda. With this logic in mind, Europe 2020 has been organised around three integrated pillars as shown in Figure 1.1 (European Commission, 2010 and 2010a):

1. *Macro-economic surveillance*, which aims at ensuring a stable macro-economic environment conducive to growth and employment creation. In accordance with Integrated Guidelines 1 to 3 (see Table 1.1), it covers macro-economic and structural policies to address macro-economic imbalances, macro-financial vulnerabilities and competitiveness issues which have a macro-economic dimension. It is the responsibility of the EU "Economic and Financial Affairs" (ECOFIN) Council.

2. *Thematic coordination*, whose focus is on structural reforms in the fields of innovation and R&D, resource-efficiency, business environment, employment, education and social inclusion (Integrated Guidelines 4-10; see Table 1.1). Policies pursued in this context are expected to deliver smart, sustainable and inclusive growth and employment creation at EU and national levels and also to help remove obstacles to achieving the objectives set in the Guidelines. Thematic coordination combines EU priorities, EU headline targets (and national targets that underpin them) and EU flagship initiatives (see Sections 1.2.1, 1.2.2 and 1.2.3 below). It is conducted by the sectoral formations of the EU Council of Ministers (thus including, for social protection and inclusion matters, the EU "Employment, Social Policy, Health and Consumer Affairs" (EPSCO) Council). It "reflects the EU dimension, shows clearly the interdependence of Member States economies, and allows greater selectivity on concrete initiatives which push the strategy forward and help achieve the EU and national headline targets" (European Commission, 2010).

3. *Fiscal surveillance under the Stability and Growth Pact*, which should contribute to strengthening fiscal consolidation and fos-

tering sustainable public finances. It is expected to help to ensure the overall consistency of EU policy advice by identifying the fiscal constraints within which Member States' actions are to be developed.

Figure 1.1: The three pillars of the Europe 2020 Strategy

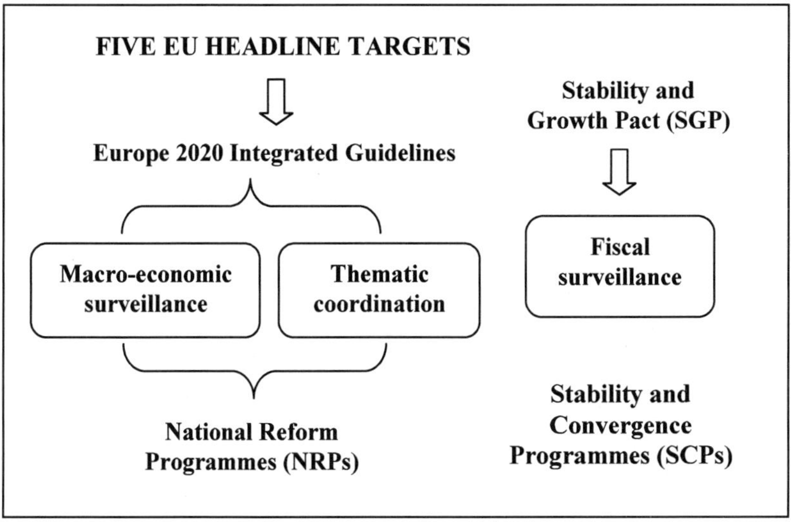

```
┌─────────────────────────────────────────────────────────────────────┐
│                                                                       │
│   FIVE EU HEADLINE TARGETS                                            │
│                                          Stability and                │
│              ⇩                           Growth Pact (SGP)            │
│   Europe 2020 Integrated Guidelines                                   │
│                                                   ⇩                   │
│            ╭─────────╮                                                │
│   ╭──────────╮  ╭──────────╮           ╭──────────────╮              │
│   │ Macro-economic │ Thematic │        │   Fiscal     │              │
│   │ surveillance   │ coordination │    │ surveillance │              │
│   ╰──────────╯  ╰──────────╯           ╰──────────────╯              │
│            ╰─────────╯                                                │
│                                          Stability and                │
│       National Reform                    Convergence                 │
│       Programmes (NRPs)                  Programmes (SCPs)            │
│                                                                       │
└─────────────────────────────────────────────────────────────────────┘
```

Source: Figure based on European Commission, 2010a

Integrated Guidelines were adopted at EU level to cover the scope of EU priorities and targets (see Section 1.2.4). Country-specific recommendations will be addressed to countries. Policy warnings could be issued in case of an inadequate response. The reporting of Europe 2020 and the Stability and Growth Pact evaluation will be done simultaneously to bring the means and the aims together, but keeping the instruments and procedures separate and maintaining the integrity of the Pact.

Figure 1.2 summarises the complex architecture of Europe 2020 which should contribute to a coordinated response to largely common challenges (European Commission, 2010 and 2010a).

Figure 1.2: Overall architecture of Europe 2020

EU priorities	Smart growth	Sustainable growth	Inclusive growth
		Ten Integrated Guidelines	
		Five headline targets	
EU level tools		Monitoring and guidance (*)	
		Annual Growth Survey	
		Annual policy guidance and recommendations	
		Seven flagships	
		EU levers for growth and jobs (**)	
		European semester	
National level tools		National reform Programmes	
		(with national targets)	

Notes: (*) Macro, thematic and fiscal surveillance; (**) The three levers are: Single Market relaunch, Trade and external policies, EU financial support.

Source: Figure based on European Commission, 2010a

1.2.1 Three mutually reinforcing priorities

The March 2010 European Council agreed to the European Commission's proposal to launch a new Strategy for jobs and growth, Europe 2020, based on enhanced socio-economic policy coordination. Europe 2020 is organised around three priorities expected to be mutually reinforcing (European Commission, 2010):

- smart growth, i.e. "strengthening knowledge and innovation as drivers of our future growth";
- sustainable growth, i.e. "promoting a more resource efficient, greener and more competitive economy"; and
- inclusive growth, i.e. "fostering a high-employment economy delivering social and territorial cohesion". This priority is about "empowering people through high levels of employment, investing in skills, fighting poverty and modernising labour markets, training and social protection systems so as to help people anticipate and manage change, and build a cohesive society".

1.2.2 Five EU headline targets
to be translated into national targets

To that end, the June 2010 European Council agreed to set "five EU headline targets which will constitute shared objectives guiding the action of Member States and the Union" (European Council, 2010):

- to raise to 75% the employment rate for women and men aged 20-64;

- to raise combined public and private investment levels in research and development (R&D) to 3% of EU's Gross Domestic Product;

- to reduce greenhouse gas emissions by 20% compared to 1990 levels, increase the share of renewables in final energy consumption to 20%, and move towards a 20% increase in energy efficiency (i.e. the "20/20/20" climate/energy targets); and to increase to 30% the emissions reduction if the conditions are right[5];

- to improve education levels, in particular by aiming to reduce school drop-out rates to less than 10% and by increasing the share of 30-34 years old having completed tertiary or equivalent education to at least 40%;

- to promote social inclusion, in particular through the reduction of poverty, by aiming to lift at least 20 million people out of the risk of poverty and exclusion. This target is based on a combination of three indicators: the number of people at risk of poverty[6], the number of people "materially deprived"[7], and the number of people aged 0-59 who live in "jobless" households (defined, for the purpose of the EU target, as households where none of the members aged 18-59 are working or where members aged 18-59 have, on average, very limited work attachment). So, the target will consist of reducing the number of people in the EU (120 million) who are at risk of poverty and/or materially deprived and/or living in jobless households by one sixth.

In light of these interrelated targets, Member States have to set their national targets "taking account of their relative starting positions and national circumstances and according to their national decision-making procedures. They should also identify the main bottlenecks to growth

---

[5]   "The EU is committed to taking a decision to move to a 30% reduction by 2020 compared to 1990 levels as its conditional offer with a view to a global and comprehensive agreement for the period beyond 2012, provided that other developed countries commit themselves to comparable emission reductions and that developing countries contribute adequately according to their responsibilities and respective capabilities." (European Council, 2010).

[6]   According to the EU definition, people "at risk of poverty" are people living in a household whose total equivalised income is below 60% of the median national equivalised household income (the equivalence scale is the so-called *OECD modified* scale).

[7]   Based on the limited information available from the EU Statistics on Income and Living Conditions (EU-SILC) data-set, this indicator focuses on the number of people living in households who cannot afford at least 4 items out of a list of 9.

and indicate, in their National Reform Programmes (NRPs), how they intend to tackle them." Member States have to submit their draft NRPs to the Commission in November 2010 and their final NRPs in April 2011. It is important to highlight that the European Council has stressed that "all common policies, including the common agricultural policy and cohesion policy, will need to support the Strategy", and that "progress towards the headline targets will be regularly reviewed".

1.2.3 Seven flagship initiatives

To underpin these targets and "catalyse progress under each priority theme", the Commission has suggested seven *flagship initiatives* which should encompass a wide range of actions at national, EU and international levels: "Innovation Union", "Youth on the move", "A digital agenda for Europe", "Resource efficient Europe", "An industrial policy for the globalisation era", "An agenda for new skills and jobs" and "European platform against poverty" (EPAP). Unlike the other flagships announced by the Commission, there was no prior consideration given to what the EPAP would be and how it would relate to the existing EU coordination and cooperation in the social field. It was a top-down initiative without much apparent coherent thought and lacking any consultation with stakeholders. Several chapters in the present volume discuss the potential role and added value of the EPAP in creating a more Social EU.

1.2.4 Ten Integrated Guidelines for employment and economic policies

Finally, ten *Integrated Guidelines* for implementing the Europe 2020 Strategy have been adopted by the Council in October 2010 – six broad guidelines for the economic policies of the Member States and the EU, and four guidelines for the employment (and in fact also social) policies of the Member States (Table 1.1). These Guidelines were adopted on the basis of the Treaty on the functioning of the EU – Article 121 for the former and Article 148 for the latter. Their aim is to provide guidance to Member States on defining their NRPs and implementing reforms, reflecting interdependence and in line with the Stability and Growth Pact.[8]

---

[8] The "broad guidelines for the economic policies of the Member States and of the Union" were adopted by the Council in July 2010 (EU Council of Ministers, 2010), whereas the "guidelines for the employment policies of the Member States" were adopted in October 2010 (EU Council of Ministers, 2010a).

Table 1.1: Ten integrated guidelines for Europe 2020

Guideline 1	Ensuring the quality and sustainability of public finances
Guideline 2	Addressing macroeconomic imbalances
Guideline 3	Reducing imbalances in the euro area
Guideline 4	Optimising support for R&D and innovation, strengthening the knowledge triangle and unleashing the potential of the digital economy
Guideline 5	Improving resource efficiency and reducing greenhouse gases emissions
Guideline 6	Improving the business and consumer environment, and modernising and developing the industrial base in order to ensure the full functioning of the internal market
Guideline 7	Increasing labour market participation of women and men, reducing structural unemployment and promoting job quality
Guideline 8	Developing a skilled workforce responding to labour market needs and promoting lifelong learning
Guideline 9	Improving the quality and performance of education and training systems at all levels and increasing participation in tertiary or equivalent education
Guideline 10	Promoting social inclusion and combating poverty

Source: EU Council of Ministers, 2010 and 2010a

It will be important for the EU and Member States to mobilise all the potentialities provided by several of these Guidelines, and in particular by Guideline 10 (on "Promoting social inclusion and combating poverty") which reads as follows:

"The extension of employment opportunities is an essential aspect of Member States' integrated strategies to prevent and reduce poverty and to promote full participation in society and economy. Appropriate use of the European Social Fund and other EU funds should be made to that end. Efforts should concentrate on ensuring equal opportunities, including through access for all to high quality, affordable, and sustainable services, in particular in the social field. Public services (including online services, in line with Guideline 4) play an important role in this respect. Member States should put in place effective anti-discrimination measures. Empowering people and promoting labour market participation for those furthest away from the labour market while preventing in-work poverty will help fight social exclusion. This would require enhancing social protection systems, lifelong learning and comprehensive active inclusion policies to create opportunities at different stages of people's lives and shield them from the risk of exclusion, with special attention to women. Social protection systems, including pensions and access to healthcare, should be modernised and fully deployed to ensure adequate income support and services – thus providing social cohesion

– whilst remaining financially sustainable and encouraging participation in society and in the labour market. Benefit systems should focus on ensuring income security during transitions and reducing poverty, in particular among groups most at risk from social exclusion, such as one-parent families, minorities including the Roma, people with disabilities, children and young people, elderly women and men, legal migrants and the homeless. Member States should also actively promote the social economy and social innovation in support of the most vulnerable. All measures should also aim at promoting gender equality. The EU headline target, on the basis of which Member States will set their national targets, taking into account their relative starting conditions and national circumstances, will aim at promoting social inclusion, in particular through the reduction of poverty by aiming to lift at least 20 million people out of the risk of poverty and exclusion[9]." (EU Council of Ministers, 2010a)

Recitals 15, 16, 18 and 19 that accompany the Guidelines are important for the purpose of this book (EU Council of Ministers, 2010a):

- Recital 15 reminds that "cohesion policy and its structural funds are amongst a number of important delivery mechanisms to achieve the priorities of smart, sustainable and inclusive growth in Member States and regions. In its conclusions of 17 June 2010, the European Council stressed the importance of promoting economic, social and territorial cohesion in order to contribute to the success of the new Europe 2020 Strategy."

- Recital 16 requires that when designing and implementing their NRPs "Member States should ensure effective governance of employment policy. While these Guidelines are addressed to Member States, the Europe 2020 Strategy should, as appropriate, be implemented, monitored and evaluated in partnership with all national, regional and local authorities, closely associating parliaments, as well as social partners and representatives of civil society, who shall contribute to the elaboration of NRPs, to their implementation and to the overall communication on the strategy."

- Recital 18 stresses that "the Employment Guidelines should form the basis for any country-specific recommendations that the

---

[9] "The population is defined as the number of persons who are at risk-of-poverty and exclusion according to three indicators (at-risk-of poverty; material deprivation; jobless household), leaving Member States free to set their national targets on the basis of the most appropriate indicators, taking into account their national circumstances and priorities."

Council may address to the Member States under Article 148(4) of the Treaty on the Functioning of the European Union, in parallel with the country-specific recommendations addressed to the Member States under Article 121(4) of the Treaty, in order to form a coherent package of recommendations. The Employment Guidelines should also form the basis for the establishment of the Joint Employment Report sent annually by the Council and Commission to the European Council."

- Recital 19 highlights that "the Employment Committee and the Social Protection Committee should monitor progress in relation to the employment and social aspects of the Employment Guidelines, in line with their respective Treaty-based mandates. This should in particular build on the activities of the open method of coordination in the fields of employment and of social protection and social inclusion. In addition the Employment Committee should maintain close contact with other relevant Council preparatory instances, including in the field of education."

1.2.5 European semester

In terms of overall socio-economic governance, it is important to mention that in September 2010 the Council agreed to change the way in which the EU's Stability and Growth Pact is implemented in order to allow a "European semester" to be introduced, as from 2011. This change is expected to improve economic policy coordination and help strengthen budgetary discipline, macro-economic stability and growth, in line with the Europe 2020 Strategy. The European semester will start each year in March when the European Council will identify the main economic challenges and give strategic advice on policies, on the basis of a European Commission report entitled "Annual Growth Survey". Taking account of this advice, countries will review their medium-term budgetary strategies during April and at the same time draw up NRPs setting out the action they will undertake in areas such as employment and social inclusion. In June and July, the European Council and the Council will provide policy advice to countries before they finalise their budgets for the following year. The Commission's reports in the following year will then assess how well this advice has been implemented.

1.2.6 Key role of the EU Social Protection Committee in implementing and monitoring the social dimension of Europe 2020

The social goals of Europe 2020 are clear from Guideline 10 as well as other Guidelines. It should be stressed that these goals are not limited to social inclusion but also encompass social protection. The SPC, given its responsibility for EU coordination and cooperation in the social field, has a potentially major role to play in ensuring a strong social dimension for the Europe 2020 Strategy and, more generally, in implementing a more Social EU (see Section 1.2.4, Recital 16 accompanying the Integrated Guidelines). In effect, it will be critical that in the future it plays a full and equal role alongside the EU Economic Policy Committee (EPC) and the EU Employment Committee (EMCO) in the overall implementation and monitoring of the Europe 2020 Strategy.

As a first step to ensuring this, the SPC has decided to issue an annual report covering the following elements (Social Protection Committee, 2010):

- An assessment of progress towards the EU headline target on social inclusion and poverty reduction, which should: monitor progress towards the national targets and their contribution to the EU target; analyse the trends in poverty and social exclusion as well as the situation of population sub-groups (on the basis of relevant existing and yet-to-be agreed EU indicators); draw from the relevant findings of the analysis conducted under the various activities undertaken in the framework of EU coordination and cooperation in the social field.

- A monitoring of the implementation of the social aspects of the Integrated Guidelines (in particular Guideline 10), on the basis of a Joint Assessment Framework agreed upon by the Employment Committee, the SPC and the European Commission. The SPC will also contribute to assessing the social implications of the six economic Integrated Guidelines in dialogue with the Economic Policy Committee.

- Other activities to monitor the social situation and the development of social protection policies undertaken in the context of EU coordination and cooperation in the social field. This will include the results of other work conducted by the SPC in line with its Treaty-based mandate to monitor the social situation and the development of social protection policies in the EU and in Member States. This work will draw on already agreed and possible updated or new EU indicators, as well as specific analytical work such as the joint SPC/Commission EU monitoring of the social impact of the crisis.

The SPC report will be transmitted to the EPSCO Council at the beginning of each year, with a view to contributing to the EPSCO preparation of the Spring European Council as regards the Europe 2020 Strategy.

Furthermore, the SPC and EMCO have agreed that the elements of the draft Joint Employment Report concerning the implementation of Guideline 10 in relation to the EU headline target on social inclusion/ poverty reduction will be discussed and agreed by the SPC and transmitted to EMCO for adoption in the Joint Employment Report.

Further details of how the SPC's role in promoting the social dimension of the Europe 2020 Strategy can be enhanced have still to be finalised. Suggestions on this are contained in this and later chapters of this book.

1.3 Outline of the Contents

In this section, we briefly outline the contents of the individual chapters and their main messages. As mentioned above, the chapters assess the logic of the Europe 2020 Strategy and of the instruments to be mobilised for improving social policy coordination and cooperation at EU level. In doing so, many contributions reflect on and draw lessons from the Social OMC over the past decade while others consider the broader aspects of EU governance in the social field.

The analysis opens in Chapter 2 with a contribution by Maurizio Ferrera aimed at mapping the components of the Social EU and analysing its current institutional patchwork. The fundamental question he raises is whether the EU can reconcile the logic of *opening*, which drives economic integration, with the logic of *closure*, which underpins nation-based welfare arrangements. He responds positively to this question and suggests a "strategy of institutional reconciliation". He argues that the key for a successful reconciliation lies in a more explicit and effective "nesting" of the national welfare states within the overall spatial architecture of the EU. In general terms, the challenge is twofold. First, counterbalance the disruptive effects that free movement and competition rules have on nation-based social protection systems. Secondly, promote a more symmetrical balance between the economic and social spaces of the EU. More practically, Ferrera suggests that in the medium term the reconciliation agenda should focus on three priorities: a) the implementation of the so-called "Horizontal Social Clause" of the Lisbon Treaty (see above, Section 1.1); b) the clarification and operationalisation of the Social Protocol; and c) the introduction of the most urgent "social complements" of the internal market, building on the recommendations of the Monti Report on the re-launching of the internal market and the Barca Report on the reform of cohesion policies.

The key focus of Chapter 3, by Roger Liddle, Patrick Diamond and colleagues, is on the social aftershocks of the crisis. The chapter develops four main arguments. First, there are five interlocking potential social crises, which in the main reflect long term trends apparent in Europe before the crisis, but the crisis has made the context in which they need to be addressed more difficult, particularly as a result of fiscal austerity. At the same time, the long term challenges have not gone away (e.g. tackling the public spending implications of an ageing demography). Secondly, the crisis has highlighted the issue of social and economic inequality. This forces a re-assessment of the "Lisbon Agenda" policy consensus established before the crisis – i.e., more flexible labour markets, higher employment participation, social investment, getting a job as the best answer to poverty. Thirdly, the EU's economic policy response to the crisis highlights the zero sum risks of Member States seeking to gain competitive advantage against each other through a brand of welfare nationalism which transmutes into a "race to the bottom" in social standards. And fourthly, a full blown Euro-Keynesian response to these problems is politically unrealistic and anyway would prove ineffective as it ignores the need for domestic reforms to improve the resilience of national social models in face of the emergence of new social risks. However, the EU as a whole needs to develop a new policy paradigm based on a combination of social investment and regulatory intervention, the implementation of which requires both policy reforms within Member States and action at EU level. Improved policy action and coordination at EU level could provide a more favourable structural context for the evolution of social reforms.

In Chapter 4, David Natali suggests that in the post-crisis context three issues will need particular attention. The first relates to the political and economic foundation of the EU project. The Lisbon agenda represented a first attempt to find a new compromise but its limits have been obvious. Europe 2020 and the Lisbon Treaty represent important steps forward but the tight timing is a problem as the effective implementation of the new Strategy and the new Treaty requires time and political mobilisation. The crisis as well as the stricter application of budgetary stability may rapidly reduce the room for defending social entitlements. The second issue has to do with the need for effective governance: the system introduced through the Lisbon Strategy is still in need of improvement. The recent economic and budgetary crisis has shown that EU governance is still weak. Here again, Europe 2020 as well as other important parallel EU developments (e.g. the Monti and Barca Reports mentioned above) seem promising in their attempt to mobilise the various instruments available at EU level. The definition of a more ambitious strategy for the EU budget is a key part of it. Finally, the third issue is related to insufficient participation, transparency and knowledge-based governance. For Natali, EU political legitimacy has not significantly improved between 2000 and 2010. There have been advances in deliberation, sharing of information, benchmarking and learning but these have not had a decisive impact on national policies. For the Europe 2020 Strategy to change this, more emphasis on the integration of European and national parliaments and on stakeholder involvement will be needed.

Chapter 5, by Bart Vanhercke, reviews some of the main advances and limits of the implementation of the Social OMC to date. It argues that the debate on Europe 2020 and its social dimension (the future role of the Social OMC and of the European Platform against Poverty) needs to better take into account the empirical evidence of the effects of the Social OMC as it has developed between 2000 and 2010. It suggests an analysis of this evidence in terms of two key dimensions: the "adequacy" of the Social OMC (assessed against the main goals proposed at the launch of the process) and its actual "impact" on national policy-making and reforms. A first conclusion of the chapter is that in different policy areas the Social OMC has been much "harder" than might have been expected from a "soft" law. In part this is due to the fact that the Social OMC is being used strategically by national and sub-national actors as a resource for their own purposes and independent policy initiatives. A second conclusion is that the Social OMC has become a "template" for soft governance – not only at EU level but also at country level in some federal Member States. A final conclusion is that the idea of "hybrid" EU governance should be explored because of the linkages between the Social OMC and other EU policy instruments. The chapter also puts forward various proposals aimed at further improving the Social OMC's "infrastructure", such as: a) continuing a "broad" Social OMC, covering not only poverty and social exclusion but also social protection; b) developing further the set of EU social indicators (for instance in relation to *social adequacy* of benefits and *participatory governance*); and c) strengthening the link between the Social OMC and EU funding (i.e. making the use of European Social Fund (ESF) money conditional upon the achievement of the EU social objectives).

In Chapter 6, Mary Daly analyses EU engagement with poverty and social exclusion as they were conceived and operationalised in the Lisbon process between 2000 and 2010, and draws out some implications for the further elaboration of EU coordination and cooperation in the social field. She shows, first, that as a set of social policy ideas the Social OMC was both innovative and far-reaching. It contributed significantly to elaborating the relationship between poverty and social exclusion, as problems and phenomena in their own right and also as approaches to social policy. She then highlights inconsistencies or lack of coherence in the social policy substance of the OMC. While poverty and social exclusion are evolving ideas and are located in highly contested political processes both nationally and in the EU, very different approaches have appeared in the Social OMC at different times. For example, in the early stages of Lisbon social inclusion was a goal in its own right whereas the revisions made in 2005 rendered social development a by-product of economic development. The process has been quite unstable. Daly argues that all in all, the Social OMC has had significant achievements and offers numerous insights about what is possible in regard to changing social policy considerations at EU and national levels. In particular, emerging risks and target groups have been highlighted, information assembled and procedures put in place for improving policy-making at national and transnational levels. Daly also highlights the most useful role that the European Platform against Poverty (EPAP) could play. She suggests that among the functions it could undertake are investigation of innovative approaches to emerging problems, raising awareness and visibility of social issues and especially EU approaches to them at national and EU levels and promoting a much more systematic impact assessment.

A *territorialised* social agenda to guide Europe 2020 and the future EU cohesion policy is proposed by Marjorie Jouen in Chapter 7. This concept of a "territorialised social agenda" was put forward by Fabrizio Barca (2009) with a view to giving coherence to the future, post-2013 EU cohesion policy. In the light of the future EU budgetary negotiations and the Europe 2020 priorities, the chapter first examines the main messages set out in the Barca Report. Then, it discusses the various methods and tools that could be used to "socialise" cohesion policy, i.e. to reorganise the "menu" offered to the regions following 6 priorities which will deal separately with territorial and economic efficiency on the one side, and social inclusion on the other (innovation, climate change, migration, children, skills and ageing). Along with the EU indicators for monitoring the social dimension of the Europe 2020 Strategy in the broader sense, new social performance criteria should be developed at regional level immediately. As regards the "territorialisation" of the EU social objectives, which was not treated as such by Barca and which is not tackled by the Europe 2020 Strategy, it would consist of ensuring that links are developed between EU social objectives and cohesion policy. In other words, exploring the implications of the new territorial cohesion objective (introduced by the Lisbon Treaty) in the next programming regulations, ensuring that cohesion policy fully takes on board the EU social objectives and also incorporating the territorial approach as element in EU coordination and cooperation in the social field.

The aforementioned "Horizontal Social Clause" of the Lisbon Treaty should provide a more solid basis for requiring the European Commission and EU countries to mainstream the EU's social objectives into policy-making and, for this to be effective, to systematically carry out social impact assessments (social IAs) of all relevant policies. Social IA is therefore an important area where progress is urgently needed. This is the topic of Chapter 8, by Martin Kühnemund. Based on an EU study funded by the European Commission, the chapter comments that although most Member States and several regions have systems in place for an *ex ante* assessment of the likely social impacts, there are significant implementation gaps. Examples of IAs that contain an in-depth analysis of social impacts are few and far between; where they do exist, they are most often conducted on policies with specific social objectives (and therefore largely irrelevant for mainstreaming social policy objectives into policies in other areas). Nonetheless, Kühnemund shows that there are examples of good practices. At the same time, he also identifies a number of key challenges that any country or region looking to set up an effective system for social IAs, or to improve their current system, needs to be aware of and to address. Some of these challenges relate to (integrated) IAs in general: this is still a relatively new process and tool in most countries and its application tends to be far from perfect. IAs are generally difficult to reconcile and integrate with previously existing policy processes. To be fully effective, there needs to be a shift in the policy-making culture, and officials need to have sufficient time, knowledge, skills and support to make it work. In order to facilitate more effective *social* IAs, countries need to work towards establishing a *general* IA culture. In addition, they have to address *specific* challenges for social IAs that relate to three key aspects: understanding social impacts (through an agreed reasonably simple categorisation), embedding social impacts in the broad governance process (through proper guidance and support as well as screening tools), and analysing social impacts (through the development and dissemination of appropriate tools, methods and data sources).

The next chapter, by Robert Walker, discusses the potential of targets, an area where expertise also needs to be built at EU and national levels. The aim of the chapter is to draw selectively on the experience gained from the use of targets at national level to begin reflection on the challenges that will need to be overcome if the recently agreed EU targets are to drive rather than obstruct progressive EU policy-making. Targets work by adding a new dynamic – the measurement of progress – to policy-making, thereby increasing accountability and stimulating public debate and engagement that is often led by civil society organisations. Walker argues that the intention of targets is not just to set policy goals but typically also to shake up the policy-making process, to challenge ways of working and to change institutional cultures. For EU targets to be effective, powerful "champions" must be appointed at EU and country levels to monitor achievements and to encourage, facilitate and cajole the various stakeholders to take those actions necessary to meet the targets set. There may even be a case, based on the experience of implementing national targets, for establishing financial incentives that reward success. Furthermore, EU targets provide an opportunity to enhance the legitimacy of the EU's democratic institutions by bringing the role of the European Parliament to the fore, alongside that of civil society, in holding Member States to account as they endeavour through policy and institutional change to attain or, preferably, to exceed their targets by 2020. Walker warns that targets need accurately to reflect the causal mechanisms embodied in policy logic. They must measure the right outcomes in an appropriate manner so as to avoid distortion and not to encourage gaming – i.e. that targets may be met but policy objectives are forgotten or ignored. In his view, the policy logic underpinning the poverty target is unclear both at EU and country levels, which increases the scope for gaming and creaming. It is therefore essential to continue to monitor the whole set of commonly agreed social indicators to guard against both possibilities and also to better understand why some Member States may be performing worse than others against their respective national targets.

In Chapter 10, Frazer and Marlier analyse the EU's current approach to promoting social inclusion and combating poverty and social exclusion. They briefly describe the functioning of the Social OMC since 2000 and then assess the strengths and weaknesses of the process. They highlight important progress that has been made in putting poverty and social exclusion on the EU agenda, in increasing understanding, in improving data, indicators and analysis, in mobilising actors, and in developing the exchange of learning and good practice. However, they also highlight that the process has not achieved a significant reduction in poverty and social exclusion, has remained a rather "soft" and peripheral process at both (sub-)national and EU levels with insufficient interaction with the EU's economic and employment policies. Frazer and Marlier go on to suggest what needs to happen to build a stronger EU social process in the future and to bring together the patchwork of different strands that currently makes up Social EU into a more coherent whole. They suggest the importance of both building on the positive elements of the Social OMC but also using the increased status accorded to poverty and social inclusion issues in Europe 2020 to address some of the political and institutional weaknesses identified and to strengthen the central element of the Social OMC, the National Strategy Reports on Social Protection and Social Inclusion (especially the NAPs/inclusion). They make concrete proposals for setting clear EU social objectives with EU and national social outcome targets, for improved benchmarking, monitoring and evaluation, for strengthening social inclusion in the Europe 2020 Integrated Guidelines and in NRPs, for developing more effective national social protection and social inclusion strategies, for taking advantage of the Lisbon Treaty's "Horizontal Social Clause", for developing the EPAP, for building on the thematic approach (e.g. active inclusion, child poverty, and homelessness and housing exclusion), for strengthening governance, for better linking EU social inclusion and EU Structural Funds objectives and for improving exchange, learning and communication.

The final chapter, by Jonathan Zeitlin, starts by looking backward at the governance of the Lisbon Strategy since March 2000, providing a critical overview of the three principal phases of its development. It then looks forward, examining the emerging governance architecture for EU policy coordination after 2010. The argument proceeds in three main steps. The first analyses the reformed governance architecture of Europe 2020, drawing attention both to its strengthened social dimension, and to serious risks to the broader European social policy coordination and monitoring capacities developed over the past decade arising from ambiguities in the institutional design of the new Strategy. The second step advances a series of proposals to counteract these risks by incorporating into the governance architecture of Europe 2020 key components of EU social policy coordination developed under the Social OMC, notably the common social objectives, common indicators, and European monitoring, peer review, and evaluation of national social protection and inclusion strategies. The final step in the argument proposes a series of reflexive reforms aimed at overcoming weaknesses within the Social OMC itself, with a particular focus on reinforcing mutual learning and enhancing stakeholder participation.

1.4 A More Social EU

1.4.1 Overall conclusions

Increased awareness of the need for a more Social EU

One of the positive effects of the economic and financial crisis has been to increase awareness of the important role that social policy in general and social protection systems in particular can play as economic stabilisers. This in turn has reinforced the need to address the tensions between economic, employment and social objectives and to develop a more balanced and sustainable approach in the future. The Lisbon Strategy, especially since it was refocused in 2005 solely on jobs and growth, has demonstrated that an approach dominated by a "trickle down" ideology, which assumes that economic growth through increased competition will automatically benefit all, has not worked and is not sustainable. Levels of poverty, inequality and social exclusion, even before the economic crisis, have remained stubbornly high. The challenges of an ageing population and the effects of increased mobility and diversity have been seen to have very serious social consequences and to have the potential to undermine future economic progress if not addressed through strong social policies. The growing sense of many EU citizens that the EU's (primarily economic) project has not been beneficial to them and that indeed it may be endangering the social standards they aspire to has called into question the political support for the EU project and therefore its democratic legitimacy. Thus it is clear that building a stronger Social EU is both a necessary investment to support economic growth and underpin free movement and an indispensable requirement to ensure the EU's continuing political legitimacy.

Insufficient overall policy coordination under the Lisbon process

The various chapters in this book reinforce the urgent need to build a stronger Social EU. They show that the Lisbon Strategy between 2000 and 2010 played an important role in raising the importance of the EU's social dimension and promoting increased EU coordination and cooperation in the social field. In particular, the Social OMC helped to raise the importance of social policy at both EU and national levels, to develop new ideas and thinking, to deepen analysis, knowledge and expertise, to improve data collection and to mobilise a range of actors. However, although the need to find a better balance between economic, employment and social policies (particularly in the context of sustainable development) and to ensure that they are mutually reinforcing was repeatedly highlighted, in practice the Social OMC did not succeed in satisfactorily addressing the tensions between them. Social policy is still the poor relation of the Lisbon policy triangle and the disruptive effects that free movement and competition rules have had on nation-based social protection systems were not resolved. Also, social policy at EU level has remained a rather uncoordinated patchwork with insufficient integration between social protection, social inclusion, education, health, justice, housing and other policy areas.

New opportunities under the Lisbon Treaty and Europe 2020

In the light of the above, a major challenge in the next decade is to find ways of ensuring that the insights gained under the Lisbon process are built on and that a more coherent, integrated and balanced approach to sustainable development is adopted. Thus it is encouraging that many of the authors in this book highlight that the Lisbon Treaty and the Europe 2020 Strategy provide a significant, if far from perfect, opportunity to move towards a better and more mutually reinforcing balance between economic, employment and social objectives – and thus, towards a stronger Social EU. In particular, five opportunities stand out.

First, the Lisbon Treaty, through its Horizontal Social Clause, provides a legal basis for better taking into account the social impact of policies and for using this as a tool to mainstream social objectives across all relevant policy areas (including non social policies and measures) as well as to more rigorously monitor and report on the impact of policies. Secondly, the Treaty and the Europe 2020 Strategy (with its headline EU targets and its EU flagships) have increased the potential visibility and importance of social issues – especially, though not solely of social inclusion and poverty. Thirdly, the Strategy holds out the possibility of a much more integrated and coordinated approach to economic, social, employment and also environmental governance. This could ensure that policies in these areas become genuinely reinforcing. Fourthly, under the new Treaty there is an increased possibility of better safeguarding, strengthening and modernising national social protection systems and protecting non-economic services of general interests, which can contribute to restoring the balance between the EU and national levels. Fifthly, the Treaty provides the justification for EU action on a broader range of social issues than heretofore such as a high level of education and training, the protection of human health and a reduction of inequality. This may lead to greater coordination of the current patchwork of "social" policies in the broader sense than heretofore.

Risks to progress

Of course these are only possibilities and not certainties. This volume identifies some very real dangers to their achievement. There are at least five such dangers. First, there is a risk that with an increased emphasis on coordinated governance arrangements the issue of poverty and social exclusion in particular and social protection and social inclusion more generally may become swamped by economic considerations and in fact lose rather than gain importance and visibility. Secondly, there is a risk that the tendency which begun in 2005 (when the Lisbon Strategy was refocused on jobs and growth) may be reinforced; namely the risk of moving further from a multilateral and dynamic process involving and mobilising many actors to a more bilateral and technocratic process involving national and EU civil servants in limited circles of experts. This could result in less emphasis being given to the engagement by civil society and social partners as well as local and regional stakeholders. This would both reduce the extent of mutual learning and involvement, especially at sub-national levels, and would not address the challenge of building increased democratic legitimacy and support for the EU project. Thirdly, there is also the risk that in the current phase of the economic and financial crisis the growing emphasis on austerity packages and the stricter implementation of budgetary stability may rapidly reduce the room for defending social entitlements and making progress on social issues. Fourthly, it is not clear how the new governance arrangements under the Europe 2020 Strategy will connect with the broader EU coordination/ cooperation and monitoring capacities in the social field developed through the Social OMC over the past decade. Fifthly, there is a risk that the common social objectives may only be incompletely and selectively integrated into National Reform Programmes (NRPs) and that future EU monitoring of social protection and social inclusion policies may be narrowly focused on the EU social inclusion target. As rightly emphasised by the President of the European Commission, José Manuel Barroso, "the Europe 2020 agenda, in setting a social inclusion target, has highlighted three dimensions of poverty and social exclusion. It is also essential, however, that Member States – and the EU as a whole – continue to monitor performance according to the full set of commonly agreed social indicators underpinning EU coordination and cooperation in the social field." (Barroso, 2010)

1.4.2 Recommendations

Moving forward the challenge will be to ensure that the positive developments identified above are maximised and that the risks are mitigated to the greatest extent possible. The various chapters in this volume make a range of detailed suggestions as to how best progress may be achieved. Drawing on these we would particularly highlight and make recommendations in relation to nine interrelated areas. These are areas in which we consider that the Europe 2020 Strategy's institutional arrangements can be developed so as to maximise the possibility of building a more Social EU. The areas covered are: reinforcing interactions between all strands of Europe 2020 and between the various components that make up Social EU; embedding targets in national policy-making and developing leadership in their implementation; enhancing mainstreaming of social objectives through social impact assessments at EU and country levels; reinforcing social reporting and building on the Social OMC; developing complementary tools and instruments through the EPAP; mobilising EU resources to support Social EU and linking the EU's social and territorial objectives; enhancing social monitoring and strengthening analytical capacity; increasing democratic legitimacy and reinforcing stakeholder involvement; and enhancing mutual learning.

*Recommendation 1: Reinforcing interactions
between all strands of Europe 2020 and between
the various components that make up Social EU*

A key challenge will be to ensure mutually reinforcing interactions between all strands of Europe 2020 and between the various components that (potentially) make up Social EU, and to make certain that the social dimension is fully taken into account. A number of things could help in this regard. First, it will be essential that social ministers play a central role (through the EPSCO Council) in the close monitoring of the social dimension of the Europe 2020 Strategy. Secondly, the different EU Committees (in particular SPC, EMCO and EPC) but also other high level groups (in areas such as health, education and justice) should be encouraged to cooperate more systematically on a number of key issues and join forces to develop synergies between their respective areas of competence. More particularly, it is important that the SPC plays a central role in monitoring the implementation of the Integrated Guidelines. This means both taking the lead in monitoring the specifically "social" Guidelines (especially, though not solely, Guideline 10) and contributing to monitoring the social impact of the other Guidelines; this also means producing an annual Social Protection and Social Inclusion report on this for the attention of the EPSCO Council. (See also Recommendation 5.)

*Recommendation 2: Embedding targets in national
policy-making and developing leadership in their implementation*

The EU social inclusion/poverty reduction headline target is a major step forward in demonstrating the political social commitment of the EU and represents an essential element of the social dimension of the Europe 2020 Strategy. Translating the EU target into meaningful national (and possibly also sub-national) targets is essential. To ensure that appropriate targets are set we would recommend the following. National targets should clearly contribute to the overall achievement of the EU target. Targets should be evidence based. They should accurately reflect the mechanisms causing poverty and social exclusion and reflect the overall policy objectives set for increasing social inclusion. They must measure real policy outcomes and avoid the risk that, in meeting the target, policy objectives are distorted, forgotten or ignored. To ensure ongoing public and political support, targets should be set following a robust, rigorous and transparent process. Thus they should also take into account the views of stakeholders. Progress towards the EU and (sub-)national targets needs to be closely monitored and reported on. (See also Recommendations 4 and 7).

Recommendation 3: Enhancing mainstreaming
of social objectives through social impact assessments
at EU and country levels

In the light of the new Horizontal Social Clause and in view of the recommendations of the 2010 Monti Report on the re-launching of the internal market, the European Commission should systematically strengthen the role of social evaluation within its Impact Assessment system. This should be recognised as a key tool for systematically ensuring that social objectives are mainstreamed in all relevant EU policy areas. At the same time, the EPAP should be given the task of systematically monitoring and reporting on the application of social impact assessments across the Commission. In order to also promote and strengthen social impact assessment at the national and sub-national levels the SPC, in the context of the ongoing implementation of the Social OMC, should give a high priority to deepening existing work on this issue. It should promote increased understanding of this tool, encourage Member States to build its use into their policy processes from an early stage, support the development and dissemination of knowledge about the tools, methods and data sources needed to make it effective and develop a systematic process of exchange and mutual learning. At the same time, it should monitor and report regularly on the use of social impact assessments by Member States in the context of the development of the NRPs. (See also Recommendation 5.)

Recommendation 4: Reinforcing social reporting
and building on the Social OMC

The Commission has indicated its intention to continue the Social OMC as part of the new Europe 2020 Strategy. This is important as there is much that is positive to build on and it is essential that the full range of commonly agreed social objectives and indicators are maintained and taken into account into the Europe 2020 Strategy. However, in doing so it is important that a major element of the OMC, the requirement for Member States to develop national strategy reports on social protection and social inclusion (NSRSPSIs), is not abandoned. Strengthened national strategy reports (including National Action Plans on social inclusion (NAPs/inclusion)) and annual Joint Reports on Social Protection and Social Inclusion (JRSPSIs) are an essential basis for properly preparing and implementing the contribution of the social strand to the Europe 2020 Strategy. In particular, the continuation of NSRSPSIs would provide the necessary social underpinning to Member States' NRPs. This should help to ensure that the national poverty/ social inclusion targets and the social dimension of NRPs have real substance, that they are anchored in national policy-making processes and encompass the whole range of social protection and social inclusion policies. They would also provide the essential basis for continuing and deepening the involvement of all stakeholders. In addition, they would allow for the continuation and deepening of mutual learning and exchange of good practices across a broad range of policy fields relevant to social protection and social inclusion. At the same time, it will be important to maintain and build on the thematic approach (i.e. the detailed focus on key issues such as active inclusion, child poverty and well-being, housing exclusion and homelessness) to ensure that concrete progress is made on these key issues. JRSPSIs could in effect become the Annual Assessment of the social dimension of Europe 2020 and feed into the Commission's Annual Growth Survey and EU policy guidance and possible recommendations to Member States on their NRPs. (See also Recommendations 7 and 8.)

Recommendation 5: Developing complementary tools and instruments through the EPAP

While it is important that the Social OMC is continued and reinforced, the analysis in this book clearly demonstrates that it is not, on its own, a sufficient tool to develop a stronger Social EU. The EPAP could become a very important and complementary mechanism to add value to the work of the Social OMC. In this context, we would suggest that it should be given four priority tasks. First, it should provide a place which regularly brings together representatives of all the stakeholders (potentially) contributing to building a more Social EU and where they can engage and debate the effectiveness of EU cooperation and coordination in the social field (in particular, the social dimension of Europe 2020) and suggest ways in which this can be enhanced. Secondly, as already suggested, it should monitor and promote the use of social impact assessments within the Commission's impact assessment process. It could also contribute to building knowledge in this field and disseminating this to countries and to promoting the involvement of stakeholders in the process. Thirdly, it should play a key role in ensuring and proposing greater linkages between the patchwork of different components that currently makes up Social EU and in effect it should become the visible face of the Social EU. Fourthly, it should support the Social OMC and the SPC in monitoring the implementation of the social dimension of Europe 2020 and in particular the extent to which the social dimension is being taken into account not only in the "social" Integrated Guidelines but also in the other Guidelines and in Europe 2020 more generally. This should also involve systematically monitoring the extent to which real synergies are taking place between the different policy areas and the extent to which real "feeding in" and "feeding out" is being achieved. As part of this, it could also monitor and review how other EU policies (including the structural funds) are contributing to achieving the Union's common social objectives. (See also Recommendations 1 and 3.)

Recommendation 6: Mobilising EU resources to support Social EU and linking the EU's social and territorial objectives

It will be important to ensure that sufficient resources, including in terms of staff, are allocated to support the continuation and strengthening of the Social OMC and the implementation of the EPAP. As one of the key weaknesses of the Social OMC during the Lisbon process was the weak link between the commonly agreed EU social objectives and the use of EU Structural Funds, a key challenge for the Europe 2020 Strategy will be to ensure close synergies between these. Fully in line with the new EU objective of "territorial cohesion" (introduced by the Lisbon Treaty) and with the aim of the recent Budget Review[10] to concentrate cohesion funding on all Europe 2020 objectives and to strengthen cohesion policy accordingly, and building in particular on the Barca Report, the ultimate goal, which ought to be put at the heart of the next financial perspectives (for the post-2013 period), should be to ensure that the EU social objectives are fully taken into account in EU "territorial" policies and programmes. This would consist of ensuring that links are developed between EU social objectives and cohesion policy – i.e., exploiting the potential of the new territorial cohesion objective in the next programming regulations, ensuring that cohesion policy is used as a "preventive arm"[11] to promote structural and institutional reforms that enhance the achievements of the EU social objectives, and also incorporating the territorial approach as an important element in EU coordination and cooperation in the social field. It is important to highlight that an important dimension of this "territorialisation" will be the active participation of local and regional actors.

Recommendation 7: Enhancing social monitoring and strengthening analytical capacity

We have already stressed the importance of putting in place effective governance arrangements for monitoring progress on the social dimension of Europe 2020. However, if this is to be really effective it will be important that policy goals, in-depth socio-economic analysis, targets and indicators are brought much closer together. In this way, policy development, targeting and monitoring can be given a stronger evidence base.

---

[10] European Commission, 2010c.
[11] European Commission, 2010b.

It will also be important that monitoring is not confined just to the specific EU social inclusion target and related national targets. Member States and the Commission should monitor and report on EU and national performances against the full set of commonly agreed social protection and social inclusion indicators. It will also be important to ensure that possible gaps in the current portfolio of EU social indicators be identified and addressed. Developing indicators and methods for monitoring interactions between social, economic, employment, and environmental policies will be particularly important. Enhanced timeliness of social indicators is also an important condition for effective monitoring of the social dimension of the Europe 2020 Strategy. As highlighted in Recommendation 9 below, EU indicators have also an important role to play in boosting mutual learning. (See also Recommendations 2 and 4.)

Recommendation 8: Increasing democratic legitimacy and reinforcing stakeholder involvement

To avoid the Europe 2020 Strategy becoming a technocratic and remote high level process and to safeguard the social dimension of the Strategy it will be important to increase the visibility and accountability of the process. This will mean among other things strengthening the role of EU, national and possible sub-national parliaments in the process as well as extending the possibilities for the active involvement of EU and (sub-)national stakeholders (including social partners and civil society) and of all levels of governance (local and regional as well as national). One possibility in this regard would be to establish stakeholder fora linked to the EPAP and the Social OMC at both EU and (sub-)national levels and to actively use these fora as a means of ensuring stakeholder participation in the preparation, implementation, and assessment of NRPs and NSRSPSIs/NAPs. There is now a sufficient body of good practice available to enable the SPC and the Commission to prepare and agree guidelines for the involvement of stakeholders. These could then be promoted with other EU Committees (e.g. EPC and EMCO) and with Member States. Member States' performance on mobilising and involving stakeholders in the development, implementation and monitoring of the Europe 2020 Strategy in general and the NRPs in particular should then be monitored and reported on the basis of these guidelines. (See also Recommendation 4.)

Recommendation 9: Enhancing mutual learning

One of the strengths of the Social OMC to date has been to promote the exchange of good practice and mutual learning between Member States. However, this could be made more extensive and effective in the future. In particular it will be important to improve coordination so as to allow for more systematic and in depth exchanges built around specific priorities and themes. The dissemination of policy analysis and learning in ways that will make it more specific and relevant for domestic actors needs to be enhanced. In particular, the outcomes of peer reviews, policy studies and exchange projects need to be fed back into the policy-making process in a clearer way. A more extensive and systematic involvement of civil society organisations, local and regional authorities and independent experts in exchange and learning will also be necessary. Finally, the (potential) key role of the EU social indicators as mutual learning tools tends to be largely underestimated. Here, we find it useful to highlight two important applications where progress is needed. First, EU indicators can be used in a more diagnostic manner to undertake (properly "contextualised") benchmarking and to help to identify and understand the impact (both positive and negative) of policies on differences in Member State performance.[12] Secondly, they can serve as a point of reference for countries. Countries should obviously not rely solely on these EU indicators in reporting on progress towards national/ EU social objectives but the national indicators they develop and use for this purpose should be linked back to the common indicators as far as possible – again, with a view to facilitating mutual learning.

1.4.3 A final word

Suggestions and recommendations in relation to many of the areas described above are developed in more detail in the following chapters in this book. There are also many additional and helpful ideas put forward on specific aspects which are too detailed to cover in this introductory chapter. However, we hope that we have outlined a number of practical steps that can be taken to ensure that EU coordination and cooperation in the social field will take a significant step forward under the Europe 2020 Strategy and that we will indeed move to a more Social EU.

At the same time, we are also very aware that progress will not be easy. The experience of the last decade has shown that building political support and commitment for a strong social dimension will be an ongoing challenge and will continue to require the active involvement and efforts of all stakeholders.

As argued at the beginning of this opening chapter, EU integration is in many respects at a critical juncture. On the one hand, issues of legitimacy persist and there is a growing danger of an increasingly uni-

---

[12] To date, the only EU example of such an exercise is the SPC report on child poverty and well-being (2008).

dimensional focus on economic competitiveness and financial austerity as a response to the economic and financial crisis. This could further marginalise social questions. On the other hand, Europe 2020 and its social dimension could be a window of opportunity. However, this is not certain and it will be important to ensure that the new Europe 2020 governance arrangements, including the new social inclusion/ poverty target and the EPAP, do not lead to narrowing the EU's social dimension and limiting the type of flexible initiatives that were developed under the Social OMC. Political leadership will therefore be required to open this window and to seize the opportunity to redefine Social EU, to frame solidarity across national borders while maintaining strong national social protection systems and to avoid a race to the bottom in the search for economic competitiveness.

Thus we would end with a warning. If progress is not made in building a stronger Social EU as part of developing a fairer and more equitable model of development then the success of the whole Europe 2020 Strategy will be put at risk and popular support for the EU project is likely to be increasingly withdrawn.

References

Barca, F. (2009), *An agenda for a reformed cohesion policy: A place-based approach to meeting European Union challenges and expectations*, Independent Report prepared at the request of Danuta Hübner, Commissioner for Regional Policy, Brussels: European Commission. Available at: http://ec.europa.eu/regional_policy/policy/future/pdf/report_barca_v0306.pdf.

Barroso, J. M. (2010), Foreword to A.B. Atkinson and E. Marlier (editors), "Income and living conditions in Europe", Luxembourg: Office for Official Publications of the European Communities.

EU Council of Ministers (2010), *Recommendation for a Council Recommendation on broad guidelines for the economic policies of the Member States and of the Union*, Document 11646/10 dated 7 July 2010, Brussels: EU Council of Ministers.

EU Council of Ministers (2010a), *Council Decision on guidelines for the employment policies of the Member States*, Document 14338/10 dated 12 October 2010, Brussels: EU Council of Ministers.

European Commission (2010), *Europe 2020: A strategy for smart, sustainable and inclusive growth*, Communication COM(2010) 2020, Brussels: European Commission. Available at: http://ec.europa.eu/eu2020/pdf/COMPLET%20EN20BARROSO%20%20%20007%20-%20Europe%202020%20-%20EN%20version.pdf.

European Commission (2010a), *Governance, Tools and Policy Cycle of Europe 2020*, Brussels: European Commission. Available at: http://ec.europa.eu/

eu2020/pdf/Annex%20SWD%20implementation%20last%20version%2015-07-2010.pdf.

European Commission (2010b), *Enhancing economic policy coordination for stability, growth and jobs – Tools for stronger EU economic governance*, Communication COM(2010) 367/2, Brussels: European Commission. Available at: http://ec.europa.eu/economy_finance/articles/euro/documents/com_2010_367_en.pdf.

European Commission (2010c), *The EU Budget Review*, Communication COM(2010) 700 final, Brussels: European Commission. Available at: http://ec.europa.eu/budget/reform/library/communication/com2010700en.pdf.

European Council (2010), *European Council 17 June 2010: Conclusions*, Brussels: European Council.

European Council (2000), *Lisbon European Council 23 and 24 March 2000: Presidency Conclusions*, Brussels: European Council.

Monti, M. (2010), *A New Strategy for the Single Market*. Available at: http://ec.europa.eu/bepa/pdf/monti_report_final_10_05_2010_en.pdf.

Social Protection Committee (2010), *SPC opinion on the Social Dimension of the Europe 2020 Strategy*, SPC/2010/10/7final. Available at: http://ec.europa.eu/social/main.jsp?catId=758&langId=en.

Social Protection Committee (2008), *Child Poverty and Well-Being in the EU: Current status and way forward*, Luxembourg: OPOCE. Available at: http://ec.europa.eu/social/main.jsp?catId=751&langId=en&pubId=74&type=2&furtherPubs=yes.

2. Mapping the Components of Social EU:

A Critical Analysis
of the Current Institutional Patchwork

Maurizio FERRERA[1]

2.1 Introduction

By the end of 2010 the welfare state will have celebrated its centennial in several European Union (EU) Member States. A genuine European invention, public protection schemes were introduced to respond to the mounting "social question" linked to industrialisation. The disruption of traditional, localised systems of work-family-community relations and the diffusion of national markets – based on free movement and largely unfettered economic competition within the territorial borders of each country – profoundly altered the pre-industrial structure of risks and need. The regulation of the new national labour markets, by establishing common standards, rights and obligations (through labour laws, unemployment and more generally social insurance, national labour exchanges etc.), was one of the fundamental institutional and political responses that European states gave to the big "social question" which confronted them.

In his ground-breaking historical analysis of modern citizenship, T.H. Marshall suggested that the evolution of the national welfare state involved a two-fold process of fusion and of separation (Marshall, 1950). The *fusion* was geographical and entailed the dismantling of local privileges and immunities, the harmonisation of rights and obligations throughout the national territory concerned, and the establishment of a level playing field (the equal status of citizens) within state borders. The *separation* was functional and entailed the creation of new sources of nationwide authority and jurisdiction as well as new specialised institutions for the implementation of that authority and that jurisdiction at a decentralised level. The development of national markets, accom-

---

[1] This chapter builds on previous work, partly carried out with Stefano Sacchi; I am grateful for the fruitful collaboration. I also warmly thank the editors of the book for their precious inputs and suggestions. Address for correspondence: maurizio.ferrera@unimi.it.

panied by the creation of new "social" entitlements and public protection schemes, triggered off – at least in liberal democracies – a phase of unprecedented economic growth and social progress, while strengthening at the same time the political loyalty of citizens and the overall legitimacy of the state.

To a large extent, the present historical phase is witnessing the emergence of a new (a "second") social question in Europe, which is reproducing under new guises the double challenge of fusion and separation already experienced between the 19th and the 20th centuries. Historical parallels are always slippery and can be misleading when taken too literally, yet they may serve a useful heuristic function. As was the case one hundred years ago at the domestic level, the Europeanisation ("fusion") of national markets through freedom of movement and competition rules is (already has been) a tremendous trigger for growth and job creation in the EU's economy, enhancing life chances and welfare for European citizens. But it is also a source of social and spatial disruptions. Again, economic "fusion" requires the introduction of some common social standards, rights and obligations through a socially-friendly institutional re-articulation of the novel Europeanised space of interaction.

We can think of at least three reasons which make such a socially-friendly re-articulation desirable[2]. First, the re-articulation is needed in order to secure a fairer, more equitable distribution of life chances for EU citizens, both within and between Member States. This is the "social cohesion", or "social justice" rationale. Unless one believes in a naive version of the trickle-down effect of growth, the pursuit of economic prosperity through efficient and open markets should be accompanied by an agenda for social progress, resting on key values (such as "social justice and protection, equality between women and men, solidarity between generations and protection of the rights of the child" – now enshrined in Article 3 of the Lisbon Treaty) which are widely shared and deeply rooted in Europe's political cultures. While there can be no doubt that this agenda includes areas and policies which legally come under national jurisdiction, it should be equally clear that the EU can play an important role, both directly (by exercising its legal powers to sustain and complement national social justice agendas) and indirectly (by "mainstreaming" social cohesion/ justice considerations within its entire array of policies). Second, a more Social EU is desirable in order to improve the very functioning of the internal market, and thus generate more growth and jobs (this is the "economic efficiency" rationale). A wealth of political economy research has in fact shown that social

---

[2] For a more expanded discussion and references see Ferrera and Sacchi (2009).

policies can play an important role not only as redistributive instruments, but also as "productive factors" (Fouarge, 2003). Thirdly, and possibly most importantly, a more Social EU is needed in order to secure continuing support for the integration process itself on the part of increasingly worried national electorates (this is the "social and political legitimacy" rationale). There is indeed growing evidence that the EU is now perceived as a potentially dangerous entity by a majority of its citizens, as a threat to national labour markets and social protection systems, as a "Trojan horse" serving the malevolent interests of globalisation. As noted above, post-war social protection systems have built extraordinary bonds between citizens and their national institutions, bringing about a very robust form of allegiance, based on the institutionalised exchange of material benefits for electoral support. The EU, conversely, has been rather weak in terms of identity and allegiance building. If voters' anxieties vis-à-vis markets and competition are not alleviated, if voters are not convinced that "the EU cares" (through direct and indirect action, or non-action), the integration process as such may be seriously de-legitimised and jeopardised by xenophobic sentiment and neo-protectionist demands voiced by those social groups that are most directly affected by economic opening – and the economic crisis has undoubtedly intensified this challenge.

The institutional re-articulation which is required in order to build a stronger Social EU (better: a fully fledged "EU social model") is much more complex and difficult than the organisational separations that took place within the nation states about a hundred years ago. In late 19th century Europe, social rights emerged on a *tabula rasa* (or at least almost *rasa*): there was not much to "fuse" and there were wide margins for creating *ex novo* in terms of social policies. In today's EU, the institutional material to be integrated is very thick and very solid in the welfare realm, and decision making rules at the EU level are inherently biased against efforts of positive integration. But there is an even more fundamental obstacle: the institutional clash between the logic of closure, which underpins nation-based social programs, and the logic of opening which drives the integration process. By its very nature, the welfare state presupposes the existence of a clearly demarcated and cohesive community, whose members feel that they belong to the same "whole" and that they are linked by reciprocity ties vis-à-vis common risks and similar needs. Since the 19th century (or even earlier in some cases) the nation-state has provided the closure conditions for the development of an *ethos* of social solidarity and redistributive arrangements within its geographical territory. By contrast, EU integration is clearly guided by a logic of "opening", aimed at fostering free movement (in the widest sense) and non discrimination by weakening or tearing apart those spatial demarcations and closure practices that nation-states have historically built around themselves, especially in the social sphere.

Finding a well-designed and viable institutional response to EU's "second social question" means, essentially, addressing the clash between the logic of closure and the logic of opening. Can the Union reconcile these two logics and transform the encounter between nation-based welfare and EU-based economic unification into a "happy marriage", i.e. into an institutional engine for further expanding and strengthening the life chances of its citizens? This chapter argues in favour of a positive answer and discusses possible pathways towards the "happy marriage" scenario. Section 2.2 presents the main argument by illustrating the programmatic contrast and growing tensions between the welfare state, on the one hand, and the EU, on the other. Section 2.3 outlines a possible strategy of institutional reconciliation. It argues that the key for a successful reconciliation lies in a more explicit and effective "nesting" of the national welfare state within the overall spatial architecture of the EU. The next two sections try to identify and discuss some possible building blocks (and even some ongoing developments) which may promote the formation and consolidation of the new architecture and thus activate a virtuous nesting scenario, in which the economic and the social spaces of Europe will be able not only to co-exist without colliding, but also to re-enforce each other. Section 2.6 concludes.

2.2 The Challenge: Closure vs. Opening

As has been shown by a large scholarship in sociology and political science[3], welfare state formation can be seen as the last phase or step in the long term historical development of the European system of nation states: the step through which territorially bounded political communities came to introduce redistributive arrangements for their citizens, thus transforming themselves into self-contained and inward-looking spaces of solidarity and inaugurating novel and original models of state-mediated social sharing.

While this transformation was being completed within each domestic arena, during the so-called *Trente Glorieuses*, a new institutional development took off in the inter-state or supranational arena: the process of EU integration. Even though originally meant to "rescue the nation-state" (Milward, 2000) by boosting economic growth, the Rome Treaty

---

[3]   I have reconstructed and discussed this strand of scholarship in Ferrera, 2005. One of the most prominent Founding Father of this tradition is of course Stein Rokkan (Flora, 1999).

pulled a strong brake on the long-term dynamic of nation- and state-building in Europe.

The original EU Treaties envisaged a division of labour between supranational and national levels: the European Community was to be instrumental in opening up markets and helping to achieve otherwise unattainable economies of scale, so as to fully exploit Europe's (initially, the Six's) economic potential. Member States could use part of the extra surplus in the institutionalised exchange of social benefits – flowing from their national welfare institutions – for "anchoring" support on the part of their domestic political communities. "Keynes at home, Smith abroad", as Robert Gilpin aptly dubbed this kind of embedded liberalism arrangement (Gilpin, 1987, page 355). This justified the weakness of the social provisions in the Rome Treaty: from equality of treatment for men and women to the coordination of social security regimes, all the social provisions and articles contained therein were instrumental in the dismantling of non-tariff barriers to trade and the creation of a higher economic order featuring unconstrained economic trade flows. However, this supranational liberal order rested upon, or rather was embedded into national welfare states that were to be equally unconstrained in terms of social regulation capabilities, and in particular would not be constrained by the supranational authorities. This division of labour implied separating jurisdiction between the supranational and national levels, thus establishing "mutual non-interference" between market-making and market-correcting functions. EU competition law and the four freedoms (free movement of workers, capitals, goods and services) were not supposed to impinge upon Member States' sovereignty in the social sphere (Giubboni, 2006).

This did not last. Firstly, since the 1970s, international political economy conditions have changed, and the embedded liberalism compromise has floundered. Moreover, and more importantly still as regards EU integration, the Community legal order has been constitutionalised (Weiler, 1999). The supremacy of Community law over domestic legislation has, along with direct effect, torn the initial division of labour to pieces: if Community law trumps national law, then provisions geared to foster free movement and unconstrained competition (i.e., the Treaty provisions) trump social regulation, as enshrined in national constitutions and laws, and EU Court of Justice (CJEU) judges, contrary to national constitutional judges, will be constrained in balancing economic and social interests whenever these clash (Scharpf, 2009). To be sure, the CJEU has not always operated as a "market police force", and has on several occasions granted some degree of "immunity" against EU market law to national welfare institutions and practices. However, in the absence of a Treaty "hook", it has done so on the grounds of judicial doctrines that lack a stable legal anchoring and may well be overridden in other rulings or legislative acts.

The de-bounding and opening logic of EU integration has raised increasingly severe problems for the welfare state, as it has put in question two central tenets of this institution: the territoriality principle and the principle of compulsory affiliation to state-controlled insurance schemes. More specifically, through the four freedoms, competition rules and the rules of coordination of national social security systems, the EU law has launched two basic challenges to nation-based welfare:

- A challenge to its territorial closure, through the explicit prohibition of (most) cross-border restrictions regarding access to and consumption of social benefits and to some extent also the provision of services. The nationality filter has been neutralised for admission into domestic sharing spaces and some core social rights (such as pensions) have become portable across the territory of the whole EU.

- A challenge to the very "right to bound", i.e. the right of each national welfare state to autonomously determine who can/must share what with whom and then enforce compliance through specific organisational structures backed by coercive power (e.g. setting up a compulsory public insurance scheme for a given occupational category).

These challenges have manifested themselves gradually and incrementally over time, affecting in different ways and with different intensity the various risk-specific schemes and the various tiers and pillars of provision in different countries (Martinsen, 2005 and 2005a). So far the two challenges have not caused major organisational upheavals. But during the last two decades the institutional status quo has been explicitly and directly attacked on several occasions in some of its founding properties: for example the link between legal residence and the right to enjoy means-tested social assistance benefits or the public monopoly over compulsory insurance (see Box 2.1).

Box 2.1: Examples of effects of EU law on national social spaces

• Nationality/citizenship no longer a legitimate instrument of "closure" in the access to social benefits → Equal treatment for all "legal residents"

• Increasing top-down harmonisation of criteria for obtaining "legal residence"

• Compulsory membership to public social insurance schemes ("monopoles sociaux") legitimate only if certain conditions apply

• Patients legally residing in a EU Member State can seek medical care abroad at the expenses of national schemes

• Liberalisation of "second pillar" pension schemes

• Right to industrial action/strike and application of collective agreements challenged if clashing with freedom of movement (Laval, Viking, Rueffert cases)

• Closure rules in higher education challenged if clashing with freedom of movement

---

During the last couple of decades, Member States have been investing a lot of energy in cushioning their social protection systems against challenges stemming from EU law, e.g. by not complying with rulings, agreeing among themselves to change EU law, or even failing to introduce new social programmes that could subsequently become the object of EU Court of Justice (CJEU) action. This may well be one of the reasons why such issues have not yet come to the fore of public debate at EU level and remain confined to restricted insider circles: their potentially disruptive outcomes have so far been (relatively) buffered by Member States' reactions. But how long can this last? What risks are involved in terms of social and political consensus?

The new situation of social "semi-sovereignty" (a term originally coined by Leibfried and Pierson, 1995) has already prompted in recent years a growing politicisation of the "opening" issue and, in some countries more than others, of the integration process as a whole. The most evident manifestation of this politicisation occurred in spring 2005, during the campaigns for the French and Dutch referendums, which rejected the EU Constitutional Treaty (and the Irish referendum on the Lisbon Treaty held in June 2008 confirmed that popular fears about "opening" have certainly not abated). Not surprisingly, questions regarding the social sharing dimension (who shares what, and how much? Is it appropriate for the EU to interfere in such decisions? More crucially still, is the EU undermining national welfare arrangements and labour markets?) have been playing a central role in this process of politicisation, while national governments find themselves increasingly sandwiched between the growing constraints imposed by the EU on the one hand and the national basis of their political legitimacy on the other – a legitimacy which remains highly dependent on decisions in the social protection domain.

As witnessed, again, by the referendum debates, the vast majority of ordinary citizens and a good number of policy-makers think that the growing friction between the welfare state and the EU has or could have an easy solution: the two institutions should be put back on "separate tracks", as they were in the first couple of decades after the Rome Treaty. Anyone that has some familiarity with institutional theory knows, however, better: macro-historical trends cannot be reversed (Pierson, 2004). The welfare state and the EU – which can undoubtedly be regarded as the two most important achievements of the 20th century in Europe – have now encountered each other and are bound to remain on the same track of development: there is no going back to separate tracks. If, as is here argued, the logic of integration does have a high destabilising potential with respect to national social protection, then can we think of ways to mitigate this potential and imagine a strategy of compromise and "institutional reconciliation"?

2.3 A New "Nested" Architecture

Our answer to such question is: "Yes, we can". As mentioned in the Introduction, the key for a successful reconciliation lies in a more explicit and effective "nesting"[4] of the national welfare state within the overall spatial architecture of the EU. Figure 2.1 shows how the nesting between the welfare state and the EU could be achieved. Let us illustrate and discuss the underlying rationale and the various elements of this Figure in some detail[5]

As can be seen, the national welfare state is placed at the very centre of Figure 2.1. For responding to the big social risks of the life-cycle, the broad-based national insurance schemes remain today the most efficient and equitable institutions at our disposal. These schemes must be updated and modernised, of course, in order to respond to a host of endogenous transformations (see below). But they must also be safeguarded as precious instruments to promote distributive equity (the

---

[4] I have discussed the concept of "nesting" and its use in the social sciences in Ferrera (2009).

[5] An earlier version of this Figure is included in Ferrera (2005). I re-propose here a slightly modified version: not only do I still consider it a useful heuristic tool, but my impression is that a number of developments since 2005 have made that nesting scenario more feasible, i.e. have brought it within an easier reach.

"social justice rationale"), cohesion and social consensus (the "legiti-macy rationale") and even a smooth and correct functioning of market transactions (the "economic efficiency" rationale).

Figure 2.1: The nesting of nation-based welfare within the EU

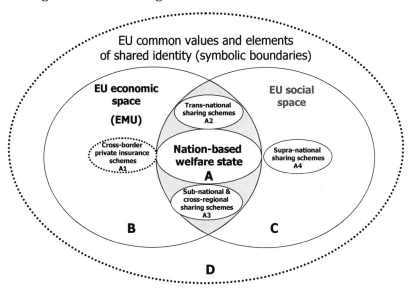

In the wake of half a century of supranational integration, the wel-fare state is already inserted – as shown in the previous section – within the economic spaces of the EU: space B consists of the Economic and Monetary Union (EMU), resting on free movement provisions, competi-tion law, the fiscal rules of the Growth and Stability Pact – and, in the Euro-zone, a common currency and monetary policy. Space B has been the very epicentre of the opening waves of the integration process. We know that such waves were well-meant, so to speak, and that they have brought unquestionable advantages from an economic point of view. The EMU project was elaborated during the 1980s and 1990s in order to respond to the threats of stagnation and Euro-sclerosis, with a view to revamping "growth, competitiveness and employment": the EU Gross Domestic Product (GDP) is now significantly larger than it would have been without enhanced market integration. Liberalisations have made many goods and services more affordable to consumers (let us think of low-cost air fares), increasing the range of options available to them (including cross-border private insurance schemes, as shown by the Figure). In certain areas (e.g. health and safety), market integration has also brought about more consumer protection and higher labour standards. In addition, the tighter coupling between economic integration and national welfare states has prompted several countries to undertake much needed functional and distributive "recalibrations" of their social protection systems (Ferrera and Hemerijck, 2003; Ferrera and Gualmini, 2004).

However, as explained in the previous section, space B has also increasingly become a source of instability for national welfare state programmes: its principles and policies are eroding the foundations of the "nest", i.e. those closure preconditions which are necessary from an institutional and political point of view for sustaining social solidarity over time. As convincingly argued by Fritz Scharpf, this process of erosion is largely driven by decision-making rules that systematically favour negative over positive integration, but is also intensified by a sort of general pro-integration bias on the side of supranational authorities (and in particular the CJEU) "that treats any progress in mobility, non discrimination and the removal of national obstacles to integration as an unmitigated good and an end in itself" (Scharpf, 2009, page 15). In other words, the destabilising pressures of space B are linked to institutional and ideational dynamics that often push the logic of opening well beyond the functional and normative requirements (and overall rationale) of economic integration *per se*.

A strategy of reconciliation thus calls for the formation within the EU architecture of a second circle, which Figure 2.1 calls the EU "social space" and whose main function should be to safeguard or re-construct those institutional preconditions (the "boundary configuration") that underpin domestic sharing arrangements. To be sure, especially after the Amsterdam and Nice Treaties (not to speak of the Lisbon Treaty: see below), various important steps have already been taken in this direction: in space C we now have a Charter of Fundamental Rights, hard laws on some common labour and social security standards and soft laws on employment, social inclusion, pensions as well as healthcare and long-term care. In recent years, the Spring European Councils have also agreed on a number of grand "Pacts"[6] that have reaffirmed the EU's recognition of fundamental social objectives, its commitment to the "caring" dimension of the Union. These are all steps in the right direction, but, as will be argued below, some key and strategic elements are poorly defined or altogether missing. Before discussing what is to be improved, let us however complete the description of the nested architecture of Figure 2.1.

---

[6]   Pact on "Youth policies and youth mainstreaming" (2005); Pact on "Equal opportunities and work-life balance" (2006); and Alliance on "Family policy" (2007).

As mentioned earlier, an institutional reconciliation between the welfare state and the EU implies not only mutual acknowledgement, as it were, but also some mutual concessions. A strengthened Space C can be seen as the concession that the EU makes to the welfare state, recognising the fundamental role played by nation-based sharing programmes in enriching and stabilising citizens' life chances. But the national welfare state must make concessions too. First, it must learn how to live with (and hopefully take advantage of) some of the opening spurs coming from space B – a learning process that seems to be already under way, as we have seen. But the welfare state must also be ready to delegate or transfer some of its traditional social sharing functions to novel post-national forms of risk-pooling and redistribution.

More specifically, Figure 2.1 indicates three new possible types of sharing spaces:

1. trans-national sharing spaces, centred on specific risks and occupational sectors and resting on novel functional alignments;

2. sub- and cross-regional sharing spaces, possibly addressing a plurality of risks or social needs and resting on new territorial alignments; and

3. supranational sharing spaces, i.e. novel redistributive schemes directly anchored to EU institutions and based on EU citizenship (or "denizenship") alone, i.e. without the filter of national institutions and politics.

In the "virtuous nesting" scenario envisaged by the Figure, the spatial architecture of the EU must become more protective of the institutional core of the national welfare state, but at the same time it must make room and encourage innovation and experimentation on each of these three post-national fronts. What kind of institutional reforms, specifically, could be introduced in order to make progress in both directions?

2.4 A More Social EU: Reconfiguring the Patchwork

Let us first address the issue of how to introduce stronger protections for the core social schemes operating at the national level, enabling them to withstand the destabilising challenges originating from space B. As is well known, such challenges rest on the strongest base that the EU constitutional framework can offer: primary law, i.e. explicit and binding Treaty clauses on free movement and competition. In order to be effective, the institutional buffers which must be provided by space C should rest on an equally strong legal basis. Identifying these buffers is far from easy and requires a delicate balancing act. The general goal is however sufficiently clear: the EU constitutional framework (in the wide sense) ought to explicitly define the content and the boundaries of "social protection" as a distinct and relatively autonomous space, and specify the limits of free movement and competition rules in respect of this space.

Ever since the landmark rulings of the CJEU in the 1990s (especially the *Poucet-Pistre* and *Albany* rulings, which had to adjudicate on some foundational questions regarding the balance between "opening" and "closure")[7], we know that this goal has been on the EU agenda: not only the social agenda, but also the wider agenda of broad institutional reform, and some progress has indeed been made. A detailed reconstruction of the winding road of such progress from the Single European Act to the Lisbon Treaty would fall far beyond the scope of this chapter: let us therefore focus on the latter only.

The Treaty on the Functioning of the European Union (TFEU) does contain a series of provisions that could significantly strengthen space C and offer a promising basis for a (more) virtuous nesting between social welfare and economic integration. A highly competitive social market economy, full employment and social progress have been explicitly included amongst the Union's objectives. The coordination of Member States' economic policies and employment policies is now within the sphere of competence of the Union, which allows for the possible coordination of Member States' social policies as well. Fundamental rights have also been explicitly recognised by the Lisbon Treaty through the incorporation of a legally binding reference to the "Nice Charter of Fundamental Rights". The latter contains a section on solidarity, which lists a number of rights and principles directly relevant to the social field, such as the right to information and consultation within undertakings, the right to negotiate collective agreements and to take collective action, the right of access to free placement services and protection against unjustified dismissals, and the right to have access to social security and social assistance. With the new Treaty, the EU has also acceded to the European Convention for the Protection of Human Rights and Fundamental Freedoms, which shall constitute general principles of the Union's law (Article 6).

---

[7]   In the *Poucet-Pistre* joined cases (C-159-91 and C-160-91) the Court had to establish whether the state monopoly over social insurance in France was legitimate according to EU law. In its ruling the Court found that the freedom of service and competition norms could not be invoked to justify exit from mandatory public insurance schemes. In the *Albany* case (C-67-96) the Court had to establish whether a textile company in the Netherlands was obliged to pay the contributions requested by its industrial pension fund, as envisaged by collective agreements. The Court ruled in favour of the pension fund. These cases and the political contexts under which they occurred are reconstructed in detail in Ferrera (2005).

Possibly the most important innovation of the Lisbon Treaty is however the so-called "Horizontal Social Clause" (Article 9), which states that: "In defining and implementing its policies and activities, the Union shall take into account requirements linked to the promotion of a high level of employment, the guarantee of adequate social protection, the fight against social exclusion, and a high level of education, training and protection of human health." It must be added that two other "horizontal clauses" (Articles 8 and 10) extend the scope of what might be called "social mainstreaming" to the reduction of inequality and the fight against discrimination[8]. The horizontal clauses and the recognition of fundamental rights mark the appearance within the EU constitutional arena of two potentially strong anchors that can induce and support all EU institutions (including the Court of Justice of the EU) in the task of finding an adequate (and more stable) balance between economic and social objectives.

There are at least two additional provisions of the Treaty which deserve to be highlighted for their "re-bounding" potential. The first is Protocol 26 on services of general interest, included as an Annex to the TFEU (especially in the wake of Dutch, French and Belgian pressure). Article 2 of this Protocol explicitly says that "the provisions of the Treaties do not affect in any way the competence of Member States to provide, commission and organise non economic services of general interest". As can be immediately appreciated, this is an important statement, that seems to grant to these services a sort of "constitutional" immunity from the opening logic of the integration process and in particular from the competition regime that pervades space B. The article is very short and its wording is not very precise. But, as specified by various European Commission documents (see in particular European Commission, 2008), non economic services of general interest definitely include "social services", which in turn comprise the institutional core (and also some of the periphery) of national welfare programmes, namely: 1) health care; 2) statutory and complementary social security schemes covering the main risks of life; and 3) personal social

---

[8]   Interestingly, the Horizontal Social Clause did not exist in the Treaty establishing the European Community (TEEC), which only dealt with equality between men and women and non discrimination. Article 9 thus represents a genuine "social improvement" achieved during the Intergovernmental Conference, especially in the wake of effective mobilisation of the former members of the Social Europe Working Group of the European Convention (Vandenbroucke, personal communication). It also owes much to the direct efforts of civil society and in particular to EAPN's intervention with the Irish Presidency to highlight the importance of such a clause.

services (such as social assistance, employment and training services, social housing, childcare and long term care services)[9].

The second provision of the Lisbon Treaty that deserves to be highlighted is Article 48 (TFEU). This article (which in "euro-treaty" parlance is known as the "social security emergency brake", a term apparently coined by UK negotiators) recognises to each Member State the right to suspend the adoption of a legislative proposal related to the social entitlements of migrant persons if its implications are considered to negatively affect "important aspects of its social security system, including cost, scope, financial balance or structure". If a Member State requests the suspension, the matter is referred to the European Council where the proposal can be blocked[10]. Under the pre-Lisbon status quo, Member States did have the possibility of ultimately blocking a proposal in this delicate sphere: the co-decision procedure that regulates legislation on the social security rights of migrants envisaged unanimity for Council decisions. But a blockage that can be exerted (or threatened) at the very beginning of a legislative process – as in the new Article 48 procedure – is likely to be much more effective than a blockage that is attempted at its very end, possibly after a lengthy and controversial conciliation process between Parliament and Council. Article 48 is, in other words, a second important innovation of the Lisbon Treaty that puts back into the hands of the nation state some "gating" powers in respect of its own sharing spaces and thus strengthens its capacity to respond to the destabilising potential linked – in this case – to free movement provisions.

---

[9] Steps to formalise such definitions are already under way on the side of the Commission.

[10] The European Council has four months for either referring back the draft legislative proposal to the Council (in which case the ordinary legislative procedure will continue) or requesting the Commission to submit a new proposal (in which case the act originally proposed will be considered as non adopted). There is also a simpler solution for the European Council: "taking no action", which means that the proposed act falls without the need for further initiatives. This simpler option was not envisaged by the Constitutional Treaty and has been inserted during the Lisbon negotiations. A declaration agreed by all Member States specifies that the European Council shall decide "by consensus" in the procedure envisaged by Article 48.

**Box 2.2: Impact assessment in the EU
and the Horizontal Social Clause**

- 2002: The European Commission establishes a new system of integrated Impact Assessment (IA) to consider the effects of policy proposals in their economic, social and environmental dimension

- 2005: Better Regulation Action Plan, European Strategy for Sustainable Employment and Lisbon Strategy adopt IA

- 2009: External evaluation of IA → revision of the guidelines and extension of IA to all legislative initiatives

- 2009: Lisbon Treaty enters into force: Horizontal Social Clause

- 2010: European Court of Auditors presents own evaluation of IA and recommends enhancement and more publicity

- 2010: The Belgian Presidency (2nd semester 2010) launches a debate on strengthening the social dimension within the IA in the wake of the new Horizontal Social Clause (→ generating evidence-based knowledge for its systematic implementation)[11]

The new provisions of the Lisbon Treaty will obviously require time, intellectual and political mobilisation, litigation and jurisprudence in order to become effective as re-balancing tools. But if we compare the current climate with that which prevailed at the time of the Single European Act (SEA) there are some reasons for moderate optimism about the "virtuous nesting" scenario outlined in Figure 2.1. Could more have been achieved with the new Treaty? Certainly, yes: various interesting proposals did in fact emerge during the work of the Convention and the Treaty negotiations (from the constitutionalisation of the Open Method of Coordination (OMC) to the introduction of qualified majority voting for the social issues on which the EU has legislative powers). Without entering into the merit of such proposals, it can be generally said that the goal of reaching a full (or at least quasi-full) symmetry between Economic and Social Europe still remains to be attained[12]. For the time being, the best strategy is that of a full

---

[11] Under the spur of the Belgian Presidency, the EPSCO Council has already started a reflection on strengthening social mainstreaming in the follow up of the Horizontal Social Clause (see http://www.eutrio.be/pressrelease/informal-meeting-epsco-council-social-security-and-social-inclusion).

[12] On the persistent conditions of asymmetry and bold proposals (through political action by the European Council) for breaking the negative integration bias of the EU and in particular the CJEU, see Scharpf, 2009. The European Trade Unions have proposed further amending the Lisbon Treaty with a "Social Progress Protocol" clearly stating that "Nothing in the Treaties and in particular neither economic freedoms nor competition rules shall have priority over fundamental rights (...). In case of conflict

exploitation of the existing building blocks for a better balancing. There are three more obvious critical priorities for moving in this direction. The first and possibly top priority has to do with the new "Horizontal Social Clause" of the Lisbon Treaty, which needs to be clarified in its meaning and scope and made operative as soon as possible, especially by linking it with the already existing procedural framework for the impact assessment of EU policies (see Box 2.2). The clause can serve as a leverage for systematically and transversally identifying and, if possible, quantifying, the social impact of all EU policies, thus encouraging (or even making possible) a better balancing (see discussion in chapter by Kühnemund).

Box 2.3: Workers' rights in the internal market:
Key recommendations of the Monti Report

- Clarify the implementation of the Posting of Workers Directive and strengthen dissemination of information on the rights and obligations of workers and companies, administrative cooperation and sanctions in the framework of free movement of persons and cross-border provision of services

- If measures are adopted to clarify the interpretation and application of the Posting of Workers Directive, introduce a provision to guarantee the right to strike modelled on Article 2 of Council Regulation (EC) No. 2679/98 and a mechanism for the informal solutions of labour disputes concerning the application of the directive.

The second priority is that of working on the Social Protocol and transforming its general principles into more detailed and operational regulations. The third priority is finally the introduction/ strengthening of what might be called the "social complements" of the internal market (Ferrera and Sacchi, 2009), i.e. positive measures that are capable of offsetting the specific negative social implications of free movement and cross-border competition as they clearly manifest themselves (as, for example, in the case of the Laval, Viking and Rueffert rulings of the CJEU, which seem to have challenged three fundamental rights of the modern EU institutional order, i.e. freedom of association, freedom to strike and freedom to establish and enforce collective agreements: see Bueckert and Warner, 2010). Interesting proposals on this front have been recently advanced by Mario Monti's Report on the re-launching of

---

fundamental social rights shall take precedence". See Bueckert and Warner, 2010, pages 143-145.

the internal market, especially as regards the posted workers regime and the right to strike (Monti, 2010: see Box 2.3). It is to be noted that the Monti Report also calls for a strengthening of social evaluation within the European Commission's impact assessment exercises.

But what about the other element of this scenario, i.e. the formation of post-national sharing spaces? On at least two of these fronts some signs of innovation and experimentation are already clearly visible.

As far as trans-national sharing spaces are concerned (space A1 in Figure 2.1), the most significant development is the formation of the so-called "cross-border institutions for occupational retirement provision" (IORPs). An EU directive adopted in 2003 has laid down the legal framework for the establishment of occupational pension funds covering workers of different Member States[13]. Closely linked, as they are, to contributions, second pillar pension schemes incorporate limited amounts of redistribution and solidarity; they still are, nevertheless, recognisable sharing spaces, with the potential for activating a modicum of "bonding" among their affiliates. The Commission's doctrine already counts second pillar pension schemes among "social services of general interest" (European Commission, 2008). A number of cross-border schemes were already operating prior to the 2003 directive, mostly based in the UK. The directive has however given a significant spur to new establishments of this kind. In the years since the implementation of the directive (which entered into force in 2005), the number of cross-border pension schemes has increased from 9 to 61 (Guardiancich, 2009).

These are very new developments on which reliable data are lacking and empirical research is urgently needed. It would thus be imprudent and unwarranted to make bold evaluative statements. For the time being and for the purposes of this chapter, it is sufficient to conclude that the institutional landscape is in flux, that a new phase of trans-national experiments in the field of social protection has clearly dawned and that the EU seems to be providing at least some of the correct incentives and supports.

The same holds true for the other front, that of cross-regional experiments providing jointly some types of services (space A2 in the Figure). Here, especially in the wake of the INTERREG initiatives of the European Commission, a growing number of interesting experiences have been taking place during the last fifteen years, in the context of a wider process of sub-nationalisation of welfare provision within the

---

[13] Directive 2003/41/EC of the European Parliament and the Council of 3 June 2003 "on the activities and supervision of institutions for occupational retirement provision".

domestic arenas and the activation of what has been called "competitive region building" (Keating, 1998; McEwen and Moreno, 2005). Virtually all these experiences include a social policy component, typically in the field of health, employment or care services and all of them have set up permanent institutional structures for the managing and monitoring of cooperation (Pancaldi, 2010). Full use should be made of the potential of the European Grouping for Territorial Cooperation (EGTC), a promising instrument aimed at facilitating economic and social cohesion through cross-border, trans-national or inter-regional initiatives (Regulation 1086/2006). A host of public and non public actors are allowed to join forces and establish the EGTC through direct agreements, within a general legal framework set up by the EU – a framework which recognises the legal personality of the "grouping". Though not exclusively centred on social sharing objectives, this instrument is likely to encourage the coming together of sub-national territories belonging to different Member States and thus open up channels and opportunities for spatial reconfigurations above and beyond the established boundaries of nation states – including their social boundaries (Spinaci and Vara-Arribas, 2009). The Barca Report on the reform of cohesion policies contains several insights and proposals for "place-based" measures and incentives that may facilitate this process, with a view to "socialising" the territorial agenda of the EU as well as "territorialising" the social agenda (Barca, 2009). The place based approach may play an important role also for promoting and underpinning sub-national policies and social agendas. The Europe 2020 Strategy should be improved in this respect, as suggested by the Committee of the Regions (2010) and by Marjorie Jouen in her contribution to the present volume.

Finally, what about innovation and experimentation on the third front of post-national solidarities (space A4 in the Figure), i.e. supranational sharing schemes directly anchored to the EU? The last two decades have indeed witnessed an increasingly richer and imaginative debate on possible institutional "pioneers", such as a pan-European minimum income scheme for the needy (dubbed as Euro-stipendium by Schmitter and Bauer, 2001), a child or birth grant payable to all (or needy) newly born Europeans[14], an "EU minimum income for children" (Atkinson and Marlier, 2010), or the establishment of a supranational social insurance scheme for migrant workers (a proposal originally put

---

[14]   The proposal to establish an EU Capital Grant for Youth was presented by Julian Le Grand at a seminar of the Group of Social Policy Advisors to the European Commission, held in Brussels on 8 September 2006. See Barrington-Leach, Canoy, Hubert and Lerais (2007).

forward in the 1970s under the name of "13th state scheme" and recently resurrected by the French debate) (Lamassoure, 2008)[15].

As is known, a number of redistributive funds are already operative at the supranational level for broad social cohesion purposes. None of these funds and programmes qualifies, however, as a genuine pioneer for supranational social sharing. The fault line that needs to be crossed is that which separates forms of territorial or inter-level redistribution from inter-personal redistribution. Even the last addition to the long list of EU "social policy" funds, the Globalisation Adjustment Fund, has not made this quantum leap, as the Fund does not grant benefits to individual workers, but limits itself to transferring funds to the local-level collective actors that have applied for assistance (Novaczek, 2007). Crossing this critical fault line will not be easy from a political and institutional point of view, as witnessed by the experience of all historical federations in the 20th century (Obinger, Leibfried and Castles, 2005).

A more realistic medium-term target for the consolidation of the EU's social space could be the strengthening of binding regulatory standards and possibly the establishment of some "social snakes" (to use the jargon of the 1970s and 1980s: see Pennings, 2001) forcing the Member States to loosely align themselves to a European "norm" regarding certain areas of social protection. The setting of precise and measurable targets within the Social OMCs (a goal that has already been on the agenda for some time: see European Commission, 2008a) could be the first concrete step in this direction, in the wider framework of the newly launched "Europe 2020" Strategy.

2.5 Europe 2020 and Its Institutional Potential

Europe 2020 must certainly be appreciated as a promising governance tool for the strategy of institutional reconciliation discussed in the previous section. A number of critics at both national and supranational

---

[15] The Monti Report discusses this proposal in respect of occupational pensions and health insurance schemes: "The Commission should prioritise the issue of obstacles to transnational labour mobility in its forthcoming consultation on the pensions systems in Europe. In this context, an option to explore would be to develop a 28th regime for supplementary pension rights. This would be a regime entirely set by EU rules but existing in parallel to national rules, and thus optional for companies and workers. A worker opting for this regime would be subject to the same rules for its non statutory benefits wherever it goes in Europe. To make things easier, a sub-option would be to limit the possibility to opt in this regime only to workers taking up their first work contract. This would serve as an incentive for the mobility of certain young workers, who are the keenest on international mobility." (Monti, 2010, page 57).

level have already started to dismiss it as "cheap talk", taking it for granted that it is doomed to the same destiny of (alleged) failure of its soft and wet predecessor, the Lisbon Strategy[16]. As noted by other contributors to this volume, such sweeping negative judgements are definitely unwarranted: programmatic pessimism is itself "cheap". To begin with, significant empirical evidence signals that the Lisbon Strategy has not been a failure, even acknowledging its many shortcomings and limitations, especially in respect of its over-ambitious original goals (see chapter by Natali). The impact of Lisbon is clearly detectable also as regards employment and social objectives (Heidenreich and Zeitlin, 2009). More importantly, Europe 2020 does contain some significant improvements compared to Lisbon on the specific front which interests us, namely the relationship between Economic and Social EU.

First, there is improvement at the ideational level (which is anything but "cheap" in political matters). As it clearly emerges from all the "soft" and "hard" acts that have launched the new strategy, its overall blueprint for a "smart, sustainable and inclusive growth" offers a wealth of normative and functional justifications for both the protection ("nesting", in our language) and the ameliorative recalibration of the nation-based welfare state. In line with a vast literature, we have noted above that welfare programmes are in urgent need of modernisation and updating in the wake of the changed structure of risks and needs (in particular demographic ageing). Three out of the seven so-called flagship initiatives ("Youth on the move", an "Agenda for skill and jobs", and in particular the "European platform against poverty") of Europe 2020 are geared towards this task and, if correctly developed and articulated, can provide precious ideational resources for national "puzzling" around welfare reform. A significant step forward in respect of Lisbon is that the Europe 2020 Integrated Guidelines for the annual cycles of the strategy will integrate the economic policy and the employment policy dimensions and – via the latter – the social policy dimension as well (see opening chapter). Guideline 10 is entirely devoted to "promoting social inclusion and combating poverty", with the headline target that will consist of "promoting social inclusion, in particular through the reduction of poverty by aiming to lift at least 20 million people out of the risk of poverty and exclusion" (based on three indicators: poverty risk, severe material deprivation and very low work attachment)[17]. Needless to say, the ideational component of Europe 2020 will be able to make a difference only if accompanied by a deliberate strategy of

---

[16] A good source for the Europe 2020 debate is Euroarchiv (www.euroarchiv.com).

[17] The significance of this guideline is discussed in this volume by Daly and by Frazer and Marlier; on the issues raised by targets, see also chapter by Walker.

both "communicative" and "coordinative" discourse on the part of EU institutions, the Commission in particular[18].

Second, there is improvement at the practical, operational level. The addition of "thematic coordination" to the overall governance of the strategy (i.e. focussed monitoring on growth enhancing reforms, including welfare state modernisation, with the possibility of issuing recommendations based on Article 148 not only on employment but also "other selected thematic issues", presumably including social policies), the launch of the European semester, the institutional re-location and procedural refinement of the Social OMC: these are all promising innovations that can contribute to a more effective "nested" delivery of the strategy's array of policies. It is to be noted that the Horizontal Social Clause has already played a role in fostering and underpinning the operational definition of Europe 2020, especially as regards the enhancement of horizontal coordination and mainstreaming of the Lisbon common social objectives – which will be hopefully firmed up and articulated through pertinent indicators.

Referring back to Figure 2.1: Europe 2020 does seem to have the adequate institutional potential for steering the Union's architecture towards a more virtuous nesting, both between nation-based welfare and its wider supranational spaces and between space B (economic Europe) and space C (social Europe). Acknowledging the potential of Europe 2020 does not mean, of course, that the strategy has no weaknesses – both substantive and procedural – that ought to be addressed (as recommended by all the chapters of this book). With appropriate "institutional gardening" in the years to come, coupled with some political ambition, imagination, and consensus-building, Europe 2020's social agenda could be used to lay the conditions not only for creating a somewhat stringent social snake binding Member States to remain within certain quantitative "bands" after reaching the headline targets (e.g. in terms of social inclusion levels) but also for establishing a fully fledged "EU system of social protection" consisting of coordinated and correctly nested national, sub-national and post-national sharing spaces.

2.6 Conclusion

The national welfare state and the EU are probably the most salient and distinctive institutional legacies that the 20th century has bequeathed to our continent: two institutions that have given an invaluable contribu-

---

[18] According to Vivien Schmidt, discourse is the interactive process of conveying ideas throughout a political system. It comes in two forms: the coordinative discourse among policy actors and the communicative discourse between political actors and the public (Schmidt, 2006).

tion to enriching and expanding the life chances of millions of ordinary people, in a context of economic growth, social security, cohesion and peace. The 21st century has however opened with some turbulence and tension regarding, precisely, the mutual relationship between these two institutions. As argued in the previous sections, this tension ought to (and can) be contained. The search for a strategy of institutional reconciliation must become a top priority for the political agenda and the most promising point of departure should be a rapid definitional and procedural "operationalisation" of the Horizontal Social Clause, in parallel with a cleared definition of the scope and legal implications of the Social Protocol. The challenge ahead of us is that of imagining and then engaging in the actual construction of a recognisable EU social model: not just and generically "European", but a distinctive "EU" social model, resting on a well-designed and protective nesting of social sharing goals and practices (including nation-based practices) within the overall legal framework of the Union. The prime institutional rationale behind this new model should be that of promoting a virtuous and dynamic balance between the logic of opening and the logic of closure, in order to effectively underpin the self-sustaining production of both individual opportunities and social "bonds", i.e. the two sides of life chances European style.

References

Atkinson, A.B. and Marlier, E. (editors) (2010), *Income and living conditions in Europe*, Chapter 1 in Atkinson, A.B. and Marlier, E. *Income and living conditions in Europe*, Luxembourg: Office for Official Publications of the European Communities (OPOCE).

Barca, F. (2009), *An agenda for a reformed cohesion policy: A place-based approach to meeting European Union challenges and expectations*, Independent Report prepared at the request of Danuta Hübner, Commissioner for Regional Policy, Brussels: European Commission. Available at: http://ec.europa.eu/regional_policy/policy/future/pdf/report_barca_v0306.pdf.

Barrington-Leach, L., Canoy, M., Hubert, A. and Lerais, F. (2007), *Investing in youth: An empowerment strategy*, Brussels: European Commission, Bureau of European Policy Advisers.

Bueckert, A. and Warner, W. (2010), *Viking-Laval-Rueffert: Consequences and Policy Perspectives*, Brussels: European Trade Union Institute.

Committee of the Regions (2010), *Consultation: Your Voice on Europe 2020: Final Report*, Brussels: Committee of the Regions. Available at: http://portal.cor.europa.eu/europe2020/news/Documents/Your%20Voice%20on%20Europe%202020%20Final%20Report.pdf.

European Commission (2008), *Biennial Report on Social Services of General Interest*, SEC 2179/2, Brussels: European Commission.

European Commission (2008a), *Commission Recommendation on the active inclusion of people excluded from the labour market*, Brussels: European Commission.

Ferrera, M. (2009), "The JCMS Annual Lecture: National Welfare States and European Integration: In Search of a 'Virtuous Nesting'", *Journal of Common Market Studies*, Volume 47, 2: 219-233.

Ferrera, M. (2005), *The Boundaries of Welfare. European Integration and the New Spatial Politics of Social Protection*, Oxford: Oxford University Press.

Ferrera, M. and Gualmini, E. (2004), *Rescued by Europe*, Amsterdam: Amsterdam University Press.

Ferrera, M. and Hemerijck, A. (2003), "Recalibrating European Welfare Regimes", in J. Zeitlin and D.M. Trubeck (editors) *Governing Work and Welfare in A New Economy*, Oxford: Oxford University Press.

Ferrera, M. and Sacchi, S. (2009), "A More Social EU: Issues of Where and How", in S. Micossi and G.L. Tosato (editors) *The European Union in the 21ˢᵗ Century. Perspectives from the Lisbon Treaty*, Brussels: Centre for European Policy Studies.

Flora, P. with Kuhnle, S. and Urwin, D. (editors) (1999), *State Formation, Nation Building and Mass Politics in Europe: the Theory of Stein Rokkan*, Oxford: Oxford University Press.

Fouarge, D (2003), *Costs of Non-Social Policies. Towards an Economic Framework of Quality Social Policy and the Costs of Not Having Them*, Brussels, Report prepared for the Employment and Social Affairs DG. Available at: http://www.temaasyl.se/Documents/ETG/Cost%20Of%20Non%20 Social%20Policy.pdf.

Gilpin, R. (1987), *The political economy of international relations*, Princeton: Princeton University Press.

Giubboni, S. (2006), *Social Rights and Market Freedom in the European Constitution: A Labour Law Perspective*, Cambridge: Cambridge University Press.

Guardiancich (2009), *Report on Cross-Border IORPs: The Implications for the Creation of Pan-European Pension Plans of Directive 2003/41/EC of the European Parliament and of the Council of 3 June 2003 on the Activities and Supervision of Institutions for Occupational Retirement Provision (IORP Directive)*, Department of Labour and Welfare Studies, University of Milan, mimeo.

Heidenreich, M. and Zeitlin, J. (editors) (2009), *Changing European Employment and Welfare Regimes: The Influence of the Open Method of Coordination on National Reforms*, London: Routledge.Keating, M. (1998), *The New Regionalism in Western Europe: Territorial Restructuring and Political Change*, Cheltenham: Edward Elgar.

Lamassoure, A. (2008), *Le citoyen et l'application du droit communautaire*, Paris: La Documentation Française.

Leibfried, S. and Pierson, P. (editors) (1995), *European Social Policy between Fragmentation and Integration*, Washington D.C.: Brookings Institution.

Marshall, T.H. (1950), *Citizenship and Social Class and Other Essays*, Cambridge: Cambridge University Press.

Martinsen, D.S. (2005), "The Europeanization of Welfare: the Domestic Impact of Intra-European Social Security", *Journal of Common Market Studies*, Vol. 43, 5: 1027-1054.

Martinsen, D. S. (2005a), "Social Security Regulation in the EU: the De-Territorialisation of Welfare?" in G. de Búrca *EU Law and the Welfare State: in Search of Solidarity*, Oxford: Oxford University Press.

McEwen, N. and Moreno, L. (editors) (2005), *The Territorial Politics of Welfare*, London: Routledge.

Milward, A. (2000), *The European Rescue of the Nation State*, London: Routledge, second edition.

Monti, M (2010), *A New Strategy for the Single Market*. Available at: http://ec.europa.eu/bepa/pdf/monti_report_final_10_05_2010_en.pdf.

Novaczek, K. (2007), "The European Globalization Adjustment Fund: A Social Pilot Project between Political and Economic Realms", *European Governance*, Vol. 1, 1: 21-24. Available at: http://www.urge.it/eg.html# publications.

Obinger, H., Leibfried, S. and Castles, F. (editors) (2005), *Federalism and the Welfare State. New World and European Experiences*, Cambridge: Cambridge University Press.

Pancaldi, F. (2010), *The Spaces Between. Interregional Cooperation in the EU: evidence on Cross-border Social Policies*, Milan, Graduate School of Social, Economic and Political Studies, WP 1/2010.

Pennings, F. (2001), *Introduction to European Social Security Law*, The Hague: Kluwer.

Pierson, P. (2004), *Politics in Time. History, Institutions and Social Analysis*, Princeton: Princeton University Press.

Scharpf, F. (2009), "Legitimacy in the Multi-level European Polity", *European Political Science Review*, Vol. 1, 2:173-204.

Schmidt, V. (2006), *Democracy in Europe*, Oxford: Oxford University Press.

Schmitter, P.C. and Bauer, M.W. (2001), "A (modest) proposal for expanding social citizenship in the European Union", *Journal of European Social Policy*, Vol. 11, 1: 55-66.

Spinaci, G. and Vara-Arribas (2009), *The European Grouping of Territorial Cooperation (EGTC): New Spaces and Contact for European Integration?*, Maastricht, Eipascope 2009/2.

Weiler, J.H.H. (1999), *The Constitution of Europe*, Cambridge: Cambridge University Press.

3. Aftershock: The Coming Social Crisis in the EU and What Is to Be Done

Roger LIDDLE and Patrick DIAMOND[1],
with Simon LATHAM and Tom BRODIE

3.1 Introduction

The focus of this chapter is on the social aftershocks of the economic crisis of 2008-2009. This crisis will have fundamental implications for the future of the European Union (EU). It has called into question the political economy of the preceding two decades. Not only has it knocked the "Anglo-Social model"[2] (Dixon and Pearce, 2005) of a once elevated pedestal that now appears to have distinctly weak foundations. It has simultaneously thrown the Eurozone into turmoil, exposing fault lines in its governance that raise doubts about the Euro's long term viability as presently constituted. In redrawing the boundaries between states and markets, the crisis is initiating a major structural transformation of the EU economy, throwing up new social challenges for the EU in the decades ahead.

Section 3.2 discusses the nature of this crisis and highlights the links between three central framing arguments of the chapter: the multidimensional nature of the crisis, the challenge it poses to solidarity and the present ambiguity of EU integration. The first framing argument is that current crisis aftershocks originate not just in the financial sector crash itself, but in long term structural trends relating both to profound social changes in the life expectations, aspirations and risks that EU citizens are experiencing as well as the changing shape of the productive economy in the West, in part as a result of globalisation. These pose major long term challenges that have not gone away. For example, coping with the public spending consequences of an ageing demogra-

---

[1] Addresses for correspondence: rliddle@policy-network.net and pdiamond@policy-network.net.

[2] "Anglo-Social" was first coined by Nick Pearce to describe how the New Labour policies of public intervention and social inclusivity were modifying the Anglo-American, Thatcherite model which aimed for a purer form of capital, product and labour market flexibility.

phy, or tackling climate change, may prove as big a fiscal challenge as the present need for consolidation to reduce indebtedness. The second of our framing arguments is that these aftershocks in combination put social and economic inequality back at the centre of the public policy agenda, alongside the emerging problems of the "squeezed middle". This forces a reassessment of the strengths and weaknesses of the pre-crisis policy consensus based on the Lisbon agenda principles: more flexible labour markets, higher employment participation, social investment and getting a job as the best answer to poverty. This is not to say these principles are wrong, but they certainly need refinement as experience suggests that social investment strategies for welfare reform will only work when combined with more effective regulatory intervention.

The third framing argument concerns what the authors see as the ambiguity of the EU's own role in this social crisis: how on the one hand, the existing path of EU integration might be intensifying the social challenge and on the other, the potential of the EU to present itself as a positive strategic actor, facilitating the return of EU's economy and welfare regimes to stability and good health. For at present EU's economic policy response highlights the zero sum risks of Member States seeking to gain competitive advantage against each other through a brand of welfare nationalism which transmutes into a "race to the bottom" in social standards.

Section 3.3 amplifies the multidimensional nature of the crisis. The paper argues that it is not just one crisis that the EU faces, but five interlocking social crises: rising unemployment and the social consequences of the global financial crash; the long-term crisis of winners and losers that originates in economic globalisation; the structural trends of demography and rising life expectancy that bear down on the welfare state; the impact of migration, integration and identity on social citizenship and cohesion; and growing divergence throughout the EU, as countries seek alternative paths to entrenching macro-economic stability and coping with new structural pressures.

Section 3.4 expands on the role of the EU in these aftershocks. It highlights the present trade offs between economic integration and a socially inclusive modernisation (not a retrenchment) of EU's welfare states and considers how a strengthening of the EU's social dimensions might help resolve these tensions. It argues that a Euro-Keynesian solution is both simplistic and unrealistic as individual Member States need to pursue distinctive reform strategies in order to improve their resilience in coping with present challenges and future social risks. However, the EU as a whole needs to develop a new policy paradigm based on a combination of social investment and regulatory intervention, the implementation of which requires both policy reforms within Member States and action at EU level.

Section 3.5 concludes with some pointers to how improved policy action and coordination at EU level could provide a more favourable structural context for the evolution of social reforms and how, following Ferrera's argument in this volume, the development of the EU "social space", through for example the poverty target agreed by the European Council in June 2010, could provide some safeguard against a destructive "race to the bottom".

3.2 The Multidimensional Nature of the Crisis, the Challenge It Poses to Solidarity and the Present Ambiguity of EU Integration

In the wake of the crash, intellectual and political attention has unsurprisingly focused on immediate crisis management, in particular restoring stability and resilience to the financial sector and handling the rise in public indebtedness. But major questions about the sustainability of EU social protection regimes and the models of capitalism which underpin them, still remain unanswered.

The term "crisis" remains somewhat nebulous and should be used within a specific structural context. It is clear that every major crisis has a political dimension, as well as an economic one (Gamble, 2009). We use the term crisis to denote major adjustments in existing institutions and policy regimes as the result of new structural forces and pressures. Crises are not only moments of catastrophe, but create unprecedented opportunities for social and economic reform. Of course, the current crisis has thrown up many challenges, but it also presents a window in which to transform the existing social and economic order. It needs to be acknowledged, however, that crises do not necessarily lead to major ideological and political shifts. There is always the possibility that the previous order will be restored, in this instance the neo-liberal order that prevailed prior to the financial crisis in 2008-2009. In particular the leadership of Germany, which has been forced reluctantly by events once again to assume the role of economic hegemony within the Eurozone, and for the moment is itself basking comfortably in an export boom, may well believe that tighter financial regulation, tougher fiscal rules and better crisis management capabilities will be sufficient in themselves to resolve the problems with the current EU economic and social order. The reforms we argue for in this chapter are therefore not inevitably bound to happen: they will require a significant change in the prevailing orthodoxy.

The present structural context of the EU makes the term "aftershock" just as appropriate as the notion of "crisis": EU countries are confronted by the prospect of a series of aftershocks that will delay or even jeopardise the recovery, and constrain the options available to governments in the future (Proissl, 2010). Unless concrete steps are taken to deal with the fall-out of after-shocks, EU's ability to overcome the social impact of the global financial crash will be seriously impaired.

The first of our three central framing arguments is that the aftershocks of the current crisis originate in long-term structural trends relating to demography, life expectancy, globalisation, and the changing shape of the productive economy in the West, not just the financial sector crash itself. These trends are clearly visible in all the Member States of the old EU15, despite the diversity of their "social models". They also have relevance in the EU27 despite the much wider differences in living standards and stages of economic development within the EU which have been the consequence of the 2004 and 2007 enlargements. In some respects these trends have been exacerbated by the global shocks of 2008-2009, which in particular have underlined the global shift in economic power away from the EU and the rest of the developed world, as shown by the remarkable recent resilience of the emerging Asian economies since the crisis. By contrast, within the EU, the shock to growth and the public spending consequences of the resulting need for fiscal consolidation will make it even harder to address long-term social and economic challenges. For example some estimates of the scale of the fiscal challenge posed by EU's ageing demography suggests that this could be as large as the formidable scale of fiscal consolidation ultimately required in several Member States as a result of the financial crisis.[3] Equally significant is the long term challenge of tackling climate change. The failure of the Copenhagen Summit and the impact of the economic crisis itself, in reducing, then delaying the upward path of carbon emissions, have reduced the immediate political pressure for action. But it is inconceivable that climate change will not at some stage burst back into prominence as a policy priority. And there will be major public finance implications. While the EU could do far more to set a more robust economic framework of carbon pricing that would incentivise private actors to invest in carbon reduction, major infrastructure investments will require at the minimum costly public guarantees and welfare states will face a new challenge in ameliorating the impact of much higher energy prices on the poor (Giddens, 2009; Liddle and Latham, 2009).

---

[3] DG ECFIN in conjunction with the ECOFIN Council carried out a series of detailed studies on the fiscal consequences of the ageing society in the mid-2000s.

Many EU governments have struggled to implement immediate crisis management measures and have had to deal with the fall-out of the sovereign debt crisis. In the meantime, hastily conceived fiscal austerity measures are beginning to bite. The danger is that during an era of serious fiscal retrenchment, existing welfare policy regimes will be frozen as governments struggle to reassure citizens and protect people from the adverse consequences of the crisis. It is precisely at this moment, however, that reform is needed most, not only to manage new financial pressures, but to make welfare states more resilient for the future and prevent the crisis from further damaging the life-chances of the least advantaged in society.

The second central framing argument is that crisis aftershocks put social and economic inequality back at the centre of the public policy agenda. Recently, unequal societies were purported to do far worse on a range of important social indicators including crime rates, public health, educational achievement, work-life balance, personal well-being, and so on (Wilkinson and Pickett, 2009). There is much debate among experts as to whether inequality is generally on a rising long term trend in the EU, as opposed to there having just been episodic shocks that have led to large increases in inequality within (some) Member States. Tony Atkinson in examining trends in inequality in Europe has argued, for example, that a large rise in inequality in the United Kingdom occurred in the late 1980s and can be explained by the combined impact of labour market reforms, a big rise in worklessness and discretionary tax changes favourable to the better off, returning the UK to levels of inequality not seen since before the Second World War.[4] By comparison, the position has been relatively stable since, despite the Labour Government successes between 1997-2010 in reducing poverty among families with children and old people (Joyce *et al.*, 2010). In a 2010 study of "Income and Living Conditions in Europe", Atkinson and Marlier conclude that while "it is widely believed that income inequality was increasing globally prior to the economic crisis (...) the EU-SILC[5] data suggest that the EU picture is more nuanced, with some Member States exhibiting declining inequality" (Chapters 1 and 5 in Atkinson and Marlier, 2010). It is however the case that the at-risk of poverty rate is closely correlated with the degree of income inequality (as measured by the S80/S20 ratio and the Gini coefficient). Also there is no data yet available on what has happened to inequality since the crisis broke, though one can reasonably presume that the overall impact of spending cuts will be harsher on poorer households than the better off.

---

[4] Sir Tony Atkinson made this argument in paper for the DG ECFIN Economics Conference in 2008.

[5] "EU-SILC" stands for EU Statistics on Income and Living Conditions.

The inequality debate has in recent years become broader than the traditional focus on economic inequality and the relationship between the top and bottom of the distribution. A new focus in the debate relates to the stagnation of the "squeezed middle" and the downward pressure on wages created both by globalisation, and internally-driven pressures such as deregulatory labour market reforms undertaken with the objective of "making work pay" and raising employment participation rates (Hans Boeckler Stiftung, 2006). The relative position of low skilled men in jobs at the margin of the labour market appears to have declined. The impact on household incomes of these trends will in part have been offset by the widespread sharp rise in female employment participation in the last decade, for example in Germany, though a large gender pay gap still adversely affects the position of women in the labour force in many Member States.

The question of inequality cannot be separated from the wider debate about the nature of capitalism in the West, which in the UK has led to a revival of interest among economic and social commentators in the German coordinated social market economy regime. Also throughout the crisis, the globally-orientated Nordic social democracies have continued to be successful in combining efficiency and equity, though Sweden has experienced particularly high youth unemployment.

The final argument of the chapter concerns the capacity of the EU to present itself as the strategic actor best placed to deal with the fall-out of crisis aftershocks, and help facilitate the return of EU's economy and welfare regimes to stability and good health. This optimistic view of the EU's potential role underestimates the extent to which the EU itself has accentuated the scale of the social challenges facing the EU principally through the dynamics of the internal market. Combined with EU enlargement, the single market has contributed to the increasingly adverse fortunes of the lowly skilled in the labour market and the erosion of labour standards. There is also the issue of whether the established EU policy framework, with its emphasis on fiscal discipline, national competitiveness and labour market reforms has contributed to the rise of zero sum competition between Member States. Whereas before the crisis social policy experts imagined that membership of the EU contributed to a positive "race to the top" dynamic for its national welfare states, the real impact of the crisis has been to exacerbate economic and social divergence in the EU, as Member States find themselves with widely differing room for manoeuvre and therefore seek different remedies to the challenges presented by the crisis. The ethic of solidarity between EU countries is weakened as a result. The very legitimacy of the EU as a social and political actor is put in question. These issues are more fully debated in Ferrera's contribution to this volume which points out how national welfare states within the EU operate both within a clearly defined "EU economic space" and a more imprecise "EU social space". The parameters of this social space could now be strengthened, not least as the practical application unfolds of the new social provisions of the Lisbon Treaty through its Horizontal Social Clause, the Social Protocol covering "services of general economic interest" and the incorporation of the Charter of Fundamental Rights.

This raises the question of what the common principles of solidarity are that should mould a collective EU approach in future and what concrete steps might be taken by the EU institutions. Proposals on this theme are contained in the contributions to this volume by Frazer and Marlier on ensuring a stronger approach in the new Europe 2020 Strategy and by Vanhercke in his review of the Social OMC's adequacy and impact. While the authors of this chapter recognise the importance of these policy initiatives, we advocate a broader brush approach: what is needed in the EU is a new model of social investment and regulatory intervention. The social investment paradigm as developed by policy-makers in the last decade has rightly focused on making pro-active contributions to human and social capital, instead of relying on the passive income redistribution mechanisms of the post-war welfare state. However this strategic approach did not sufficiently acknowledge that the success of social policy itself rests on how effectively national governments and international institutions are able to regulate global capital, labour and product markets. Investment in training or education programmes, for example, cannot protect disadvantaged citizens from the impact of financial shocks that lead to the drying up of capital, and weaken public provision by depriving governments of tax revenues.

One of the central lessons of the crisis, particularly in countries such as Britain, Ireland, and Spain, is that social policy cannot adequately compensate for the effects of models of capitalism that tend to strongly amplify inequality and risk. This is also a lesson for some of the new Member States, for example the Baltics. In the future, social investment and regulatory intervention have to be seen as two sides of the same coin. Social policy has to operate within the context of robust regulation of markets, instead of relying solely on the *post hoc* cushioning provided by the central state. A deregulated financial sector, for example, will impair social investment, as well as the resilience and stability of the wider economy. In tackling the crisis aftershocks analysed in this article, social policy has to help shape market outcomes as a positive productive factor, instead of seeking only to correct adverse consequences after the event. This clearly has implications for how the EU conceives its future policy for the Single Market, not simply as an instrument of liberalisation and deregulation, but as a common set of rules designed to combine greater economic efficiency with better social outcomes.

3.3 The Multidimensional Nature of the Crisis

To understand the full implications of the crisis, one has to distinguish between five interlocking aftershocks which are at work.

3.3.1 Aftershock I: Rising unemployment and the social consequences of the financial crisis

An immediate consequence of the financial crisis has been the increase in Eurozone unemployment, which currently stands at 10%. This reverses the progress made in reducing unemployment from 2004 to 2008 when the EU was more successful than the United States in creating new jobs.[6] However, one of the positive features of the current crisis is that in the core EU countries – Britain, France and Germany – unemployment has risen significantly slower than was forecast. This suggests that government-led labour market interventions and stimulus policies have in the short term been effective. A good example is the German subsidy to support temporary short time working. However despite these positive interventions, the diverse impact of unemployment on national labour markets in the EU is reflected in its diverging severity across Member States. Averages mask a deeper malaise in some Member States. Contrast Spain that suffers from over 20% unemployment or Estonia from 18.6%, with the figure in Germany at 6.9%. Even in France, unemployment is much lower at 9.6%[7]; the rate in Austria is only 3.8%.[8] There is a clear contrast between the core of the Eurozone and a periphery of countries in which there are severe problems. This raises the question of how unemployment is affecting social and geopolitical cohesion among various age groups and Member States within the Eurozone.

Crucially, the young are disproportionately affected. Across the EU, youth unemployment (defined as ages 15-24) stands at 19.6%, rising to 41.5% in Spain and 39.5% in Latvia.[9] The Netherlands is the only

---

[6] http://epp.eurostat.ec.europa.eu/statistics_explained/index.php/Unemployment statistics#Youth_unemployment_trends_in_Europe.

[7] http://epp.eurostat.ec.europa.eu/cache/ITY_PUBLIC/3-31082010-BP/EN/3-3108 2010-BP-EN.PDF

[8] http://www.bbc.co.uk/news/business-11138110.

[9] http://epp.eurostat.ec.europa.eu/cache/ITY_PUBLIC/3-31082010-BP/EN/3-31082 010-BP-EN.PDF.

Member State whose youth unemployment is ranked below 10%.[10] The severe impact of the crisis on the young raises major social concerns about the long term "scarring" effects of youth unemployment as well as the loss of productive potential for the future.

Similarly, unemployment has increased faster amongst workers on temporary contracts than those with permanent positions. The Spanish case is the most extreme. In 2009, fixed term employment fell by a staggering 35% in the Spanish construction sector, while at the same time the country's permanent workers' wages actually increased by 4%.[11] This suggests that the pattern of rising unemployment and its social impact in the immediate aftermath of the financial crisis reflects the existence of two-tier labour markets where those at the margins have proved most vulnerable. But this has been offset in those countries unlike Spain that have enjoyed the fiscal policy space to intervene directly to save jobs. Clearly however, in the second round of the crisis, where measures are now being taken to execute "exit strategies" from public indebtedness, the social consequences will differ greatly in scale and social impact as Member States face a wide divergence of fiscal challenges. A central indicator is how levels of public debt vary between Member States. In 2009, Ireland's budget deficit was 14.3% of GDP and Spain's 11.2%, but in contrast Germany's was only 3.3%, and Austria's 3.4%.[12] The imperative of fiscal consolidation varies widely.

Whereas the UK government is committed to £113 billion of savings over the next four years,[13] the current "masochistic" reductions in Ireland's debt as a proportion of GDP would amount in equivalent terms to 150 billion sterling[14] and the Irish now face the need for a second round of cuts. Meanwhile, the scale of the UK Coalition Government's onslaught on the national budget is itself significantly more ferocious than the German government's austerity regime. Germany is a larger economy than the UK, with over 20 million more citizens. The German government has announced 80 billion Euros of cuts over 4 years[15] – equivalent only to £67 billion in sterling terms. Moreover, while the German government intends to cut 15,000 public sector jobs over the

[10] http://epp.eurostat.ec.europa.eu/statistics_explained/index.php/Unemployment _statistics#Youth_unemployment_trends_in_Europe.

[11] http://www.voxeu.com/index.php?q=node/5289.

[12] http://www.bbc.co.uk/news/10150007.

[13] http://www.bbc.co.uk/news/10390823.

[14] http://www.guardian.co.uk/world/2010/may/26/ireland-economic-collapse.

[15] http://www.independent.co.uk/news/world/europe/germany-pledges-record-euro80bn-of-budget-cuts-1994087.html.

next four years,[16] while the UK government anticipates a cull close to a staggering 500,000 by 2015 on current projections.[17]

Despite these differences, common themes do emerge across the EU. Welfare spending on transfer payments is being cut in many Member States, though there are exceptions so far such as Belgium. For example, 30 billion Euros have been slashed from the budget in Germany,[18] with parents on unemployment benefits losing their entitlement to *Elterngeld* of 300 Euros a month.[19] In the UK, 11 billion pounds of cuts to benefits have been announced, with another 4 billion planned.[20] Commentators have noted that the predominant impact of the welfare changes so far announced will be on poor families with children, despite the Coalition Government's commitment to tackle child poverty. 760 million Euros are being cut from social welfare in the Republic of Ireland.[21] Further major cuts are expected in the December 2010 EU budget as Ireland has agreed with the EU to reduce spending in 2011 by a minimum of 3 billion Euros, though there is every chance this could become a considerably higher figure. These cuts tend to fall on the most politically marginalised; above all, they affect the young much more than the electorally influential elderly. It is telling that the UK government, for example, has displayed great caution in cutting funding for the National Health Service (NHS), free travel cards for the elderly and the winter fuel allowance. The danger is that fiscal retrenchment will reinforce the elderly bias that has predominated in Western welfare state regimes (Esping-Andersen, 2009).

3.3.2 Aftershock II: The long-term globalisation crisis of "winners" and "losers"

Greater divergence *between* Member States at the macroeconomic level is accompanied by the increasing polarisation of labour markets between "winners" and "losers" *within* Member States. The labour market has been increasingly hollowed out, squeezing real wages for those in the middle and low deciles of the wage distribution, as Maarten Goos and Alan Manning's cogently argue in their seminal work, *Lousy and Lovely Jobs* (Goos and Manning, 2007). Since the 1990s, employment as a share of the total workforce has declined by more than 7.5%, while the share of both low- and high-skilled jobs increased (Goos

---

[16] http://www.thelocal.de/money/20100608-27715.html.
[17] http://www.bbc.co.uk/news/10457352.
[18] http://www.alertnet.org/thenews/newsdesk/LDE65625L.htm.
[19] http://www.thelocal.de/money/20100608-27715.html.
[20] http://www.bbc.co.uk/news/uk-politics-11287172.
[21] http://www.bbc.co.uk/news/10162176.

et al., 2009). Lower skilled workers are also increasingly vulnerable to the threat of redundancy and unemployment. While 84% of highly skilled Europeans have a job, more than half of low-skilled workers are currently unemployed.[22] In France, 72% of those with Bac+2 qualifications have full time jobs, whilst the figure for those without a diploma is 43%.[23] Downward pressure on wages and fear of unemployment have heightened economic insecurity for those on lower and middle incomes, compounded by the growth of income volatility. Across the OECD, median income households experience much sharper changes in incomes over time than was the case thirty years ago (OECD, 2008).

While the poorest 10% of the UK population have on average seen a fall in their real incomes over the previous decade, after deducting housing costs[24] and the wealthiest 10% by contrast have seen much larger proportional rises in income than other social groups,[25] the interesting development in the last decade is how those in the middle of the income distribution have lagged behind as well. Overall, wage share as a proportion of national income has declined sharply since 1980 in the EU15, Japan and the United States, implying that average wages have failed to keep pace with labour productivity. In seventeen out of twenty countries in the survey, earnings at the top of the wage distribution rose sharply relative to those at the bottom after the early 1990s. There is also evidence of higher levels of income volatility and wage instability in the major industrialised countries (OECD, 2008).

The City of London appears to be recovering rapidly from the initial impact of the financial crisis, with the return of extravagant bonuses (£6.8 billion forecast for 2010[26]) and even a return to the irrational exuberance of the boom decade in the late 1990s.[27] There were twice as many financial sector job vacancies in the spring of 2010 than the previous year,[28] in stark contrast to the 50% fall in the UK manufacturing sector (Diamond and Liddle, 2009). The decline of "good working class jobs" is grimly illustrated by the rise in poverty rates among households where both parents are working: in 1999, 40% of children classed as living in poverty came from families with at least one working parent; by 2009, this had increased to 50%.[29] In Germany, the

---

[22] http://www.dw-world.de/dw/article/0,5218569,00.html.

[23] http://understandingsociety.blogspot.com/2009/03/inequalities-in-france.html.

[24] http://www.poverty.org.uk/09/index.shtml.

[25] http://www.guardian.co.uk/money/2010/jan/27/pensioners-poverty-ons-inequality.

[26] http://www.guardian.co.uk/business/2010/apr/23/city-bonuses-forecast-to-rise.

[27] http://www.guardian.co.uk/business/2009/nov/01/city-parties-again.

[28] http://www.ft.com/cms/s/0/ad3deabe-5df5-11df-8153-00144feab49a.html.

[29] http://campaigns.dwp.gov.uk/asd/asd5/rports2009-2010/rrep549.pdf, p. 7.

National Institute for Economic Research calculated that domestically 11.5 million individuals were living in poverty; a third more than a decade previously.[30] Vital in this regard was the increase from the early 1990s to 2008 of the proportion of jobs paying only basic wages, from slightly over a quarter, to over a third of the total.[31] "Work doesn't protect against poverty" cried the German *Stern* newspaper's headline. The situation in the EU is of course characterised by diversity. Some Member States have sought to cope with structural challenges by maintaining strong protections for those in work at the cost of a higher unemployment and inactivity, while others have put employment activation first and tolerated more widespread low pay and in-work poverty. There has been a tendency to increased dualism in both labour markets and the design of welfare states, with employers on the one hand restructuring their operations to offer near lifetime opportunities to a highly skilled core, whereas on the other hand welfare states have needed to adjust to the risks of in-work poverty among increasingly excluded groups of low-paid and low-skilled workers (Palier and Thelen, 2010). Of all Member States the Nordics have by far the best record in finding a way through this dilemma.

Access to the necessary skills for an individual to succeed in the global knowledge economy also remains unequally distributed. In the UK, the class divide in educational achievement between children from high and low income households remains stubborn and persistent. According to Professor Anne West of the London School of Economics, "There is an achievement gap between children from poor family backgrounds and others; this is not unique to the UK, but found in all other countries of the OECD" (West, 2009). It appears that family, income and material resources are highly significant, although schools also play an important role in reproducing such inequalities.

These educational inequalities exacerbate the polarisation between "lovely" and "lousy" jobs, ensuring that existing social inequalities in ethnic and class terms are hardwired into this diverging labour market. This has wider social ramifications, as the decline of stable working-class jobs fuels a loss of self-esteem and identity particularly among younger and older men, leading to the rise of social pessimism across the EU and even disengagement from politics itself (Liddle and Lerais, 2007). It also raises the issue of a potential cultural cleavage in the EU between the "cosmopolitan" liberal middle classes, who have done well

---

[30] http://www.focus.de/finanzen/news/untersuchung-armut-trifft-zunehmend-junge-menschen_aid_481122.html.

[31] http://www.stern.de/panorama/armutsbericht-arbeit-schuetzt-nicht-vor-armut-620763.html.

as a result of globalisation, and the "communitarian" traditional work-ing-classes who feel left out and left behind, their living standards increasingly imperilled.

3.3.3 Aftershock III: Demography and life expectancy – the long-term viability of the "European Social Model"

The threat to social cohesion created by the polarisation of the EU labour market is heightened by the increasing strains imposed on the post-war welfare state by changing patterns of longevity and life expec-tancy, as the Commission has recently recognised in a green paper on pensions (European Commission, 2010a). For example, one in five Italians are now of pensionable age; Italy is projected to have at least one million individuals over the age of 90 by 2024 (2020 Public Ser-vices Commission, 2010). The March 2000 Lisbon European Council estimated that Italy's workforce will be 16% smaller in 2030 than in 2005.[32] Whereas in contemporary Germany there are roughly 2.6 people of working age for every over 60 year old, this ratio is projected to decline to 1.4 by 2030.[33] Similarly in Britain, it is estimated that by 2034, 23% of the population will be aged over 65, in comparison to 16% in 2009.[34] Today three workers support every older Briton; by 2025, just over two will have to manage the load.[35]

Whether post-war welfare regimes in the EU can survive these struc-tural pressures is still unknown. The 2020 Public Services commission report published on 14 September 2010 warns that UK public services are "increasingly unsustainable" in the light of an ageing population, requiring an annual funding increase from 4 to 6% of GDP in the long term.[36] A profound tension is emerging between the increasing long-term costs of welfare provision, and Member States' immediate drive for fiscal austerity. In simplistic terms, once the painful fiscal consolida-tion resulting from the events of 2008 is complete, Member States face the challenge of having to do it all over again to meet the spending costs of EU's demographic crisis.

Moreover, an ageing population is likely to be accompanied by ris-ing social inequalities. In the UK, for example, for every 100 people dying in the wealthiest areas, 199 die in the poorest places: this is the

---

[32] http://www.ft.com/cms/s/0/eaf2c538-57af-11df-855b-00144feab49a.html.
[33] http://www.goethe.de/ges/soz/dos/dos/age/dgw/en1274578.htm.
[34] http://www.statistics.gov.uk/cci/nugget.asp?id=949.
[35] http://www.independent.co.uk/news/uk/home-news/why-an-ageing-population-is-the-greatest-threat-to-society-656997.html.
[36] http://www.localgov.co.uk/index.cfm?method=news.detail&id=91763.

largest divide recorded since 1921.[37] Male life expectancy in the northern town of Blackpool is 73.6 years, whereas in affluent Kensington and Chelsea it is 84.3.[38] Even in Germany, women who are among the highest 10% of earners live three years longer on average than those in the bottom 10%.[39] In addition, to straining the capacities of national welfare systems, the ageing of EU's populations threatens to widen the gulf between rich and poor.

There is also the aftershock of the financial crisis in pensions – the sharp fall in equity markets has seriously affected the level of pension fund assets, squeezing pensioners' incomes in countries with large private sector provision (Hemerijck *et al.*, 2010). Whereas in the UK in 1977, the state pension made up 53% of a retired person's income, and occupational pensions 18%, by 2007/08, the state pension had declined to 37% and occupational pensions risen to 36%.[40] Whatever the design of the pension system, nearly a fifth of Europe's older people are still prone to poverty in old age, particularly where they have an inadequate occupational pension and live alone. Single elderly women are particularly at risk, with 22.1% over-65 living in poverty in Germany.[41]

The favoured policy response to the sustainability of the welfare state in face of an ageing demography is to raise the retirement age and promote higher employment participation rates among the active older worker. Clearly the financial crisis, recession and rise in unemployment pose a potential threat to this strategy. While the first signs are that employers and unions are not following the restructuring strategies of the 1980s and 1990s in laying off older workers and encouraging early retirement, the costs of which are now much higher and more transparent, it is unclear whether the welcome rise in the employment participation rate among the over-50 in the last decade will be sustained. For example, in August 2010 in the UK were witnessed the highest levels of over-50 unemployment since June 1997.[42]

---

[37] http://www.guardian.co.uk/uk/2010/jul/23/uk-health-gap-widest-ever.

[38] http://www.guardian.co.uk/society/2010/jul/02/poor-in-uk-dying-10-years-earlier-than-rich.

[39] http://www.faz.net/s/Rub8EC3C0841F934F3ABA0703761B67E9FA/Doc~E E313C38A84EF44C6BE8F86874C578271~ATpl~Ecommon~Scontent.html.

[40] http://www.guardian.co.uk/money/2010/jan/27/pensioners-poverty-ons-inequality.

[41] http://www.prb.org/Journalists/Webcasts/2008/olderwomen.aspx.

[42] http://www.guardian.co.uk/money/2010/aug/11/older-workers-long-term-unemploy ment.

3.3.4 Aftershock IV: Migration, integration and identity

As demographic change poses profound questions about the future sustainability and structure of the welfare state in the EU, an obvious answer would be for the Union to be the welcoming recipient of younger migrants both from its economically less well developed regions and from outside. Internal migration was a huge driver of economic growth in EU in the past, both in the movement from rural village to urban town and city and in the massive population shifts from poorer regions such as the Italian South and Andalusia in Spain. From the 1960s on, migrants came to the EU from Turkey, North Africa and former colonies throughout the world. In the last decade and half there has been a huge growth in migration to southern Europe from Africa, the Balkans and Latin America, while the UK and Ireland saw a large influx of East Europeans after EU enlargement in 2004.

Economically however the EU has failed to make the most of this potential talent pool and it is likely that the aftershocks of the economic crisis both on job opportunities and social provision will worsen this situation markedly. In Germany, only 12.2% of boys and 14.8% of girls from a Turkish background attend an elite *Gymnasium*, in comparison to 41.7% and 47.4% of their native contemporaries.[43] Turkish pupils are by contrast disproportionately represented at the lower end of the school system; with 44.3% of "Turkish" boys attending a *Hauptschule*, as opposed to only 16.7% of German males.[44] Similar ethnic inequalities are present in France, where according to a 2003 study, 10.1% of second generation Turkish pupils attend university, in contrast to 18.6% of those from the "French working class" (Windle, 2008). In some countries, such as the UK, children from some ethnic minorities do better at school than their white working class equivalents, though the children of other minorities such as Afro-Caribbeans, Bangladeshis and some Pakistanis fare much worse. However a recent study showed that only in Sweden does the second generation of migrants enjoy the same educational opportunities for their children as the native community (OECD, 2008).

There are growing concerns about the social and political impact of migration across the EU, despite the many economic and cultural benefits which migrants bring to Member States. The 2009 European Parliament elections witnessed significant success by far-right political parties standing on an anti-immigration agenda. Geert Wilders' anti

---

[43] http://www.bildung.koeln.de/schule/artikel/artikel_05149.html?PHPSESSID =188603ef2f272941edc2dd11b5ff9337.

[44] http://www.bildung.koeln.de/schule/artikel/artikel_05149.html?PHPSESSID =18860 3ef2f272941edc2dd11b5ff9337.

Islamic party came second in the Netherlands with 15% of the vote,[45] with Jobbik, a Hungarian anti-Semitic party antagonistic towards Sinti and Roma, winning 3 of the country's 22 seats.[46] Austria's two main far-right parties claimed over 28% of the vote in the 2008 general election.[47] The British National Party is strong in disadvantaged areas of Northern England, winning seats in the European Parliament for the North West and Yorkshire and Humberside in 2009.[48] With high levels of unemployment due to the financial crisis, it seems that hostility to immigrants has plenty of fuel to hand. It can hardly be coincidental that the neo-Nazi National Party of Germany is most entrenched in two former eastern *Länder*, Mecklenburg-Western Pomerania and Saxony, possessing seats in their regional parliaments.[49]

Beyond these alarming successes by extremist parties, there are new concerns about the integration of Muslim communities. Whilst Thilo Sarrazin has been forced to resign from the Bundesbank due to his polemical attack on the impact of Islamic immigration in Germany, the debate he initiated is infinitely more difficult to dispel.[50] The Swiss People's party, the largest in parliament, received popular backing via referendum for a constitutional ban on the building of minarets.[51] Symbolically, the first question posed during the UK's first ever televised Leaders' debates in the 2010 election concerned immigration.[52] The Sarkozy government's much publicised debate regarding national identity has been widely criticised as an attempt at right-wing populism,[53] as has the recent forced repatriation of Sinti and Roma.[54] This increasingly defensive discourse concerning immigration and identity may propel mainstream parties towards a tougher stance.

The capacity of migration to emerge as a major political issue is greatly exacerbated by divergences between the richer and poorer Member States in the EU after the financial crisis. If the "Polish plumber" emerged as a major issue in the French referendum of 2005, at a time of relative economic stability and prosperity, how much greater

45 http://www.guardian.co.uk/politics/2009/jun/05/european-elections-the-netherlands-far-right.
46 http://ceeuropeaninfo.blogspot.com/2010/04/rising-rightwing-extremism-in-eastern.html.
47 http://www.ft.com/cms/s/0/a4cc3cf0-be9f-11de-b4ab-00144feab49a.html.
48 http://news.bbc.co.uk/1/hi/8088381.stm.
49 http://www.spiegel.de/international/germany/0,1518,614209,00.html.
50 http://www.spiegel.de/politik/deutschland/0,1518,715836,00.html.
51 http://news.bbc.co.uk/1/hi/8385069.stm.
52 http://www.guardian.co.uk/commentisfree/2010/apr/18/general-election-2010-immigration.
53 http://www.time.com/time/world/article/0,8599,1963945,00.html.
54 http://www.bbc.co.uk/news/world-europe-11020429.

will the impact be at a time of increasing unemployment and social austerity?

3.3.5 Aftershock V: The impact of EU divergence

While much of the EU's half century history has been a positive story of increasing convergence between Member States, the present crisis is forcing divergence. To take an extreme example, in the second quarter of 2010, Greece's GDP fell by 1.5%[55], while Germany's grew in stark contrast by 2.2%.[56] Several of the new Member States have witnessed much more dramatic falls in GDP. For example, Romania's economy shrunk by 8.7% in the second quarter of 2009.[57] This is in a country where the average standard of living of its weakest regions is little more than a quarter of the EU27 average. However, solidarity among Member States might become more limited and may begin declining in line with the pressures of domestic austerity.

The diverging impact of the economic crisis across the European continent is also exacerbating regional divisions within EU countries. Whereas London is forecast to recover its pre-recession employment peak in 2013 due to strong private sector presence, Wales will not do so until after 2025.[58] Cuts to public sector jobs, a source of employment for over 27% of the Welsh workforce, are expected to produce an unemployment rate of over 10%.[59] Research commissioned by the BBC indicates that within England, deprived northern communities are at far greater risk from government cuts than wealthier counterparts in the south. Middlesbrough is ranked as most vulnerable, Elmbridge in Surrey as the least.[60]

The threat to national solidarity produced by such polarisation has been revealed in Germany, where FDP finance expert Frank Schäffler advocated in August 2010 the abolition of "solidarity" payments by West German citizens to fund investment in the former east.[61] In January 2010, unemployment in eastern *Länder* stood at 13.5% in contrast to 7.4% in the west.[62] The irony is that higher wage settlements in Germany would help to boost domestic consumption, strengthening the

---

[55] http://www.guardian.co.uk/world/2010/aug/12/greece-recession-gdp-unemployment.

[56] http://www.bbc.co.uk/news/business-10962017.

[57] http://www.ft.com/cms/s/0/2207f1ca-a9cc-11de-a3ce-00144feabdc0,dwp_uuid=cfff5f9a-a803-11de-8305-00144feabdc0.html.

[58] http://www.ft.com/cms/s/0/0f1a58a0-90bc-11df-85a7-00144feab49a.html.

[59] http://www.bbc.co.uk/news/uk-wales-11151909.

[60] http://www.bbc.co.uk/news/uk-england-11141264.

[61] http://in.reuters.com/article/idINIndia-50988720100821.

[62] http://www.dw-world.de/dw/article/0,5265094,00.html.

German economy as well as helping lower paid workers. However, wage share as a proportion of GDP in Germany has fallen rapidly over the last decade, as it has across many other major industrialised nations. Employers, especially in tradable sectors that face fierce foreign competition, have been able to enforce lower wage settlements.

3.4 The Role of the EU and How Its Social Dimension Might Be Strengthened

While a strong case in principle can be made for greater EU economic integration in the wake of the crisis, at the level of domestic politics, the major Member States appear to be reverting to welfare nationalism and "beggar thy neighbour" policies in labour market regulation and welfare spending. Crucially, major EU Member States are currently committed to allying domestic austerity, based on the notion of a balanced household budget, with the cultivation of export surpluses as their route to economic recovery. A host of experts have lined up to criticise the detrimental reverberations of such an approach across the Eurozone. Leading *Financial Times* commentator Samuel Brittan describes such policies as "beggar-my-neighbour" in their scope, highlighting that: "Do I have to add that not every country can have an export surplus?" before noting pessimistically that "countries now in surplus, including China and Germany, are not going to spend their way into payments deficit because of exhortations by the UK or even the International Monetary Fund."[63]

Yet, such criticism has had little impact on policy-makers. Many economists are incredulous about the universal export-centric approach to the recovery as all the economies cutting back on public spending hope to compensate for the negative impact on growth by increasing exports – in the EU maybe into shrinking markets. But Germany looks likely to emerge the sure-fire winner in this contest. With the euro's exchange rate depressed by worries about debt default in parts of the Eurozone, Germany's hidden bonus from the creation of the Euro is a much greater export competitiveness than if the Deutschmark had remained an independent currency. The result is that while these exports and ensuing growth benefit Germany, the country's chosen path to recovery bulldozes those of weaker Eurozone economies. Beyond therefore the widely publicised threat of a double dip recession, leading Member States' economic policies display a dangerous focus on their own narrowly defined interests, to the detriment of the broader EU economy and solidarity. As The Guardian's economic editor put it, "what we are seeing is a race to the bottom. Every country is being

---

[63] http://www.ft.com/cms/s/0/fca56f34-b154-11df-b899-00144feabdc0.html.

urged to tighten fiscal policy and every country is being forced to emulate Germany's downward pressure on labour costs. This is the recipe for deflation and depression."[64]

These developments are detrimental to the future cohesion and stability of the EU in a globalising world. There are strong arguments for greater economic coordination at the EU level as well a social policy framework that would constrain the present tendency towards a negative welfare nationalism where each Member State's struggle to secure competitive advantage results in a social "race to the bottom". There are some who yearn in the wake of the crisis for an EU Keynesian state that recreates the powers of economic intervention that nation-states were able to exercise at the height of the post-war consensus based on capital and exchange controls, expansionary fiscal policies, the imposition of import quotas and external tariffs, and so on. These interventionist policies would then provide the basis for a wider and deeper framework of social protection across the EU, based on the revival of the traditional post-war welfare state.

However, the crisis has underlined why the model of full blown Keynesian interventionism at EU level would be unlikely to succeed. There is little sign of significant political support for it: rather the political mood is currently one of a reversion to national sovereignty and a rejection of the idea that a stronger EU offers a way forward. But even if the political support did exist, such a prescription would not deal with the major structural trends alluded to in this chapter, which will dramatically transform patterns of need and dependency in the welfare state for generations to come and need to be tackled through national reforms.

As we noted earlier, what the Union needs is a new policy paradigm based on a combination of social investment and regulatory intervention, given the multiple risks of the demise of the social investment paradigm in the post-crisis period (Hemerijck, 2010). Policies of social investment require welfare state reforms which in the main have to be delivered at the level of the individual Member State. But they will not work unless they are coupled with stronger regulatory interventions designed to shape market outcomes, rather than simply attempting to correct the social consequences of the market. This imperative for national action should however be complemented by a stronger social framework at the EU level which conditions national reforms to Member State economic and social models. This is urgently needed because the liberalisation enforced by the single market and European Monetary Union (EMU) requires ongoing and wrenching economic adjustment. A

---

[64] http://www.guardian.co.uk/business/2010/sep/20/liberal-democrats-eurozone-policy.

strong social model is required to handle the ensuing shocks and transitional costs such as redundancy and downward pressure on wages, particularly for the most disadvantaged. Second, effective social policies help to increase employment participation which makes the EU more economically efficient, adds to the EU's long-term growth potential and improves the sustainability of the social model. Finally, if it is to sustain popular legitimacy with EU citizens, the EU cannot be reduced to a neoliberal project which is simply concerned with enabling markets to function more efficiently. The EU needs a coherent vision based on greater equity and personal well-being which advances collective solidarity. For all these reasons we agree with the conclusion of the EU's 2010 Joint Report on Social Protection and Social Inclusion (JRSPSI): "The crisis has emphasised the added value of policy coordination through the Open method of Coordination on Social Protection and Social Inclusion and provided further incentive to reinforce and exploit its potential fully" (European Commission, 2010).[65]

But action at EU level also has a strengthened role to play in shaping more socially acceptable market outcomes. A good example of what we have in mind is contained in many of the recommendations of the recent report on the future of the Single Market (Monti, 2010). Monti's purpose is to reinvigorate the Single Market and he is not himself an enthusiast for the notions of Social EU that some favour that would imply large scale transfers of competence for setting social standards from national to EU level. However he does recognise that EU policies have a key role to play in shaping socially fairer market outcomes and thereby contributing to the greater acceptability of further market liberalisation, for example through stronger tax coordination to brake a social "race to the bottom" and a strengthened Posting of Workers Directive as a counterpart to free movement of labour. It is this combination of structural market shaping and EU guidelines to promote social investment that we favour.

3.5 Conclusion: Pointers for the Future

Solidarity at the EU level is problematic, given that many traditional forms of solidarity have waned within Member States. But there are practical and concrete steps the EU can take to shape more positive social outcomes.

First, as referred to above, one important area concerns free movement of labour within the EU. The EU could do more to promote an acceptance of the free movement of labour which adds to both economic

---

[65] This was adopted in March 2010 by the European Commission and the EPSCO Council of Ministers.

efficiency and personal freedom. It could ensure greater portability of social rights within the EU. At the same time it could ease potential tensions from internal migration by revising the Posted Workers Directive in order to strengthen its protection of established domestically based terms and conditions of employment in host countries. This is essential to remove popular fears of wage undercutting by migrant workers.

Secondly, the EU could also strengthen the capacity of its Member States to fund a decent welfare state through new tax measures. In the new circumstances of post-crisis fiscal austerity, Member States should look more favourably on an ambitious tax agenda. This should include strengthened tax coordination to clamp down on tax evasion and abuse. The combined power of the EU should be brought to bear in order to tighten regulation of tax havens. Member States should coordinate more closely their approach to business taxation in order to prevent tax competition eroding the business tax base to the ultimate disadvantage of all. Member States should welcome proposals for new taxes levied at EU level for example for a financial activities levy and carbon tax. Such taxes will only raise decent amounts of revenue if imposed at an EU level. Otherwise if levied at Member State level their effectiveness will be diluted by fear that business will migrate to elsewhere in the EU.

Thirdly, the EU should develop and finance a low carbon transition plan. This will require huge public-private investments in cross border energy grids and transport infrastructure. By this means EU wide measures could be taken to stimulate growth and employment across the whole EU. This will be of particular – though not exclusive – benefit to those Member States where the degree of fiscal austerity they are currently required to pursue, precludes the possibility of them making sensible low carbon investments of their own. This low carbon investment plan would be financed by the issuance of bonds at EU level. Far from being a radical step towards a federal EU that pro-sovereignty fear, this would simply extend the practice of the European Investment Bank in issuing bonds for productive purposes, taking advantage of the lowest possible interest rates at which money can be borrowed within the EU. All that is needed is an extension of that principle.

Fourthly, the EU Structural Funds could be used more effectively to mitigate the impact of economic shocks on dislocated regions across the EU. Structural fund transfers ought to be sustained, but with greater conditionality attached. Member States should use EU finance for EU purposes. That should include the pursuit of EU social objectives, as the Barca report recommends (Barca, 2009). Structural funds can also help to promote positive policy "synergies", bringing together employment policy, welfare provision, education, health, and so on.

Fifthly, the EU should focus far greater attention on key social policy targets such as child poverty, school drop-out rates, ethnic minority integration, and employability. The Europe 2020 Strategy rightly focuses on these issues. However, a major development in EU policy is the agreement by the June 2010 European Council to reduce poverty and social exclusion by 20 million by 2020. This is a significant breakthrough for Social EU and should assume great importance, precisely because it will be particularly difficult to meet because of the crisis aftershocks that the EU is experiencing. If made operational and effective, it also offers the potential to act as an EU wide brake on the more extreme consequences of increasing welfare nationalism and a social "race to the bottom" of which this paper has warned.

The framing of the new poverty target in terms of three dimensions of relative poverty, absolute material deprivation and worklessness will require much detailed technical work. But it could enable a broader policy framework to be developed that addresses the nature of the new social risks of poverty. This should include serious examination of the structure of the labour market, the problems of addressing low wage equilibria, the effectiveness of minimum wages and in work benefits, and the need to modernise EU's welfare states to cope with new social challenges as well as the adequacy of existing social protection arrangements. We note the grim conclusion of the 2010 JRSPSI: "The crisis has highlighted great diversity within the EU. Its scope, magnitude and effects vary as does the capacity of national welfare systems to provide adequate protection. Not all Member States have the financial means to meet rising demand and some have large gaps in their safety nets. Narrowing these gaps is now a priority" (European Commission, 2010).

The 2008-2009 financial crisis is unlikely to transform the economic and social landscape of the EU, and it poses many threats to the most vulnerable. But the crisis also presents new opportunities for social and economic reform. In the past, change has been very difficult to achieve in EU welfare regimes, precisely because many groups have effectively defended the current constellation of social rights as being in the public interest. Periods of upheaval and stress on existing frameworks of provision can help to unblock frozen welfare landscapes. The crisis aftershocks that the EU is currently experiencing may be the catalyst for rebuilding the collective solidarities that a strong EU social model entails.

References

Atkinson, A.B. and Marlier, E. (editors) (2010), *Income and living conditions in Europe*, Luxembourg: Office for Official Publications of the European Communities (OPOCE).

Barca, F. (2009), *An Agenda for Reformed Cohesion Policy: A place-based approach to meeting European Union challenges and expectations*, Brussels: European Commission.

Diamond, P. and Liddle, R. (editors) (2009), *Beyond New Labour: The future of social democracy in Britain*, London: Politico's Publishing.

Dixon, M., and Pearce, N. (2005), "Social Justice in a Changing World: The Emerging Anglo-Social Model" in N. Pearce and W. Paxton (editors) *Social Justice: Building a Fairer Britain*, London: Politico's Publishing.

Esping-Andersen, G.E. (2009), *The Incomplete Revolution: Adapting Welfare States to Women's New Roles*, Cambridge: The Polity Press.

European Commission (2010), *Joint Report on Social Protection and Social Inclusion*, Brussels: European Commission. Available at: http://ec.europa.eu/ social/main.jsp?catId=757&langId=en.

European Commission (2010a), *Green Paper – towards adequate, sustainable and safe European pension systems*, Brussels: European Commission. Available at: http://ec.europa.eu/social/main.jsp?langId=en&catId=89& newsId=839&furtherNews=yes.

Gamble, A., (2009), *The Spectre at the Feast: Capitalist Crisis and the Politics of Recession*, Basingstoke: Palgrave Macmillan.

Giddens, A., (2009), *The Politics of Climate Change*, Cambridge: The Polity Press.

Goos, M. and Manning, A., (2007), "Lousy and Lovely Jobs: The Rising Polarization of Work in Britain", *The Review of Economics and Statistics*, MIT Press, Vol. 89(1), pages 118-133, 01.

Goos, M., Manning, A., Fraumeni, B., Salomons, A., (2009), "Job Polarization in Europe", *American Economic Review*, American Economic Association, Vol. 99(2), pages 58-63.

Hans Boeckler Stiftung (2006), "Arbeitskosten in Deutschland bisher ueberschaetzt", Hans Boeckler Stiftung Report Nr 11, June 2006, Düsseldorf: Hans Boeckler Stiftung. Available at: http://www.boeckler.de/pdf/p_imk_ report_11_2006.pdf.

Hemerijck, A. (2010), "The End of an Era: economic crisis and welfare state transformation", paper presented at the Conference on "Economic governance in the Eurozone and the EU: Drawing lessons from the crisis", Joint event ELIAMEP and Bruegel, Athens, 10-13 June.

Hemerijck, A., Knapen, B., Van Doorn, E. (2010), *Aftershocks: Economic Crisis and Institutional Choice*, Amsterdam: University Press.

Joyce, R., Muriel, A., Phillips, D., Sibieta, L. (2010), *Poverty and Inequality in UK: 2010*, IFS Commentary C116, London: Institute for Fiscal Studies.

Liddle, R. and Latham, S. (2009), "How can the response to climate change be socially just?" in Giddens, A., Latham, S. and Liddle, R., (editors) *Building a low-carbon future: the politics of climate change*, London: Policy Network.

Liddle, R. and Lerais, F. (2007) *Europe's Social Reality*, BEPA, European Commission. Brussels: European Commission.

Monti, M. (2010), *A New Strategy for the Single Market: At the Service of Europe's Economy and Society*, BEPA, European Commission, Brussels: European Commission.

OECD (2008), *Growing Unequal? Income Distribution and Poverty in OECD Countries*, Paris: OECD.

Palier, B. and Thelen, K. (2010), Institutionalizing Dualism: Complementarities and Change in France and Germany, *Politics & Society*, Sage Publications, Vol. 38(1): pages 119-148.

Proissl, W. (2010), "Why Germany fell out of love with Europe", 1 July 2010, Brussels: Bruegel.

The 2020 Public Services Commission (2010), From Social Security to Social Productivity: a Vision for 2020 Public Services. London: The 2020 Public Services Commission.

West, A. (2009) "Poverty and educational achievement: why do children from low-income families tend to do less well at school?", Bristol: The Policy Press. Available at: http://teachfirstfiles.co.uk/Documents/Poverty%20and %20Educational%20Achievement%20paper,%20Anne%20West.pdf.

Wilkinson, R. and Pickett, K. (2009) *The Spirit Level: Why More Equal Societies Almost Always Do Better*, London: Allen Lane.

Windle, J.A. (2008) *Ethnicity and Educational Inequality: An Investigation of School Experience in Australia and France*, Joint PHD: University of Melbourne, University of Bourgogne.

4. The Lisbon Strategy, Europe 2020 and the Crisis in Between

David NATALI[1]

4.1 Approaching Europe 2020: the Lisbon Strategy and the Crisis

The Lisbon Strategy launched in 2000 represented a twofold ambitious goal for the European Union (EU): to transform the EU economy of the 21st century (and make it the most competitive and knowledge-based economy in the world, capable of sustainable economic growth with more and better jobs and greater social cohesion) and to make innovations in EU governance through developing new forms of interaction between national practices and EU objectives.

A lively multi-disciplinary debate has developed since the early 2000s amidst much controversy between scholars and experts. This chapter provides a brief overview of the Lisbon Strategy, its political and economic rationale, and its main advances and limitations. This is essential for asking some analytical and political questions on the post-Lisbon phase and the launch of the Europe 2020 Strategy.[2] In the following sections, the reference is to the broad logic of the new Strategy and the role of social policy coordination in it.

The present contribution is organised in four parts. The first part looks at the normative political and economic foundations (the complex interplay of social and economic goals) and the key aspects of the governance (especially through the Open Method of Coordination – OMC) of the Strategy launched in Lisbon. The second part sheds light on the ongoing economic-financial crisis (and its social consequences). This is understood as the sum of the global challenges the EU is facing and the Lisbon Strategy was supposed to deal with. The third part refers to "shadows" and "lights" of the Lisbon Strategy. Some open questions on the design of the new Europe 2020 Strategy will be asked. The reference will be to two broad tensions (and seven critical points) that

---

[1] Address for correspondence: david.natali@unibo.it.
[2] For a systematic review of the literature, see Natali (2009).

require more political and analytical attention. A short conclusion summarises some key promising strategies to improve EU socio-economic governance.

4.2 The Lisbon Strategy: Logics and Promises

When the Lisbon Strategy was launched many academic and political commentators viewed its agenda and the related governance tools as a promising step to improve EU socio-economic performance while also legitimising EU integration. The Strategy was widely interpreted to be a "fundamental transformation" of the EU project in economic, social and environmental dimensions (Sapir, 2004; Rodrigues, 2002; Zeitlin, 2008).

4.2.1 The economic and political rationale of the Lisbon Strategy

The conclusions of the Lisbon Summit of 2000 were based on the assumption that EU economic models needed to change to be competitive in the global economy. Such an assumption was based on a critical understanding of the EU development trajectory since the 1970s: EU problems in productivity and innovation (and the increased gap with US dynamism) were largely interpreted to be the result of economic and social rigidities (Alesina and Giavazzi, 2006).

In the words of Begg (2008), a systematic lack of competitiveness was made evident by the deteriorating economic performances, persistent unemployment and delay in developing knowledge-intensive sectors. To remedy the EU shortcomings some key reforms had to be implemented. From a micro-economic perspective, structural reforms had to be introduced to boost productivity and employment rates. More investment on information technologies, fewer obstacles to the freedom of services provision and the liberalisation of transport and energy markets were some of the innovations to be introduced (Daveri, 2002). In order to achieve the objective of a competitive and dynamic economy, the EU had to achieve results in reforming social and environmental policies (Begg *et al.*, 2007).

Economic reasoning was also at the basis of the perceived need for more economic and social coordination (Collignon, 2008). In line with Pisani-Ferry and Sapir (2006) two types of reasoning justify embarking on EU coordination. First, interdependence may render independent decision making undesirable. Spill over effects of national decisions may be active in the policy areas where benefits are not confined to the country where decisions are taken (e.g. research and development), and in policy domains where complementarities exist (as is the case of product market and employment policies). Secondly, policy-makers may learn from each other. Policy learning may be improved through cross-country comparisons and benchmarking.[3] In addition, common programmes may represent a reform lever for national policy-makers through a shared understanding of the needed reforms.

Yet, as argued by Rodrigues (2002) – one of the architects of the Lisbon agenda – the emphasis of this new EU Strategy was political more than economic. While the need to ensure peace within the EU borders was taken for granted by new generations, a more "forward-looking" approach to socio-economic development had to be stressed. The new impetus for EU integration had to be based on sustaining EU citizens' living conditions, making the Union a key player in globalisation and on the improvement of the EU institutions' legitimacy. Structural reforms had to be paralleled by a new focus on multilateralism and democratic deepening for new Member States (Rodrigues, 2010).

One of the key targets of the Strategy was the European social model, its reform and the contribution it could make to the broader revamping of economic growth (Ferrera *et al.*, 2000). In such a context, social and employment policy moved higher up on the EU agenda. Social protection was defined as a productive factor and part of the "Lisbon triangle". The latter consisted of the mutual reinforcement of economic competitiveness and growth, social protection and inclusion, and employment. All this was consistent with a higher commitment to a Social EU.

The coordination of social policy (both social protection and social inclusion) was part of this attempt to redefine the EU integration project. On the one hand, the Lisbon Strategy (through the OMC) was intended to address growing imbalances between national welfare states and an increased EU role (or interference) in the social domain. Such a new mode of governance had to combine the respect for national competences while allowing for the EU coordination of welfare states. On the other hand, the Strategy and social policy coordination in it was expected to secure "structural coupling" between economic integration and the defence of social rights (see Pochet, 2006; see also chapter by Ferrera in this volume).

---

[3]   On cross-country comparisons and benchmarking, a good practice worth highlighting is the thorough report produced by the EU Task-Force on Child Poverty and Child Well-Being almost exclusively on the basis of the commonly agreed EU social indicators (Social Protection Committee, 2008).

4.2.2 The Lisbon Strategy as a new "participatory" and "knowledge-enhancing" form of governance

While the Strategy was based on a set of policy tools including regulation, social dialogue and structural funds, the new modes of governance have attracted much of the scientific debate.[4] Terms such as "soft law", experimental governance and self-regulation have been widely used to characterise the OMC – that is, the new governing instrument agreed upon at the European Council of March 2000 (Falkner *et al.*, 2005).

For political scientists, international relations theorists and lawyers the OMC represented an important change in EU policy-making. In line with Scott and Trubek (2002), the OMC was characterised by experimentation and knowledge creation, flexibility and revisability of normative and policy standards, and diversity and decentralisation of policy-making (Héritier, 2002). The revised EU toolkit was assumed to represent a promising instrument to face up to common EU challenges while at the same time respecting national diversity and sovereignty. It was also intended as a means to use the diversity of national policies as a resource to find solutions to "intractable problems".

Another key dimension of the Strategy consisted of participation. Stakeholders (i.e. business and trade unions, civil society (NGOs), etc.) in the EU and national arenas have been encouraged to participate in all stages of the process and have been in particular called upon to take an active role in the elaboration of national reports and of common guidelines to be followed for drafting them (Natali and de la Porte, 2009). According to the "input legitimacy" perspective, the Lisbon Strategy was intended to ensure the concrete implementation of the principles of participation, transparency and openness. In this case, the reference is to the theory of directly deliberative polyarchy that stresses the importance of the participation of different citizens in a bottom-up process (Sabel and Zeitlin, 2007).

The Lisbon Strategy was the source of new forms of multi-level governance through: the exchange of information among policy-makers; learning from each other's experience, practices and intentions; national ownership and the exertion of peer pressure to galvanise governments into taking appropriate policy action (Ioannou *et al.*, 2008, page 13).

---

[4] Zeitlin (this volume) rightly argues that the OMC was never intended to serve as the sole governance instrument for the Lisbon Strategy, but was always supposed to be combined with the full set of EU policy tools, including legislation, social dialogue, Community action programmes, and the structural funds.

4.3 Economic and Financial Crisis: A Three-Step Process

While early research viewed the Strategy as a promising project for the EU, more recent contributions have contributed to a more complex and nuanced understanding. Much criticism (of both the Lisbon Strategy and the new Europe 2020) has increased after the huge financial, economic and then budgetary crisis affecting most advanced western economies (see Pochet, 2010).

This section sheds light on the key aspects of the crisis and the most evident questions raised by experts, scholars and policy-makers on the coherence of the Lisbon policy agenda and its capacity to face socio-economic challenges, especially after the crisis (see Liddle in this volume for an encompassing summary of present and future challenges). The latter is summarised in line with the three major steps that have characterised its evolution: the financial crisis (worsened following the collapse of Lehman Brothers in 2008); the broad economic recession that hit Europe in 2009; and the Greek crisis and the consequent budgetary tensions in the EU in 2010.

4.3.1 Financial crisis in 2008

In its early stages, the crisis manifested itself as an acute liquidity shortage among financial institutions as they experienced ever stiffer market conditions for rolling over their short-term debt. The inter-bank market virtually closed and risk premiums on inter-bank loans soared. Banks faced a serious liquidity problem. In this phase, concerns over the solvency of financial institutions were increasing, but a systemic collapse was deemed unlikely (European Commission, 2009).

It was also widely believed that the European economy, unlike the US economy, would be largely immune to the financial turbulence. This belief was fed by perceptions that the real economy, though slowing, was thriving on strong fundamentals such as rapid export growth and sound financial positions of households and businesses. This perception dramatically changed when major investment banks defaulted in September 2008. Confidence collapsed, taking down major US and EU financial institutions. The crisis thus began to feed on itself, through: credit cuts, economic activity plummeting, loan books deteriorating and so on. The downturn in asset markets snowballed rapidly across the world.

Western governments did introduce emergency measures to prevent collapse of the financial system, while the debate about the regulation of financial markets increased.[5] As far as the Lisbon Strategy is concerned, it has been largely criticised for the weakness of the "better regulation" approach to financial markets. Some authors assume the crisis to have been the result of a twin failure, namely the ineffective regulation of the global financial markets and excessive financial liquidity due to historically low interest rates (Quaglia, 2010; Natali, 2010).

4.3.2 Economic recession in 2009

From then onward the EU economy entered the steepest downturn since the 1930s. The transmission of financial distress to the real economy evolved at record speed, with credit restraint and sagging confidence hitting both investment and demand. The cross-border transmission was also extremely rapid through global financial and product markets (European Commission, 2009, page 27; Pisani-Ferry *et al*, 2008). As can be seen in Table 4.1, potential growth decreased across western countries: the negative trend was particularly severe in the US, but Europe was hit too.

Table 4.1: World economic projections 2009-2010

	2009	2010
World Output	-1.3	1.9
Advanced Economies	-3.8	0.0
United States	-2.8	0.0
Euro Area	-4.2	-0.4
Japan	-6.2	0.5
United Kingdom	-4.1	-0.4
Canada	-2.5	1.2

Source: International Monetary Fund (2009)

New risks have emerged and have made many economists fear that it may still weigh on economic performance for some time to come and that a recovery will only be in sight after a protracted period of time. Labour markets in the EU started to weaken considerably in the second half of 2008, deteriorating further in the course of 2009. The EU unemployment rate has increased by more than 2 percentage points, and a further sharp increase is likely in the future. In the second quarter of 2009 the unemployment rate increased by 2.2 percentage points.

Progress made in bringing the unemployment rate down vanished in about a year. A major challenge stems from the risk that unemployment

---

[5] As for the EU, in 2008, European Commission President Barroso set up the so-called Larosière Group to give advice on the future of European financial regulation. This high-level group has reported on its main goals for increasing financial market stability.

may not easily return to pre-crisis levels once the recovery sets in. This could threaten EU welfare states, which are already under strain as a result of ageing populations (European Commission, 2009).

Economic downturn and its consequences on the labour market have contributed to the criticism of the Lisbon Agenda. Many scholars have questioned the belief that economic deregulation and flexibility in labour markets is the right path for more economic growth and for reducing the impact of the crisis (Amable, 2009). Others have stressed that inequality and the adequacy of welfare benefits have been largely neglected in the implementation of the Strategy even though they contribute to reducing the negative impact of the economic cycle through promoting a more inclusive society (Pochet, 2010).

4.3.3 Growing budgetary tensions in the Euro-zone in 2010

The condition of the EU economy prevailing in this crisis corresponds almost exactly to the textbook case for a budgetary stimulus. The fiscal stimulus adopted by EU governments as part of the EU Strategy for coordinated action, has weighted heavily on public budgets. As a consequence, the International Monetary Fund (2009) projects an increase in the average debt-to-GDP ratio in the euro area of 30% and that this will reach 90% of GDP by 2014. This average disguises substantial increases for some Member States. Part of the budgetary deterioration is cyclical, but part is permanent. In the years following a shock, growth rates often recover to the pre-crisis pace but the loss in output level typically remains permanent, implying a parallel fall in public revenues (Von Hagen *et al.*, 2009).

According to the Commission's autumn economic forecast, as a result of automatic stabilisers and discretionary measures to enhance social benefits, social expenditure in the EU is expected to increase by 3.2 percentage points of GDP between 2007 and 2010. A Commission estimate shows that spending on overall recovery measures varies from less than 1% of GDP to more than 3.5% (Social Protection and European Commission, 2009).[6]

Many EU countries have thus started to show increased financial stress. Greece has represented a special case: no other euro-area country exhibits a similar combination of budgetary misreporting and misbehaviour (Marzinotto *et al.*, 2010). Throughout the 2000s, the country has been running an expansionary budgetary policy while attempting to hide

---

[6] Member States have also utilised resources from European Social Funds and from the European Globalisation Adjustment Fund to combat unemployment and to improve social inclusion of most vulnerable groups (Social Protection Committee and European Commission, 2009).

it. The problem it poses is therefore primarily one of enforcement of the existing provisions of the Treaty and the Stability and Growth Pact (SGP).

Yet, other EU countries have suffered increased budgetary tensions. This fiscal stimulus is estimated to amount to up to 2% of GDP on average in the EU for the period 2009-2010. With the rise in the fiscal deficit over that period estimated to average about 5% of GDP, the resulting budgetary developments thus amount to around 3%. Part of this fiscal expansion is likely to be permanent (European Commission, 2009).

The tensions mentioned above have raised some questions on the reform agenda proposed by the Lisbon Strategy and its own governance of economic and social matters. As for the former, before the crisis there was a strong belief in the EU that budgetary discipline was the "mother of all policies" (Marzinotto *et al.*, 2010, page 2). Accordingly, budgetary surveillance was deemed sufficient to prevent instability, with no reference to the private sector. The limits of such neglect started to become apparent at the beginning of the crisis, as emphasised in the European Commission report on the first ten years of the euro (European Commission, 2009). Further criticism has focused on the economic and budgetary coordination in the Euro zone through the Stability and Growth Pact and especially the Broad Economic Policy Guidelines. Both mechanisms for crisis prevention and management have been at the core of the political debate (Pochet, 2010).

4.4 The Lisbon Strategy Ten Years on: A More Complex Understanding

In the following sections we briefly summarise the main critical viewpoints on the Strategy in the light of the recent economic crisis mentioned above. We organise these open questions along the two main analytical dimensions mentioned in the first part of the chapter: the political and economic foundations of the Lisbon Strategy and its governance (see Box 4.1).

Box 4.1: Open questions on the efficacy of the Lisbon Strategy

The Political-economic rationale of the Lisbon Strategy

1) The wrong Strategy for further EU integration?
2) The wrong policy agenda? Tensions between Budgetary Stability and Structural Reforms?
3) A more central understanding of social and employment policy?

The Lisbon Strategy and its governance

4) Weak economic policy institutions?
5) A limited participation of stakeholders?
6) A more encouraging assessment of learning?
7) Some influence on national policy-making?

Some of these tensions are related to the critical understanding of the limits the Strategy has proved to have. Others are based on a more encouraging reading of its implementation and influence on Member States' reforms and performance. All these points represent key elements of the debate on the new Europe 2020 Strategy (see Vanhercke in this volume).

4.4.1 Questioning the political-economic rationale of the Lisbon agenda

1) The wrong Strategy for further EU integration?

For some authors, the Lisbon reform package did not represent a programme to "recalibrate" the European social model and that of continental European countries in particular. By contrast, it was an economic project to destabilise it. Much of the delay in the reform process and the tensions over its implementation could thus be understood in terms of an ongoing tension between the Lisbon ideology and the socio-economic compromise of many EU members (Amable, 2009).

A more institutional and historical approach to the risks for the future of EU integration (with evident links with the Lisbon agenda) seems to converge towards the same insights (Hopner and Schafer, 2007). For these authors, EU economic integration has entered a new, post-Ricardian phase in which it systematically clashes with national varieties of capitalism. Rather than enhancing competition that builds on existing comparative (institutional) advantages, the EU project is propelling convergence. Integration attempts affect liberal market capitalism and organised capitalism differently and result in a "clash of capitalisms". Convergence may thus lead to one of two different scenarios.

The first is that convergence alters the way in which continental European economies operate. The second is that political resistance in the organised economies leads to a crisis of political integration.

The EU has moved beyond the stage of technical harmonisation or purely regulatory policies. Boundary redrawing deeply affects Member States' ability to govern the economy, and governments are unable to control further integration (Ferrera, 2008). If this is the case, the indirect legitimacy of EU institutions seems an insufficient democratic basis for economic liberalisation (*ibid.*, pages 23-24). In the words of Majone (2005), "integration by stealth" has reached its limits, in that EU strategies are increasingly in conflict with national socio-economic institutions. The Lisbon process is thus interpreted as a source of political opposition and disaffection with the EU.

2) The wrong policy agenda? Tensions between Budgetary Stability and Structural Reforms

A critical reading of the Lisbon Agenda has focused on its liberal approach. On the one hand, the supposed superiority of the liberal model implemented in US has been questioned on the basis of evidence from different productive sectors (see European Commission, 2009). From a more analytical perspective, some have argued economic analysis should focus on single sectors (industry, service) rather than on broad economic models. And this revised focus may be used to provide evidence of a more complex economic dynamic. On the other hand, scholars have questioned the belief that deregulation and flexibility (in labour markets) is the right path for more economic growth (Amable, 2009).

A more direct and precise analysis of the overall Lisbon philosophy has been provided by Mabbett and Schelkle (2007). The authors have stressed the potential contradiction within the Lisbon and Economic Monetary Union (EMU) projects and have shed light on the "conflicting political economy" of the EU's simultaneous agenda (*ibid.*, page 83). While for the literature that most embraced the Lisbon Strategy, fiscal austerity had to contribute to the reform of social and employment policies (see Rodrigues, 2002). Mabbett and Schelkle agree with the opposite reading: fiscal consolidation is not expected to help structural reforms but to lead to more tensions. Reform's losers should be compensated for their losses, but austerity limits the room for that. In such a context, the Lisbon agenda may get a "double whammy" from simultaneous fiscal consolidation and welfare reforms: austerity may limit political consensus in favour of reforms and may lead interest groups to ask for compensations that obstruct the Lisbon goals. The authors conclude by challenging the political economy of Lisbon and EMU and stressing the potential contradiction between structural reforms and fiscal stabilisation.

The most recent crisis has largely reinforced such a critical reading: Pochet (2010) has stressed the persistent tensions (if not contradiction) between the different aims of the Strategy; especially between the Stability and Growth Pact and the fight against poverty. Austerity packages, largely supported by the EU, risk limiting the activation of social and employment policy to dealing with the further effects of the crisis.

3) A more central understanding of social and employment policy?

Political scientists and lawyers have shared a less critical reading of the Lisbon Strategy and its influence on both EU and national policy-making, and policies. Goetschy (2009) for instance has stressed the Lisbon Strategy's influence on the EU's role in social policies. The Strategy has been assumed to have contributed to "enlarge EU employment and social agenda on matters of national priority" (*ibid.*, page 222). And it has been argued that the broader EU agenda with explicit interaction between economic, social and environmental policies could help to overcome traditional fragmentation in EU policy-making (see Zeitlin, 2008). Others have stressed the revised political equilibrium at the base of the Strategy and the progressive shift of the original compromise between social democracy, liberalism and "Third Way" towards a more right-centred approach (see Pochet, 2006).

Open questions have recently been asked on the need for a revision of the key issues at the core of the Strategy and especially on social and employment policies. For the preparation of the new Europe 2020 Strategy, and in a context of potential long-term employment crisis, some authors have stressed the problematic implementation of the "flexicurity" principle in times of huge economic downturn. Theodoropoulou (2010) stresses "flexicurity reforms should not be abandoned (...) however the focus must be on creating the conditions to provide employment security first, before resuming the push for greater flexibility". Another issue has to do with the articulation of the social goals of the new Strategy: the fact that the EU headline target focuses on social inclusion/ poverty reduction should not lead to a reduction of both the visibility and salience of the other policy fields (pensions, healthcare and long-term care) (see chapters by Zeitlin and by Frazer and Marlier in this volume).

4.4.2 The Lisbon Strategy and its governance

Another strand of the economic literature has seen the foundations of the Strategy to be correct but has discovered major institutional short-comings related to EU governance and to the OMC in particular. Such a research effort has been based on extensive empirical evidence of the economic performance of EU countries since 2000, the political functioning of the process at national and EU level and the key "deliverables" of the process.

4) Weak economic policy institutions?

Scholars have firstly analysed the "disappointing" economic and social performance of the EU since 2000. Comparing the post-Lisbon period with the previous decade, an extensive literature has stressed that the EU has not become the "most dynamic economy in the world": GDP growth in EU-15 and the euro area has been much lower than in the US; long-term productivity has been higher in the US than in Europe; and while employment rates have improved, the labour market has become more flexible at the lower end (Collignon *et al.*, 2005; Fitoussi and Le Cacheux, 2005). Creel *et al.* (2005) follow a similar approach: the poor performance of the EU proves that the EU has not developed the coherent economic policy institutions that are needed to foster its potential growth. The EU thus lacks "the real means of a proactive macro-structural policy mix (...) implementing structural reforms without coherent macro-economic governance" appears to be an "impossible task" (*ibid.*, page 4).

Collignon (2003 and 2008) has stressed that the objectives set in 2000 will not be met as a consequence of the weak focus on economic growth and the ineffective macroeconomic management: "institutional realities and hard-nosed political considerations have often impeded the realisation of policies necessary to improve the EU's economic performance" (*ibid.*, page 5).

The most recent Greek crisis has further contributed to the critical understanding of the Lisbon governance. This is firstly the case in regards to the mechanisms implemented through the Stability and Growth Pact and its interaction with the economic and employment guidelines. The debate is focused on crisis prevention on the one hand (need for enforcing existing provisions on auditing, stress-testing of budgetary policy and incentives for budget reforms) and on crisis management on the other (e.g. financial assistance, loans, interplay between EU and International Monetary Fund, etc.) (Marzinotto *et al.*, 2010). Other contributions to the contemporary literature have then shed light on the problematic balance between the ministers of finance and social policy ministers (Pochet, 2010). And the issue is even more evident in the governance of the new Europe 2020 Strategy.

5) A still limited participation of stakeholders?

The literature with a more political science and sociological angle has further developed the analysis of new modes of governance introduced through the Lisbon project. One of the key findings has been that individual parts of the Lisbon Strategy have their own institutional dynamics and policy influence. As far as participation is concerned, in particular, recent research indicates that, in practice, participation in the whole Strategy has proved to be uneven. As indicated above, the OMC was interpreted as a particularly participatory mode of governance that emphasises subsidiarity and as an example of democratic experimentalism (Smismans, 2008; de la Porte and Nanz, 2004).

The social partners and NGOs are involved to varying degrees in the different strands of the Social OMC (i.e. social inclusion, pensions, and healthcare and long-term care) at national and supranational level. Although there is some methodological ambiguity, Tucker (2003) provided evidence (on the base of reports provided by research networks) that in general the social partners and other groups have not played a major part in the policy coordination process, but there are indications that this varies significantly across the OMC and cross-nationally. In some coordination processes, for example the OMC on social inclusion, early indications stressed improvements in facilitating new forms of meaningful participation of civil society at the domestic level. This was interpreted as a signal that the OMC "has partially matched the ambition of the Lisbon participatory governance" (*ibid.*, page 20). This is confirmed by more recent assessments of the Social OMC (see chapter by Vanhercke in this volume).

Yet, more in-depth analyses of single OMC processes have led to more sceptical understandings of the participatory dimension. In particular, much research has focused on two categories of actors: social partners and civil society organisations. Empirical evidence has shown the broad variety of access venues open at EU level: from informal meetings between EU officials and NGOs, to formal committee meetings with important differences between policies and competent Directorate-Generals (see also Obradovic and Vizcaino, 2007). But, in the words of Kröger (2008, page 31), "access for civil society organisations to policy processes at EU level is poorly regulated and does not seem to be equally open to all in all instances (…) it does not fulfil the democratic norm of both liberal and deliberative democracy".

For Smismans (2008), the European Employment Strategy (EES) to date has proved to be a "top-down" approach with an inclusion of regional and local authorities in the implementation of employment guidelines. The OMC is a technocratic process involving national and EU civil servants in limited circles of experts.[7] In the words of Kröger (2008), consultative practices seem to do little to bridge the gap between the EU and its citizens. As argued by Kerber and Eckardt (2007), in most strands of the Social OMC the participation of social partners, local actors, civil society representatives, or even national parliaments, is weak or non-existent, despite the efforts of the Commission to increase their influence.

6) A more encouraging assessment of learning?

Political scientists have contributed to the more complex understanding of the causal nexus between the Lisbon project and national reforms introduced so far. As argued by Zeitlin (2009), the national influence and effectiveness of OMC processes is difficult to assess, not only because of their variety, complexity and relative newness, but also because of the methodological problems involved in assessing "the independent causal impact" of an iterative policy-making process without legally binding sanctions.

While economists have been sharply critical of the Lisbon Strategy and have stressed its lack of efficacy, Zeitlin (2008) has put forward a more optimistic reading, defining the cognitive impact of the Strategy and the OMC governance in particular as a "qualified success" (at least in some areas). For example, in social and employment policy the Strategy is held to have helped to raise the importance of national social policy issues in many Member States, to change policy thinking and cognitive maps through the introduction in the national debate of EU concepts (social inclusion, gender mainstreaming, etc), and to redefine old concepts which have proved increasingly ineffective. The same reading is shared by Tucker (2003), Jacobsson (2004), de la Porte *et al.* (2009) and Frazer and Marlier (present volume) as far as learning processes in technical committees are concerned. Both EU and national institutional capabilities have been improved through the definition of common indicators (Social Protection Committee, 2009).

For Vanhercke (in the present volume) and Zeitlin (2008), OMC processes have helped to raise the salience and ambition of national employment and social inclusion policies in many Member States. They have contributed to changes in national policy thinking by incorporating EU concepts and categories (such as activation, prevention, lifelong learning, gender mainstreaming and social inclusion) into domestic

---

[7] For a more positive assessment of participation through the Lisbon Strategy, see Zeitlin (2007).

debates, exposing policy-makers to new approaches, and pressing them to reconsider long-established but increasingly counterproductive policies. Yet, the same authors have focused on the risk of reducing learning opportunities as a consequence of the introduction (after the mid-term revision of Lisbon) of a more bilateral (between the Commission and each Member State) rather than multilateral dynamic in the process.

7) Some influence on national policy-making?

There is also evidence from both official reports and interviews that OMC instruments have contributed to changes in specific national policies. Yet, given the active role of Member States in shaping the development of OMC processes, their relationship to national policy-making should be understood as a two-way interaction rather than a one-way causal impact. Further positive influence concerns procedural shifts in governance and policy-making arrangements; mutual learning, based on the identification of common challenges and promising policy solutions at EU level; statistical harmonisation and capacity building; and the stimulus to rethink established approaches and practices. In this context, some contributions have provided empirical evidence that the Social OMC has supported a more "consensus oriented process of policy-making" (Natali, 2009).

Other scholars (see Kerber and Eckardt, 2007) have advanced some open questions. In particular, problems with incentives within the complex process of the OMC have still to be analysed. More detailed analysis is required to assess the interaction of its many participating agents, interest groups and institutions, both at the EU and the Member State level. An important object of future research should be the complex political bargaining processes that lead to common goals, assessment criteria and policy recommendations (*ibid.*, page 241).

Frazer and Marlier (2009) have stressed the need to better link the future EU social process with other relevant EU processes so that they are mutually reinforcing. For instance a better integration of the EU's and Member States' social objectives and EU Structural Funds may improve the influence of the new Europe 2020 on national reforms. (On the latter point, see also chapter by Jouen in the present volume.)

4.5 Concluding Remarks: Some Hypothesis on the Future EU Socio-economic Governance

The Lisbon agenda has represented in many respects a decisive step in the EU approach to social and economic development. Yet, substantive and analytical questions still need to be dealt with to shed light on the present and on the future of EU integration. And the recent financial and economic crisis has contributed to put them at the core of the scientific and political debate. There are open tensions (or trade-offs) that EU integration protagonists (and scholars) have to face in the near future.

First, the tensions have to do with the political and economic foundation of the EU project, and the reform of the European social model in the global economy. The Lisbon agenda represented a first attempt to find a new compromise through a broad Strategy. Limits have been evident in its ability to adjust social cohesion and economic competitiveness; environmental policy and productive growth; fiscal stability and structural reforms. In that respect, the Lisbon Strategy appears as a mechanical addition of different aims and goals rather than the solution to such trade-offs. Specific problems have to do with the broad policy agenda of the future Europe 2020: the tensions between budget, economic, employment and welfare reforms; and the need to focus more on social and labour market policy. The latter is decisive for the improvement of the EU legitimacy, while economic integration "by stealth" does not seem an option for the future of the EU. In this respect, as argued by Liddle in this volume, Europe 2020 and the Lisbon Treaty provide room for improvements. The "Horizontal Social Clause" introduced through Article 9 of the Lisbon Treaty provides a strategic tool for reinforcing the EU social dimension. And the text of the 10 integrated guidelines and the explicit reference to a "smart, sustainable and inclusive growth" are consistent with this more integrated approach. Here the most problematic aspect is the timing of this attempt for a more balanced socio-economic agenda. As stressed by Ferrera in his chapter, these opportunities require time and political mobilisation to be effective. Yet, the crisis and the stricter implementation of budgetary stability may rapidly reduce the room for defending social entitlements.

Secondly, the governance introduced through the Lisbon Strategy is still in need of improvements. The recent economic and budgetary crisis has proved EU governance is still weak. Specifically in the Euro-zone, a more integrated approach to financial regulation, monetary and economic policy is needed in order to limit the risk of future speculative attacks against the common currency. And employment and social policies have to be largely integrated (the new integrated guidelines represent a promising base for such a comprehensive approach) (European Commission, 2010). Here again, Europe 2020 – and the parallel development of the political and institutional debate (see the recent Monti (2010) and Barca (2009) Reports) – seems promising in its attempt to mobilise the whole EU toolkit. Both the further integration of the Single Market and the revision of EU cohesion policy are important instruments to activate for improving EU socio-economic governance.

The definition of a more ambitious strategy for the EU budget is a key part of it. The aim of increased participation and transparency seems far from being attained. EU democratic legitimacy has not significantly improved through the Lisbon Strategy, even if improvements in facilitating new forms of meaningful participation of civil society at the domestic level are evident. Individual parts of the process have shown different dynamics, with the Social OMC being the most successful. If Europe 2020 wants to improve on that, more emphasis on the integration of EU and national parliaments and of stakeholders has to be assured. Political commitment is decisive for the future of the Strategy and of the EU integration process. More active participation of citizens and stakeholders is necessary for improving the visibility of the process and its legitimacy. This seems the most urgent problem to face.

It is widely recognised that there have been advances in deliberation, sharing of information, benchmarking and learning especially through EU coordination in the field of social protection and social inclusion. But they seem far from having had a decisive impact on national policies and further impetus has to be granted by the new Europe 2020 Strategy (see Frazer and Marlier, present volume). The latter should be based on a more effective integration of different policy tools, and the strict link between coordination and structural funds (EU budget in general) seems the most obvious step towards a more effective influence on national reforms (especially in employment and social policy).

References

Alesina, A. and Giavazzi, F. (2006), *The Future of Europe: Reform or Decline*, Cambridge MA: MIT Press.

Amable, B. (2009), "Structural Reforms in Europe and the (In)coherence of Institutions", *Oxford Review of Economic Policy*, Vol. 25, 1:17-39.

Barca, F. (2009), *An agenda for a reformed cohesion policy: A place-based approach to meeting European Union challenges and expectations*, Independent Report prepared at the request of Danuta Hübner, Commissioner for Regional Policy, Brussels: European Commission. Available at: http://ec. europa.eu/regional_policy/policy/future/pdf/report_barca_v0306.pdf.

Begg, I. (2008), "Is there a convincing rationale for the Lisbon Strategy?", *Journal of Common Market Studies*, 2 (46): 427-435.

Begg, I., Draxler, J. and Mortensen, J. (2007), *Is Social Europe fit for Globalization? A study on the social impact of globalization in the European Union*, Brussels: European Communities.

Collignon, S. (2008), "The Lisbon Strategy, macroeconomic stability and the dilemma of governance with governments; or why Europe is not becoming the world's most dynamic economy", *International Journal of Public Policy*, 3 (1/2):72-99.

Collignon, S. (2003), *The European Republic: Policy proposals for a Future Constitution*, Centre for Applied Research Working Papers, No. 10/03.

Collignon, S., Dehousse, R., Gabolde, J., Jouen, M., Pochet, P., Salais, R., Sprenger, R.-U. and Zsolt De Sousa, H. (2005), *The Lisbon Strategy and the Open Method of Coordination. 12 Recommendations for an Effective Multi-level Strategy*, Policy Paper No. 12, March 2005, Paris: Notre Europe.

Creel, J., Laurent, E. and Le Cacheux, J. (2005), *Delegation in Inconsistency: The "Lisbon Strategy" Record as an Institutional Failure*, Working Paper 05/07, Paris: OFCE and Institute for Political Studies.

Daveri, F. (2002), "The New Economy in Europe 1992-2001", Oxford Review of Economic Policy, 18 (3):345-362.

de la Porte, C. and Nanz, P. (2004), "OMC – A Deliberative-Democratic Mode of Governance? The Cases of Employment and Pensions", *Journal of European Public Policy*, 11 (2):267-288.

de la Porte, C., Natali, D. and Pochet, P. (2009), "Self-governance in EU employment and social policy through the Open method of coordination", in E. Sorensen and P. Triantafillou (editors), *The Politics of Self-governance*, Ashgate, 187-210.

Eberlein, B. and Kerwer, D. (2004), "New Governance in the European Union: A Theoretical Perspective", *Journal of Common Market Studies*, 42 (1):121-142.

European Commission (2010), *Europe 2020: A strategy for smart, sustainable and inclusive growth*, Communication COM(2010) 2020, Brussels: European Commission. Available at: http://ec.europa.eu/eu2020/pdf/COMPLET%20 EN%20BARROSO%20%20%20007%20-%20Europe%202020%20-%20 EN%20version.pdf.

European Commission (2009), *Economic crisis in Europe: Causes, Consequences and Responses*, European Economy series, No. 7/2009, European Commission, Brussels: European Commission.

Falkner, G., Treib, O., Hartlapp, M. and Leiber, S. (2005), *Complying with Europe. EU harmonisation and soft law in the Member States*, Cambridge: Cambridge University Press.

Ferrera, M. (2008), "European Welfare States: Golden Achievements, Silver Prospects", *West European Politics*, 31 (1-2):82-107.

Ferrera, M., Hemerijck, A. and Rhodes, M. (2000), *The future of social Europe. Recasting work and welfare in the new economy*, Oeiras: Celta Editora.

Fitoussi, J. P. and Le Cacheux, J. (2005), *L'Etat de l'Union européenne*, Paris: Fayard and Presse de Sciences Po.

Frazer, H. and Marlier, E. (2009), *Assessment of the extent of synergies between growth and jobs policies and social inclusion policies across the EU as evidenced by the 2008-2010 National Reform Programmes: Key lessons*, EU Network of Independent Experts on Social Inclusion, Brussels: European

Commission. Available at: http://www.peer-review-social-inclusion.eu/ network-of-independent-experts/2008/second-semester-2008.

Goetschy, J. (2009), "The Lisbon Strategy and Social Europe: two closely linked destinies", in M.J. Rodrigues (editor) Europe, Globalization and the Lisbon Agenda, Cheltenham: Edward Elgar, 74-90.

Héritier, A. (2002), "New Modes of Governance in Europe: Policy-making without legislation?", in A. Héritier (editor) *In Common Goods: Reinventing European and International Governance*, Boulder: Rowman and Littlefield, 185-206.

Hopner, M. and Shafer, A. (2007), "A New Phase of European Integration: Organized Capitalism in Post-Ricardian Europe", Max Planck discussion paper series, 07/04.

International Monetary Fund (2009), *World Economic Outlook*, October.

Ioannou, D., Ferdinandusse, M., Lo Duca, M. and Coussens, W. (2008), *Benchmarking the Lisbon Strategy*, European Central Bank Occasional Paper Series, No. 85/08.

Jacobsson, K. (2004), "Soft regulation and the subtle transformation of states: the case of EU employment policy", *Journal of European Social Policy*, 14 (4):355-370.

Kerber, W. and Eckardt, M. (2007), "Policy Learning in Europe: The Open Method of Coordination and Laboratory Federalism", *Journal of European Public Policy*, 14 (2):227-247.

Kröger, S. (2008), "Nothing But Consultation: The Place of Organised Civil Society in EU Policy-making across Policies", European Governance papers (EUROGOV), No. C-08-03. Available at: http://www.connex-network.org/ eurogov/pdf/egp-connex-C-08-03.pdf.

Mabbett, D. and Schelkle, W. (2007), "Bringing macroeconomics back into the political economy of reform: the Lisbon Agenda and the "Fiscal Philosophy" of EMU", *Journal of Common Market Studies*, 45 (1):81-103.

Majone, G. (2005), *Dilemmas of European Integration: The Ambiguities and Pitfalls of Integration by Stealth*, Oxford: Oxford University Press.

Marzinotto, B., Pisani-Ferry, J. and Sapir, A. (2010), "Two crisis, two responses", *Bruegel Policy Brief*, 2010/01.

Monti, M. (2010), *A New Strategy for the Single Market*, Independent report prepared at the request of President Barroso, Brussels, European Commission. Available at: http://ec.europa.eu/bepa/pdf/monti_report_final _10_05_2010 _en.pdf.

Natali, D. (2010), Pensions in turmoil owing to the crisis: key messages from the EU, in C. Degryse (editor) *Social Developments in the European Union 2009*, Brussels, ETUI/OSE, pages 121-45.

Natali, D. (2009), The Lisbon Strategy ten years on, A critical review of a multi-disciplinary literature, *Transfer: European Review of Labour and Research*, Vol. 15, 1:111-137.

Natali, D. and de la Porte, C. (2009), "Participation through the Lisbon Strategy: comparing the European Employment Strategy and pensions OMC", *Transfer: European Review of Labour and Research*, 15/1:71-91.

Obradovic, D. and Vizcaino, J. (editors) (2007), *The capacity of Central and East European interest groups to participate in EU governance*, Stuttgart: *Ibid.* Publisher.

Pisani-Ferry, J. and Sapir, A. (2006), "Last exit to Lisbon", *Bruegel Policy Brief*, 2006/02.

Pisani-Ferry, J. Sapir, A. and Von Weizsacker, J. (2008), "A European Recovery Programme", *Bruegel Policy Brief*, 2008/09.

Pochet, P. (2010), "What's wrong with EU2020?", *ETUI Policy Brief*, 2/2010.

Pochet, P. (2006), "Debate around the social model: evolving players, strategies and dynamics", in C. Degryse and P. Pochet (editors), *Social developments in the European Union 2005*, Brussels: ETUI, Observatoire social européen and Saltsa, 79-99.

Quaglia, L. (2010), *The "Old" and "New" Politics of Financial Services Regulation in the EU*, OSE Paper Series, Research Paper No. 2, April 2010.

Rodrigues, M.A. (2010), *The EU Economic Governance at the Crossroads*, Policy paper for Notre Europe. Available at: www.notre-europe.org.

Rodrigues, M. J. (2002), *The New Knowledge Economy in Europe – A Strategy for International Competitiveness and Social Cohesion*, Cheltenham: Edward Elgar.

Sabel, C. and Zeitlin, J. (2007), *Learning from Difference: The New Architecture of Experimentalist Governance in the European Union*, European Governance papers (EUROGOV), No. C-07-02.

Sapir, A. (editor) (2004), *An Agenda for Growing Europe. The Sapir Report*, Oxford: Oxford University Press.

Scott, J. and Trubek, D. (2002), "Mind the Gap: Law and New Approaches to Governance in the European Union", *European Law Journal*, 8 (1):1-18.

Smismans, S. (2008), "New Modes of Governance and the Participatory Myth", *West European Politics*, 31 (5):874-895.

Social Protection Committee (2009), *Growth, Jobs and Social Progress in the EU: A contribution to the evaluation of the social dimension of the Lisbon Strategy*, Brussels: European Commission. Available at: http://ec.europa.eu/social/BlobServlet?docId=3898&langId=en.

Social Protection Committee (2008), *Child Poverty and Well-Being in the EU: Current status and way forward*, Luxembourg: OPOCE. Available at: http://ec.europa.eu/social/main.jsp?catId=751&langId=en&pubId=74&type=2&furtherPubs=yes.

Social Protection Committee and European Commission (2009), *Second Joint Assessment of the social impact of the economic crisis and of policy responses*, SOC 715 – ECOFIN 808, Brussels, European Commission.

Theodoropoulou, S. (2010), "Addressing Europe's employment crisis: what policies for recovery and reform?", *EPC Policy Brief*, 02/2010.

Tucker, C. (2003), *The Lisbon Strategy and the Open Method of Coordination: A New Vision and the Revolutionary Potential of Soft Governance in the European Union*, paper presented at the Annual Meeting of the American Political Science Association, 28-31 August.

Von Hagen, Pisani-Ferry, J. And Von Weizshacker, J. (2009), "A European Exit Strategy", *Bruegel Policy Brief*, 2009/05.

Zeitlin, J. (2009), "The Open Method of Coordination and National Social and Employment Policy Reforms: Influences, Mechanisms, Effects", in Martin Heidenreich and Jonathan Zeitlin (editors), *Changing European Employment and Welfare Regimes: The Influence of the Open Method of Coordination on National Reforms*, London: Routledge: 214-45.

Zeitlin, J. (2008), "The Open Method of Coordination and the Governance of the Lisbon Strategy", *Journal of Common Market Studies*, 46 (2):436-450.

5. Delivering the Goods for Europe 2020?

The Social OMC's Adequacy and Impact Re-assessed

Bart VANHERCKE[1]

5.1 Introduction

In the ongoing discussions on the future of the Social Open Method of Coordination (OMC), in particular in the context of the Europe 2020 Strategy, one rather basic element seems to be missing from the debate (or at least to have been obscured) namely an assessment of the extent to which the Social OMC (with its three strands on social inclusion, pensions, as well as healthcare and long-term care), has delivered concrete results. This is a legitimate concern at a time when EU and national policy-makers are discussing the future role and content of the Social OMC and the yet-to-be created "European Platform against Poverty" (EPAP), the social dimension of the Integrated Guidelines for Economic and Employment Policies, and the institutional design of the overall Europe 2020 Strategy.

This chapter therefore assesses the results of the Social OMC with the aim of answering the question: *Has the Social OMC delivered the goods?*[2] This issue has in fact been widely debated in the last decade in the OMC research community: once the initial praise for the OMC (both by politicians and scientists) started to wane, the process was subjected to intense scrutiny and found wanting in mainstream academic literature (Vanhercke, 2007). At first sight this should not come as a surprise.

[1] The research done for this chapter benefited from funding from the Community's PROGRESS programme and was supported by the Belgian Federal Public Service Social Security (Directorate-General Strategy and Research) in the context of the "Europe 2020" research project. I wish to thank Caroline de la Porte and Timo Weishaupt for the collaborative research efforts which led to this chapter; Margherita Bussi for invaluable around-the-clock research assistance; Eric Marlier, David Natali, Jonathan Zeitlin, Egidijus Barcevičius, Peter Lelie, and an anonymous reviewer at the European Commission for their constructive criticism on earlier drafts. The views expressed in this chapter are the sole responsibility of the author. Address for correspondence: vanhercke@ose.be.

[2] This question is equally addressed in Vanhercke (2010), which presents a more in-depth assessment of the recent literature on the Social OMC.

Indeed, viewed in terms of its institutional characteristics, the absence of a "shadow of hierarchy" (legislative and executive decisions) would suggest that this mode of governance cannot deal effectively with the problems it is supposed to solve (Héritier and Lehmkuhl, 2008). Yet this chapter argues that through mechanisms such as leverage and policy learning, this "weak" policy instrument does produce real effects. The crux of the matter is this: it is not the "hardness" or the "softness" of the OMC that matters, but its capacity to stimulate creative appropriation and action by European, national and sub-national actors.

At the same time, this chapter argues that any credible assessment of the OMC should distinguish between two key dimensions. On the one hand, the *adequacy of the Social OMC* is defined as the extent to which the OMC's architecture (institutional setup) is likely to contribute to reaching its objectives at EU and national level. In other words, *adequacy* refers to the *theoretical* capacity of the OMC toolbox to produce results. On the other hand, the *impact* of the Social OMC is defined as the extent to which the Social OMC has *actually* influenced policies and policy-making processes at EU and national level. In other words: impact refers to the effects of the Social OMC "on the ground". Clearly distinguishing between these two dimensions is indeed important: at least some of the disagreement between OMC "optimists" and "pessimists" can in our view be attributed to the fact that they are looking at different aspects of the OMC. Quite often "theoretically enriched" studies assessing the OMC on the basis of its institutional architecture (adequacy) do not provide empirical evidence about whether or not these critical assessments are confirmed by the actual OMC practice.

The chapter is organised as follows: Section 5.2 explores the different dimensions of the adequacy of the Social OMC's toolbox, reviewing the Social OMC's communication strategy, its operational value in coordinating policies at EU level, the features of the OMC toolkit and its interaction with domestic processes. Section 5.3 assesses the impact of the Social OMC "on the ground", looking at substantive policy changes, shifts in domestic governance, and its impact on EU-level policies and politics. Section 5.4 aims at reconciling the apparently contradictory conclusions with regard to adequacy and impact by looking at some of the mechanisms at work. Finally, Section 5.5 concludes, providing some forward-looking perspectives with a view to further strengthening the Social OMC's adequacy *and* impact.

5.2 The Adequacy of the Social OMC's Toolbox: Mixed Evidence (at best)

This section assesses the theoretical capacity of the OMC toolbox to produce results at EU and national level (adequacy). Wherever possible, specific attention is paid to the three strands of the Social OMC (social inclusion, pensions, as well as healthcare and long-term care).

5.2.1 Adequacy of the Social OMC's communication strategy: public awareness and institutional visibility

Many authors concur with the finding by Kröger (2008) that the OMC is a process marked by its near invisibility in the media and to the citizens, which explains why labels such as "the EU's best kept secret" are attributed to it. A recent evaluation (INBAS *et al.*, 2009) of stakeholder involvement in the implementation of the OMC confirms the earlier finding (e.g. Büchs and Friedrich, 2005, page 275) that national reports are rarely, if ever, discussed in Parliament and that the OMC has not permeated public discourse or the media. What is perhaps even more worrying is that even for the "inner circle" of people involved in the Social OMC, key aspects of the process remain hidden, due to the fact that the Social Protection Committee (SPC) and its Indicators Sub-Group do not make the full panoply of their internal documents (including minutes of meetings) available online (Zeitlin, 2005, page 484; Marlier *et al.*, 2007, page 244). One of the rare examples of (ad hoc) public visibility of the OMC is provided by Norris (2007): in 2006, the recently-elected Portuguese President referred prominently to the inclusion plan in his address on Portugal's national holiday commemorating the return to democracy, resulting in considerable media coverage of the OMC/inclusion.

But what about the *institutional* awareness and visibility of the OMC, including among (sub-)national governmental actors (typically ministries of social security, pensions and health) and stakeholder organisations? According to Friedrich (2006) the Social OMC remains elite-driven and opaque and is therefore limited as regards its democratic potential. Some nuance is in order, however: several national studies of the OMC/inclusion (less is known about the pensions and healthcare strands) highlight that the Social OMC's institutional visibility (and thus the awareness of its existence) varies strongly within and across countries as well as over time. In Belgium some noticeable cases were reported by Vanhercke *et al.* (2008) of the strategic use of the OMC as a governance tool for coordinating local and regional (social inclusion and gender) policies, indicating a considerable degree of awareness at different levels of government.

In spite of these nuances (variation across countries and over time), a recent assessment of the awareness and perception of the social inclusion strand of the Social OMC[3] reaches the firm conclusion[4] that it "is clear from the experts' analysis that awareness of the social inclusion strand of the Social OMC is limited to a narrow band of actors in most Member States. [...] In most countries, there is virtually no media or public awareness of the Social OMC and no political debate about the process. In only a small number of countries does there appear to be much interest within the academic community or significant social partner engagement" (Frazer and Marlier, 2008, page 2).

5.2.2 Adequacy of policy coordination at EU level: objectives, messages and reports

A second dimension whereby the OMC can be assessed is to ask whether the OMC common objectives, messages and reports are clear, pertinent and operational. de la Porte (2008) found that the OMC/inclusion objectives are sometimes criticised and sometimes praised in the literature for their "openness". Büchs (2009) notes that the Social OMC's objectives and guidelines contain different and sometimes conflicting elements, some of which are more likely to be interpreted in ways that promote the strengthening of the welfare state whilst others are more likely to support retrenchment. For this author key concepts are open to interpretation (e.g. "activation").

As regards (the lack of) policy coherence within the OMC, de la Porte (2007) confirms that the objectives of the Social Inclusion strand reflect diverging national approaches (Anglo-Saxon, Continental and Nordic) to this issue. Hamel and Vanhercke (2009) confirm that the first Common Objective in this strand ("to facilitate participation in employment and access by all to the resources, rights, goods and services") was particularly conflictual and represented "the ultimate European compromise" since it is obvious that these are really two distinct priorities, and not one. And yet, the same authors find that the Social Inclusion Common Objectives had a significant influence in Belgian and French policy-making. This has been most visible in terms of agenda setting and promoting stakeholder involvement, which clearly facilitated

---

[3] Undertaken in the context of the assessment in social inclusion programme. See: http://www.peer-review-social-inclusion.eu/network-of-independent-experts/policy-assessment-activities.

[4] This conclusion is based on an analysis of the reports produced by the members of the EU Network of Independent Experts on Social Inclusion (unfortunately, the national contributions of these "OMC awareness" assessments were not made public): http://www.peer-review-social-inclusion.eu/network-of-independ ent-experts/policy-assessment-activities.

creative appropriation of the process in both countries (*ibid.*). Armstrong (2005) in fact doubts whether common EU objectives are all that significant in stimulating processes of policy problem identification.

The objectives under the pensions strand represent both economic and social concerns (Pochet and Natali, 2005). On a slightly more sceptical note, Lodge (2007, page 350) interpreted the principles and objectives of the pensions strand as the "least undesirable" outcome of negotiations between "economic" and "social" actors; according to Lodge the objectives were very weak (and were intended to be so) and extremely broad, and therefore had no directing capacity since they "allow any policy development to comply with such standards". Similarly, Radulova (2007) concludes that the institutional characteristics of this strand (lack of Treaty basis, Recommendations etc.) make it a "weak" OMC. It should be noted that one of the rare studies available that actually studied the impact of the Pensions OMC "on the ground" (Vanhercke, 2009) concluded that the Common Objectives did indeed influence the national as well as the EU agenda (see Section 5.3.1).

Discussing the healthcare strand, Greer and Vanhercke (2010) make the argument that the "ambiguous words" of the Common Objectives are in fact useful when there is no fundamental agreement: they create an opening for new EU competencies while stressing that there would have been greater efforts to block the common objectives (in health) had the objectives been clear. And yet the "normative" orientation of these healthcare objectives is quite clear for Flear (2009): they not only extend market rationality and facilitate governing at a distance by providing inducements for self-management, but they also promote moves away from equity and solidarity. Writing about the same OMC strand, Hervey (2008) rejects the claim that the healthcare OMC promotes neoliberal policies, while the European Centre for Social Welfare Policy and Research *et al.* (2008) find strong confirmation of pertinence of overarching objectives of the healthcare strand of the OMC.

Turning to the adequacy of the (subtle) country-specific messages, observers will recall the negative, collective response of SPC members to the Commission's implicit efforts to "rank" the NAPs/inclusion in the first (2001) Joint Report on Social Inclusion, which closed the door on anything resembling formal recommendations in the social field. Yet Hamel and Vanhercke (2009) explain how two "cold showers" from the European Commission (through its Draft Joint Reports) with regard to stakeholder involvement in the elaboration of the Belgian NAPs/inclusion, combined with the acknowledgment (through mutual learning) that perhaps Belgium was not the best pupil in the class after all, led to real procedural shifts; i.e. increased stakeholder involvement in the social inclusion OMC at the beginning of 2005 (see Section 5.3.2).

It is quite difficult to assess the adequacy of National Strategy reports and guidance notes for the reports. The latter are considered to be too technical by most scholars, who often do not even know about their existence. One of the rare reports that addresses the issue is from the European Anti-Poverty Network (EAPN, 2008), which found some evidence of an increase in specific social inclusion/poverty reduction targets and for specific groups as a result of the guidance notes. For the European Social Network the Commission's guidance note should be more explicit regarding the requirement to set targets and provide budget details (ESN, 2009).

The adequacy of the National Action Plans and National Strategic Reports on Social Protection and Social Inclusion can be considered as a proxy indicator for the quality of the guidance provided. Armstrong (2005) and Marlier *et al.* (2007) highlighted that the second NAPs/inclusion (during the 2003-2005 period) were above all reports, and called for "restructured" NAPs/inclusion that should become a "strategic planning exercise, the goal of which is to actually develop an 'action plan'". This diagnosis is confirmed by Jacobsson and Johansson (2009) as regards Sweden: the NAP/inclusion is not a strategic document, but instead a "report to Brussels" about existing activities. This view is shared by EAPN (2008), while the European Social Network contends that only a very small number of Member States have used the reports to (re)assess national social inclusion policies. An analysis of two rounds of NAPs/inclusion (2004-2006 and 2006-2008) by Sirovátka and Rákoczyová (2009) confirms this gloomy picture: the NAPs/inclusion reflect the low level of commitment to social inclusion/anti-poverty efforts in the Czech Republic, which are deemed even lower than in other new Member States, while the plans do not provide empirical evidence of how NGOs and civil society have or have not used the NAPs/inclusion. A different view can be read in Armstrong (2005), who found that the NAPs/inclusion triggered domestic responses. Norris (2007) goes even further and describes how in Ireland the processes of the National Anti-Poverty Strategy (NAPS) and the social inclusion OMC, including their targets and consultations, have largely been integrated.

The process for analysing reports, consulting with Member States/other stakeholders and drawing conclusions is, at least in part, addressed by Sirovátka and Rákoczyová (2009) who note that the Commission is harsh in its analysis of the Czech report, due to its lack of precision and commitment. Greer and Vanhercke (2010) provide illustrations of where the OMC might look "soft" but, in some cases, it feels quite hard to those who are affected by it. This was confirmed by earlier research by Jacobsson (2005), who found that the Swedish government showed strong resistance to the social inclusion policy, and to assessments by the Commission. Another example, provided by O'Donnell and Moss (2005), illustrates this point. They report that the first Irish NAP/inclusion lacked strategy, data, analysis of problems, and the identification of or focus on specific target groups. After "shaming" by the Commission, the second report was improved, and had a better strategy and analysis of problems.

A final dimension of the adequacy of policy coordination at EU level is the Social OMC's capacity to stimulate a genuine policy debate and build consensus around promising policy approaches. This issue was addressed by Horvath (2007), who found that most Member States' delegates regard it as essential for the SPC to reach a consensus or compromise at the end of all discussions. Being able to agree on "common opinions" is seen as one of the main factors which determine the success of the SPC. In sum: there seems to be a normative orientation towards consensus-oriented discussions, even if SPC members who have been representatives for less than 2 years (became delegates after the 2004 enlargement) refer less often to consensus, cooperation and common values.

5.2.3 Adequacy of features of the OMC toolkit: feeding in/out, indicators and mutual learning

The links between policy strands within the OMC and with other policy areas at EU level (mutual reinforcement, feeding in/out) can be considered rather problematic, amongst other reasons due to the lack of coordination between the strands on pensions, social inclusion and healthcare. Zeitlin (2008) argues that "by excluding the EU's social objectives from the integrated guidelines, the Union has effectively returned to the one-sided coordination of Member States' social policies in pursuit of financial sustainability and employment promotion which the Social OMC was developed to overcome". Unsurprisingly then the SPC (2009) concluded that the issues of "feeding in" and "feeding out" should be better covered by the Member States and the European Commission, in view of the finding that key social issues are not always properly acknowledged within the Lisbon agenda. This is corroborated by Frazer and Marlier (2009) who find that the links between social inclusion policies on the one hand and employment and economic policies on the other are in most cases modest and limited. Barbier (2010) refers to this lack of efficient feeding in/out as *"les promesses sociales non tenues"* (i.e. the broken social promises) of the Lisbon Strategy.

In the field of health, any attempt to strengthen the adequacy of the OMC will need to acknowledge the reality, recently spelled out by

Hervey and Vanhercke (2010), that no fewer than five different sets of actors are trying to expand their influence on the EU healthcare debate: the "social affairs", "internal market", "public health", "economic" and "enterprise" players. Together, they have created a very crowded law and policy-making space to which actors bring their conflicting agendas and understanding of health policies. According to Greer and Vanhercke (2010) this reduces the functional capacity of this OMC strand, since it entails huge competition for time and political attention with other health policy issues and processes. Others come to a similar conclusion in the area of pensions, where diverse organised interests try to influence the existing European networks (Natali, 2009; Pochet and Natali, 2005).

The consistency and adequacy of the set of common indicators as tools for measuring progress towards the common objectives, and for providing useful guidance for self-corrective action by domestic actors ("diagnostic monitoring") is another key dimension of the OMC's adequacy. In fact, there seems to be a widely shared understanding that the availability of comparable and quantifiable indicators constitutes the "litmus test for the political readiness to engage in open coordination" (Vandenbroucke, 2002). In this view, it may come as some surprise that much of the research on this topic seems to have missed the point that since the adoption of the initial set of social inclusion indicators by the Laeken European Council in December 2001 (Atkinson *et al.*, 2002), work on indicators has continued with a view to refining and consolidating the original set as well as to extending it (Marlier *et al.*, 2007). Similarly, important progress has been made with regard to pensions (including an overarching indicator on overall replacement rates of pensions) and healthcare indicators (Cantillon, 2010). As a result, the indicators of the Social OMC serve as a source of inspiration for those working on the analysis and measurement of social policies in a global context (Atkinson and Marlier, 2010; Social Inclusion Unit (2004).

Nevertheless, critical OMC scholars such as Flear (2009) argue that even indicators for access and quality of care ultimately seek to optimise performance, by providing the means to assess whether objectives are met, and thereby ensure that equity and solidarity are subordinated in a neoliberal frame. de la Porte (2007) suggested that over-reliance on key macro-level indicators (such as employment indicators) in Joint Reports may be misleading as employment/anti-poverty rates depend on multiple factors, not covered by the OMC, while there are no indicators for some of the OMC objectives (including on participation). Sacchi (2006) judges that indicators are too general and can be interpreted in different ways, although they can be seen as flexible tools to be adapted to national needs.

Clearly, political, institutional and national interests are present in the decision-making process on definitions and indicators of the Social OMC. This finding is corroborated by Jacobson (2005), who explains that while the Swedish and Danish governments are supportive of the OMC, both countries resist indicators/targets to monitor/assess poverty and exclusion, due to the norms of the universal welfare state. Similarly, Greer and Vanhercke (2010) find that difficulties in data collection and handling, as well as political risks, have slowed down the work on indicators in the healthcare OMC, and therefore this strand as a whole. More generally, the latter authors state that new governance mechanisms are intensely "political": they are shaped both by deliberative norms and through hardboiled power games between national and EU actors (and within Directorate-Generals of the European Commission). Cantillon (2010, page 2) confirms that the (political) ambiguity of the poverty concept is reflected in the overarching portfolio of social indicators agreed in the context of the OMC (on the potential role of EU indicators, see Frazer and Marlier, this volume).

The adequacy of OMC tools available for mutual learning is highly contested. OMC-sceptical researchers such as Lodge (2007) claim that the basic infrastructure for the (pensions) OMC to operate has been found wanting: standards had no directing capacity, information-gathering offered only very little truly comparative information to encourage "benchmarking" or "learning with others", and voluntary adjustment pressures seemed hardly present. This finding is confirmed by Kröger (2009), as she finds that the OMC does not satisfy requirements for a learning-friendly environment. Even though it is not entirely clear what such an environment would actually look like, serious questions can indeed be raised as regards the adequacy of the pensions OMC, *inter alia* because the process is not at all visible in the national arena, and regular peer review sessions (in the SPC) only allow for a superficial exchange of ideas. Furthermore, more "optimistic" scholars such as Greer and Vanhercke (2010) believe that learning, at least in the healthcare OMC, is of a limited kind because the wrong people will do the learning (i.e. the international units and not the line officials).

The Tavistock Institute (2006) considers that, in the context of the Transnational Exchange Programmes, learning did take place within the programme for those involved but it did not lead to more institutional changes or partnerships. FEANTSA[5] sees the OMC as a way to enhance "mutual learning" about the involvement of NGOs (from local to EU level) in the issue of homelessness; this European Federation is pushing

---

[5] FEANTSA is the European Federation of National Organisations Working with the Homeless.

for more thematic peer reviews, which they consider as having a genuine impact (FEANTSA, 2007). ÖSB Consulting (2006) concludes that peer reviews were most relevant where there were similar initiatives/ governance structures/ problems among peer countries. It seems important, finally, to stress that few of the studies concerned with this issue make explicit which "peer reviews" they actually refer to: the largely formal sessions in the plenary SPC meetings (involving all Member States), or the more in-depth reviews – in smaller groups – within the Peer Review programme[6].

5.2.4 Adequacy of the operational framework: the national level

Another way of assessing the adequacy of the Social OMC is to look at how it relates to ongoing national processes. Thus, Letzner and Schmitt (2007) find that the OMC reports are "in competition" with the three German national reports on pensions published during each legislature. Büchs and Friedrich (2005) confirm that there are only cautious signs that some German officials understand the NAP/inclusion as a "national" plan and have started to reflect upon a closer relation to the National Report on Poverty and Wealth (NARB). Similarly, Hamel and Vanhercke (2009) explain that the NAP/inclusion continues to coexist with the biannual reports on the evolution of poverty in Belgium, which the Resource Centre for the Fight against Poverty, Precariousness and Social Exclusion has been producing since 2001.

This is why Vanhercke *et al.* (2008) conclude that the social inclusion OMC and pre-existing national reporting and decision-making channels (with partly overlapping responsibilities) should be better geared to one another. In a similar vein, EAPN (2008) contends that the National Strategic Reports (NSRs) should be linked to the national planning cycle and affirmed as government policy discussed in the EU and national parliaments. The latter is already the case in Ireland: Norris (2007) found that national and EU processes have largely been integrated there.

5.2.5 Adequacy of the Social OMC: wrapping things up

Summing up, this section has presented a rather mixed picture of the theoretical capacity of the OMC toolbox to produce results (its adequacy). Due to the lack of transparency of the process, both the public awareness about and the institutional visibility of the process are weak overall, but there are also strong variations between countries and the

---

[6]   Peer Review in Social Protection and Social Inclusion: http://www.peer-review-social-inclusion.eu/.

OMC strands over time. In Section 5.3 we will see that this ('lack of openness') feature of the OMC architecture has important implications for the possibilities of "creative appropriation" by actors. The Social OMC's objectives contain ambiguous and sometimes conflicting elements, while country-specific messages are often deemed "too subtle" even to be assessed; at the same time there is evidence that the very same messages as well as the Common Objectives "bite" more than is generally acknowledged. The national reports produced in the context of the OMC are often seen as administrative documents (rather than planning devices), but here too important exceptions exist (i.e. triggering national responses, integration into domestic planning efforts). The adequacy of the linkages both *within* the Social OMC and with *other* policy areas at EU level is rather questionable: "feeding in" and "feeding out" do not work.

The adequacy of common indicators as tools for measuring progress towards the common objectives has equally been criticised by many authors, especially in the pensions and healthcare strands of the Social OMC. And yet, some prudence is in order: we pointed to fact that some of the key developments in the EU's statistical apparatus are simply ignored by a large part of the literature. There is considerable agreement that the adequacy of the healthcare and pensions strands of the Social OMC is severely constrained by the presence of other, competing EU-level processes. At the same time, the adequacy of OMC tools available for mutual learning is a subject of intense debate in the literature, not least because the wrong people would do the learning; in this context, too, we pointed to an important methodological problem: researchers should be far more precise about the type of "peer reviews" they are assessing, and take into account changes in the OMC toolbox. Finally, the discussion of the adequacy of the OMC operational framework at national level suggests that OMC reports are often in competition with (pre-existing) domestic processes.

In sum, while the Social OMC's institutional setup should allow it to produce at least some results, some important flaws are also apparent from the discussion. The question now is whether the flaws imply that the Social OMC has by and large failed to deliver the goods. The next section argues that to say so would be jumping to conclusions too fast.

5.3 Assessing the Impact of the Social OMC: Procedural and Substantive Effects "on the Ground"

This section assesses the impact of the Social OMC on domestic and EU policies and politics. This impact has been operationalised along two lines: the *substantive* impact of the OMC, i.e. changes in policy thinking and individual Member States' policies; and *procedural* changes, i.e. the impact on the process of domestic policy-making (shifts in governance and policy-making arrangements)[7].

5.3.1 Substantive policy change at the national level: enhancing commitment, agenda setting and mirror effects

A reasonable amount of evidence points to the OMC's impact on maintaining or enhancing commitment to the subject-matter of the OMC in the political agenda. Thus Zeitlin (2009) empirically demonstrates that the European Employment Strategy (EES) and the Social OMC have increased the salience of efforts to tackle long-recognised national problems: early exit from the labour market, childcare provision, gender segregation and the integration of immigrants. Others show how the EU commitment to eradicate poverty pushed the fight against poverty and the activation issue higher up the domestic inclusion agenda (Hamel and Vanhercke, 2009). Perhaps even more surprising is that such an impact has also been felt on "sticky" institutions such as pension systems. Thus, when studying the process of pension reform in Greece (prior to the economic crisis) in the context of the "soft" policy constraint emanating from the EU, Featherstone (2005) found that the OMC process lacks the strength to provide a stimulus to domestic reform; at the same time the author argues that the OMC coverage of pensions affects Greece's interest in reform (credibility, reputation). A similar finding applies to Belgium, where EU pressure on the need to reform is strongly felt, and has become an argument in political negotiations: doing nothing is no longer an option (Vanhercke, 2009). Referring to Germany, Eckardt (2005, page 263) confirms that, while the OMC's influence on actual policy transfer seems to be very slight, it may contribute to accelerating the speed at which reforms are tackled, by repeatedly putting the overall objectives on the EU and national agendas.

It seems important to underline that not all authors agree with such a "positive" account of this aspect of OMC impact. Büchs (2009) for example, concludes that it is possible that the OMC facilitated retrenching policy reforms by providing necessary discourses and justifications rendering policy reforms acceptable, e.g. with regard to "activation" frameworks: national policy actors seem on average to have interpreted and implemented them in ways that did not improve or actually worsened welfare state performance. In other words: OMC makes a difference within national social policy development, but not in the way

---

[7] For a more in-depth discussion of the substantive and procedural changes of the OMC, see Zeitlin (2009a and 2005).

promoted by the EU or hoped for by "optimistic" OMC scholars (Cantillon, 2010; Büchs, 2008).

It should be noted that some scholars have pointed out that the OMC does not merely contribute to enhancing "soft law" commitments, but is also used to enhance commitment to the transposition of "hard law". Thus, de la Rosa (2007) explains how soft-law mechanisms are used to increase the implementation of EU legal initiatives, for example in the area of non-discrimination. Amitsis (2004) describes how the political support for soft governance in the field of pensions seems to have spilled over to its use in the framework of Directive 2003/41 on the activities and supervision of institutions for occupational retirement provision, which uses OMC-type mechanisms (exchange of experience, benchmarking) to implement this piece of EU legislation. Hervey and Vanhercke (2010) make a more general point about the introduction of governance mechanisms within legislative instruments.

There is also considerable agreement about the fact that the Social OMC is putting new issues on the domestic political agenda: according to Zeitlin (2009) it has done so in a variety of countries (old and new Member States) and on a variety of topics, including activation, social exclusion and child poverty (on the latter topic, see Social Protection Committee, 2008). This finding is confirmed by Sacchi (2006), who points to a redirection of national priorities and concerns in the UK (e.g. more attention to gender issues and child poverty). Illustrating the "hard" impact of the OMC, Hamel and Vanhercke (2009), show that in spite of strong resistance in both France and Belgium against the issue of child poverty, this topic – which previously was virtually absent from the national agendas – gained a place in domestic politics in both countries. It figures among the top priorities of the Belgian Presidency of the EU in 2010, and was recently associated with a specific target (halving child poverty) in one of the country's Regions (Vanhercke, 2009a). Even more fundamentally perhaps, the OMC/inclusion put poverty on the policy agenda as a novelty for some countries: particularly in universal welfare states it was not (really) acknowledged as an issue that deserved specific attention (de la Porte, 2007). It may come as a surprise that the OMC equally put new issues on some domestic agendas in the field of pensions. Vanhercke (2009) describes how the pensions OMC contributed to the (very prudent) introduction of an entirely new element in the Belgian pensions system, i.e. that of actuarial neutrality. It should be noted that this development has not been particularly welcomed by some of the key Belgian actors: for some it "opens the door for a reduction of solidarity in the Belgian pension system" (*ibid.*, page 12).

Another way of assessing the OMC's impact at the domestic level is to trace whether its concepts, indicators and categories permeate domestic policy-making, an issue which has in part been dealt with in the previous paragraphs (e.g. the concept of "child poverty"). At a general level, it is widely accepted that the statistical efforts inspired by the Social OMC enhanced the statistical capacity of many EU Member States (for a detailed account of the French and Belgian cases, see Hamel and Vanhercke, 2009). One more concrete illustration of the permeation of pension OMC indicators into the domestic setting is the fact that the low (and decreasing) replacement rate of Belgian pensions has become an issue that for the first time is being studied by the influential Study Committee on Ageing (Vanhercke, 2009). In Germany, by contrast, EU debates about "replacement rates" have had no significant echo according to Letzner and Schmitt (2007, page 237), since they were already a salient issue in national debate. Another illustration of the penetration of EU categories is the use of the EU risk-of-poverty norm, which was developed in the context of the Social Inclusion strand of the SPSI OMC and which acquired a broader mobilising character, at least in some countries. Thus, Hamel and Vanhercke (2009) show how a significant increase in minimum income for the elderly (GRAPA) in Belgium was politically legitimised by pointing out that the benefit levels were below the EU risk-of-poverty norm.

Not so much is known about the effective take-up of EU recommended policies (reception and implementation of policy recommendations) within the Social OMC. Those authors who do engage with the question as to whether recommended policies are being followed often do so with a command-and-control yardstick, as it is the case for Ania and Wagener (2008, page 21), who see the OMC as an "evolutionary game", which "forces Member States to [...] adopt what has turned out to be the best-performing policy option". Unsurprisingly they conclude that "the plausible idea that the imitation of best practices makes policies converge to efficiency is genuinely misguided". The assessments by Lodge (2007) and Radulova (2007) discussed in Section 5.2.2 follow a similar line of thought: since there is no (or insufficient) "naming and shaming", the pensions' OMC is necessarily weak. And yet, when studying the OMC "on the ground", Vanhercke (2009) finds that the pensions OMC, in combination with pressure from the European Employment Strategy, has made the magnitude of the early-retirement problem crystal clear to Belgian social policy-makers and contributed to an important mind-shift among trade unions. In other words: "naming and shaming" may be more effective than it would appear at first glance (see also Section 5.2.2).

The literature provides a number of examples where the OMC has stimulated self-reflection on national performance. According to Letzner and Schmitt (2007) the pensions OMC has stimulated auto-evaluation in Germany. In the field of inclusion, Jacobsson and Johansson (2009, page 175) argue that the OMC/inclusion challenged the normative value of the universal welfare state, by acknowledging (and indeed framing) poverty and social exclusion as a challenge to be overcome in Sweden. While the EAPN (2008) contends that policy self-reflection is not always effective, process tracing in Belgium and France by Hamel and Vanhercke (2009) demonstrates how a "mirror effect" can trigger significant reforms in domestic policy-making arrangements. For these authors, the need to expose the national field to others, which is necessary for any comparison, gives a clearer vision of one's own practices (Hamel and Vanhercke, 2009, page 103-105).

5.3.2 Shifts in domestic governance: horizontal and vertical integration, evidence-based policy-making and stakeholder involvement

There is some – but not a lot of – evidence that the Social OMC is leading to a more strategic approach (in terms of planning, targeting, resources assigned and policy analysis) in social policy-making: for many countries "governance by objectives" was an entirely new feature in social policy-making. The impact of the OMC on horizontally-integrated policy-making seems somewhat more significant. According to Zeitlin (2009; 2005, pages 457-458) the obligation to draft National Action Plans for employment and social inclusion (and more recently also Lisbon National Reform Programmes for Growth and Jobs) has – in many countries – strengthened the horizontal integration of interdependent policy fields through the creation of new formal coordination bodies and inter-ministerial working groups. There is indeed some evidence that drafting the National Strategy Report was not "business as usual" in Germany and led to somewhat enhanced cooperation between the social and finance ministries (Vanhercke, 2009, page 4), while in Belgium the preparation of the NAP/inclusion has given rise to new bodies for coordinating and rationalising policy initiatives across sectors not only at the federal level, but also at the regional level (Hamel and Vanhercke, 2009).

Examples of vertically-integrated policy-making (national, regional and local level) through the OMC have equally been found. Thus, Sacchi (2006) finds greater coordination among regional and national actors in Italy, while Armstrong (2006) explains how regional actors in the UK are involved to varying degrees, some superficially and others taking the full OMC on board for regional policy development in anti-poverty/social exclusion policy. In France the social inclusion OMC is providing inspiration for the national administration to redefine its new (coordinating) role in the context of decentralisation (Hamel and Van-hercke, 2009). In Belgium, participation in the OMC is strengthening cooperation between (autonomous) Regions, and has increased the coordination role of the federal level (e.g. through the setting of national targets for regional competencies). This increased vertical coordination has created a significant spill-over effect, namely prudent intra-regional policy learning between Wallonia, Flanders and Brussels (Hamel and Vanhercke, 2009).

The Social OMC has equally promoted evidence-based policy-making (monitoring and evaluation, the use of indicators, data sources and analytical capacity). There is in fact widespread agreement that the EES and the Social OMC have contributed to an increased non-state and governmental actors' awareness of policies, practices and performance in other Member States; to the identification of common challenges and the development of shared problem diagnoses (Zeitlin, 2009). Letzner and Schmitt (2007, page 238) confirm that comparison with other Member States already existed in Germany, but became more systematic and institutionalised. It is widely accepted that the OMC – notably through the EU-SILC[8] statistical system – has enhanced statistical capacity-building in many countries, amongst others in Italy (Sacchi, 2006), France and Belgium (Hamel and Vanhercke, 2009).

As regards stakeholder involvement in the policy-making process, the evidence is less straightforward. The problem of late consultation has been established by a variety of sources: in several Member States, information about the NAP/Inclusion is often organised just before its submission to "Brussels". And yet, contrary to the general claim by Kröger (2009) that the Social OMC is sometimes more closed than the Community method as it involves a rather closed circle of "non-accountable bureaucrats", Preunkert and Zirra (2009) find that NGOs have been mobilised, especially in Germany and Italy, due to the OMC/inclusion process. This point is confirmed by Friedrich (2006): in Germany the NAP/Inclusion process provided social NGOs with additional arguments and political backing to strengthen their voice in domestic debates. This evidence supports a recent study on stakeholder involvement in the implementation of the Social OMC by INBAS *et al.* (2009): step-by-step, the process of involving the different stakeholders within the OMC has improved, even if wide variations persist, both between Member States and over time.

---

[8] "EU-SILC" stands for EU Statistics on Income and Living Conditions.

In addition, stakeholder involvement through the OMC is largely limited to the OMC/inclusion, while the other two strands (pensions and healthcare) remain closed shops. This is why de la Porte and Nanz (2004, page 278) raise serious questions about the democratic quality of the pensions OMC strand which "fares even worse" than the European Employment Strategy (EES) when assessed according to the criteria of transparency, public debate, learning and participation. It would indeed seem that the pension OMC only provides leverage to those policy-makers and stakeholders who are already in the "inner circle" of decision making. As national ministries have acted as gatekeepers of the pension process, it has not brought new actors to the table (Vanhercke, 2009). Writing about the healthcare OMC, Dawson (2009) equally finds that the method relies on those already within the "inner circle" of "Europeanised" participants (there is little evidence of the multiplication or "broadening" of accountable actors).

5.3.3 Impact on EU level policies and politics: enhancing commitment, changing actor constellations and instrument hybridity

A final type of impact relates to the impact of the Social OMC at the EU level, which includes an enhanced commitment to its subject matter among new sets of actors. According to Eckardt (2005) "the various OMCs, including that on pensions, make an important contribution. They provide a forum for the Commission and the various subcommittees involved in developing a commonly accepted European social-policy paradigm". Vanhercke (2009a) claims that the recognition that "the pensions challenge is not a financial challenge with some social constraints, but a social challenge with financial constraints" (Vandenbroucke, 2001) allowed for a more balanced EU discourse. The social dimension acquired a legitimate place, but also gave legitimacy to "economic" messages in the field of pensions. Similarly, Hervey and Vanhercke (2010) explain that the OMC increased the legitimacy of the ministers of finance to discuss healthcare issues considerably by giving them a place in the healthcare part of the Concerted Strategy.

The Social OMC has also had an impact on the institutional arrangements in the EU: several authors refer to the important (or even "dominant") role of the European Commission, which skilfully uses the OMC to expand its influence in sensitive (social) policy areas, as is shown, among others, by de la Rosa (2007) and Greer and Vanhercke (2010). This may explain why the Committee on Legal Affairs of the European Parliament (2007, page 4-5), warns against the "indirect legal effects" of soft law which would "allow the executive effectively to legislate by means of soft-law instruments, thereby potentially undermining the Community legal order". Note that Eckardt (2005) sees only a "mediating role" for the European Commission in the pensions OMC. Vanhercke (2009a) furthermore shows that the EU political playing field in the area of pensions was changed through the OMC, as the joint approach to pensions brought a new set of actors to the debate, namely the Social Affairs Council formation, the SPC and platforms such as the European Federation of Pensioners and Elderly People (FERPA) and AGE.

5.3.4 The impact of the Social OMC: wrapping things up

There is broad agreement that the OMC has a considerable impact both on the Member States' and the EU's policies and politics. Substantive policy changes include enhancing commitment to the subject matter of the Social OMC (also for "sticky" institutions such as pensions systems), agenda-setting effects (new issues such as "child poverty" emerge) and mirror effects (self-reflection on national performance). Shifts in domestic governance include horizontal and vertical integration (through new or reinforced structures), evidence-based policy-making and increased stakeholder involvement, at least in some countries and policy areas. The impact on EU level policies and politics includes enhanced commitment (e.g. reducing early retirement or increasing efforts in the fight against homelessness) and changing actor constellations. At least in some countries, OMC concepts, indicators, targets and categories permeate domestic policy-making, while soft-law mechanisms develop into legal instruments.

Having said this, there is far less agreement about the direction and scope of OMC impact. While many analyses point to beneficial effects, others point to undesirable effects, which for some include pushing for neoliberal solutions and policy tools, worsening welfare state performance and providing legitimacy for economic actors to exert further influence on social protection and social inclusion. Finally, this section made it quite clear that impact varies a lot between Member States. This concurs with the more general conclusion by Vandenbroucke and Vlemincxk (2011) regarding the Lisbon Strategy: that "Open coordination did not prevent national and regional governments and social partners from buying in selective bits and pieces of the new paradigm, but not its *gestalt*".

5.4 Mechanisms of Change: Explaining the Discrepancy Between the OMC's Adequacy and Impact

The rather mixed picture of the OMC's theoretical capacity to have an effect (which we called *adequacy*) as described in Section 5.2 is largely in line with the more "sceptical" literature which, on several occasions, has dismissed the OMC because of its institutional weakness as a paper tiger: the "soft" process should not have really significant effects. At the same time, there is a clear contradiction with the more optimistic assessments of the OMC "in action", which are largely corroborated by the finding of Section 5.3, namely that the Social OMC is, at least to some extent, delivering the goods.

This section is aimed at identifying certain factors that could help to bridge the apparent gap in our understanding of the OMC's adequacy versus its impact. A first, quite evident element in the explanation is that many of the studies focussing on the OMC's *potential* effect (adequacy) simply omit to look at the *actual* impact of the OMC on the outcome of policies or politics. More particularly, few of these "theoretically enriched" studies (focussing on the instruments of the tool) have looked at the extent to which the OMC has supported or complemented existing discourses of particular paths of national reform, which requires a more in-depth and diachronic analysis.

A second, related explanation is more methodological and has been addressed in Section 5.2: it seems that few of the (even most recent) studies dealing with the adequacy of the Social OMC take into account the many changes in the OMC process e.g. completion of the portfolio of indicators (e.g. extension to pensions and healthcare), enhancement of mutual learning activities (e.g. thematic peer reviews), streamlining (including the introduction of overarching objectives), etc. This is an important flaw in the literature that will need to be addressed by future OMC research. It goes without saying that researchers can only include the "state of the art" of the OMC toolbox in their analyses if these instruments are readily available, which is not sufficiently the case at this moment.

A third, and arguably the most important explanation, is the fact that the Social OMC is being used by domestic actors. Such "creative appropriation" involves the strategic use of EU concepts, objectives, guidelines, targets, indicators, performance comparisons and recommendations by national and sub-national actors as a resource for their own purposes and independent policy initiatives. It is increasingly accepted that this is the strongest mechanism of OMC influence on national social policies[9]. For domestic actors it is not so important how "hard" or "soft" these instruments of the OMC toolbox are: as long as they can be used in a credible way, they are real in their effects. This by

---

[9] Note that Baeten *et al.* (2010) describe Member States' creative adaptation in the shadow of the CJEU's case law on patient mobility. In other words: even though this is rarely acknowledged, this mechanism also applies to "hard law" contexts.

no means implies that the OMC architecture has no bearing on the "impact" of the Social OMC: as we have discussed before, the fact that the Social OMC remains a relatively closed shop and is a quasi-invisible process constitutes an important barrier for creative appropriation (see Sections 5.2.1 and 5.3.2).

A final explanation for the discrepancy between the adequacy and the impact of the Social OMC is that assessments of the former dimension do not sufficiently acknowledge "instrument hybridity", or the (necessary) interactions between the OMC and other EU instruments. Thus, the European Social Fund (ESF) Regulation for the 2007-2013 programming period explicitly refers to the OMC, which may provide important financial incentives that support the (social inclusion component of the) Social OMC. For Hervey and Vanhercke (2010) "there is no reason why in the near future certain elements of the healthcare OMC would not be taken into account by the Commission, *de jure* or *de facto*, to determine whether expenditure is eligible for assistance under the Fund" (*ibid.*). For Verschraegen *et al.* (2011) and de la Rosa (2007) it is clear that the relationship between the ESF and the OMC works both ways: if the ESF strengthens the OMC, the latter may (or at least should) influence cohesion policy (see also chapter by Jouen in the present volume).

The link between the OMC and the Community method has also received considerable attention. Thus, de la Rosa (2007) explains how the Social OMC ensures regular follow-up of certain non-discrimination Directives. Hervey (2010) provocatively examines rulings by the Court of Justice of the EU (CJEU) "in the shadow of the informal settlement". Even though the latter piece does not directly deal with the Social OMC (case studies are the European Employment Strategy and the Bologna Process on Higher Education) the findings are highly relevant, as they indicate not merely the *possibility* that the CJEU might take elements of the OMC into consideration (as already indicated by Greer and Vanhercke (2010) in the case of healthcare), but takes this one step further by illustrating that this kind of spillover is *happening already*. Again, this could help to explain why "soft governance" has more impact "on the ground" than could be expected from a purely functional reading.

5.5 Conclusions and Next Steps

In this chapter, we have tried to explain how the Social OMC, in the absence of a "shadow of hierarchy" (Héritier and Lehmkuhl, 2008), can still produce a significant impact on domestic and EU policies. An important key to this explanation is "creative appropriation", which has replaced "policy learning" and "naming and shaming" as the most important mechanism explaining the OMC impact (even if it is clear that while actors use the OMC for their own purposes, this may involve changes in their cognitive and normative frames resulting from policy learning). It is now widely acknowledged that the OMC can only have an impact if it is being "picked up" by actors at the domestic level, who use it as leverage to (selectively) amplify national reform strategies. In other words: the "infrastructure" of the processes (having "strong" recommendations, NSR, peer reviews, indicators, reporting cycle) only matters insofar as it enables or constrains actor involvement and leverage (see Section 5.2.5). The CJEU's actual (as opposed to theoretical) use of soft law mechanisms in its judgements and the integration of the Social OMC into the ESF Regulations present additional arguments to nuance views that oppose "hard" and "soft" governance.

As a consequence, the "hard politics of soft law" is not fiction: this chapter has shown that the OMC in different policy areas is felt and perceived as being much "harder" than might have been expected. This is a first conclusion of this chapter, and it has important consequences for any future analysis of the Social OMC's impact, which will have to take into account the degree to which a variety of actors at different levels have engaged in, and appeal to the OMC to pursue their objectives[10]. At the same time, this "creative appropriation" dimension calls for greater investment, including from the European Commission, in further strengthening the OMC infrastructure with a view to enhancing the involvement of stakeholders. At the domestic level, public authorities should organise national peer reviews, in which a wide variety of domestic actors discuss the Commission's "suggestions" in the Country Fiches as well as the reports written by independent experts in the framework of the peer reviews programme funded by the European Commission under the Community Programme for Employment and Social Solidarity (PROGRESS).

A second important conclusion is that the Social OMC has been institutionalised – at national and EU levels – in ways that may not have been expected: it has become a "template" for soft governance, not only at EU level, but also for coordinating social (inclusion) policies in some federalised countries. The Social OMC has become a trusted resource – admittedly, among others – for a variety of domestic and EU actors; and it has become linked to other EU policy instruments such as legislation and EU funds. Yet the linking of the Social OMC to other policy instruments needs to be strengthened. Thus, Ferrera (2009, page 231) posits that the setting of precise and measurable targets within the

---

[10]   Vanhercke and Campaert (2009) make a similar point regarding the creative use of ESF-funding for pursuing local activating policies "under the radar".

Social OMC, as recently agreed upon in the Europe 2020 Strategy, could be the first concrete step towards the establishment of binding regulatory standards (on the issue of targets, see also chapter by Walker in the present volume). Of course, we know that the pathway to such binding regulatory standards will be long and uncertain. The idea of making the EU Structural Funds (and especially the ESF) conditional on achieving the objectives of the Social OMC should be further explored in the context of the post-2013 EU Financial Perspectives. As the saying goes: "Put your money where your mouth is".

It is to be hoped that when domestic and EU decision makers decide on the next steps to be taken as regards the Social OMC, those choices will be evidence-based (rather than purely political). In spite of the flaws and pitfalls surrounding the Social OMC (with its three strands), it seems that the "more Social EU" called for by this book will need to build on a strengthened Social OMC complemented (rather than re-placed) by an efficient EPAP. It is essential to further institutionalise a "broad" Social OMC, which is not exclusively geared to poverty and social exclusion, thereby contributing to "disambiguating Lisbon" (Cantillon 2010). The Social Protection Committee and the Social Affairs ministers should safeguard a political space in which they can have their say on any EU initiative or development with potential social consequences. This of course not only includes topics such as social inclusion, but also pensions, healthcare and long-term care, services of general interest, education and climate change.

This "broad" reach should also apply to the need to strengthen "Social Impact Assessment" at national and EU levels (see chapter by Kühnemund in the present volume). In a similar vein, the existing set of indicators should be further developed so as to underpin the common objectives, more particularly by focusing resources on indicators that measure the social adequacy of a variety of benefits, including pensions, unemployment, invalidity etc. (see also Cantillon, 2010). In parallel, participatory governance indicators (including at the regional and local levels) would greatly improve the monitoring and assessment of national practices with regard to social protection and social inclusion policies.

In spite of its obvious flaws, at least in some important respects, the Social OMC has delivered the goods after all. And a strengthened Social OMC has a key role to play in "Europe 2020" if one of the objectives of the new Strategy is indeed to deliver a more Social EU.

References

Amitsis, G. (2004), *The boundaries between Directive 2003/41 and the OMC process on occupational welfare*, Paper presented at the *Public Seminar on Pensions at Risk*, European Network for research on Supplementary Pensions, Leuven, Belgium, September 17.

Ania, A.-B. and Wagener, A. (2008), "The Open Method of Coordination (OMC) as an Evolutionary Game", *Discussion Paper*, 2008.

Armstrong, K. (2006), "The 'Europeanisation' of Social Exclusion: British Adaptation to EU Coordination", *British Journal of Politics and International Relations*, Vol. 8: 79-100.

Armstrong, K. (2005), "How Open is the United Kingdom to the OMC Process on Social Inclusion?", in J. Zeitlin *et al.* (editors), *The Open Method of Coordination in Action: The European Employment and Social Inclusion Strategies*, Brussels: PIE-Peter Lang: 287-310.

Atkinson, A.B. and Marlier, E. (2010) "Analysing and Measuring Social Inclusion in a Global Context". Report produced at the request of UNDESA, New York: United Nations.

Atkinson, T., Cantillon, B., Marlier E. and Nolan, B. (2002), "Social Indicators: The EU and Social Inclusion", Oxford: Oxford University Press.

Baeten, R., Vanhercke, B. and Coucheir, M. (2010), "The Europeanisation of National Health Care Systems: Creative Adaptation in the Shadow of Patient Mobility Case Law", OSE Paper Series, Research paper No. 3 (July), Observatoire social européen: Brussels, 30 p.

Barbier, J.-C. (2010), "'Stratégie de Lisbonne': les promesses sociales non tenues", Documents de travail du Centre d'Economie de la Sorbonne, *CES Working Papers* 2010.18, Paris: Centre d'Economie de la Sorbonne.

Büchs, M. (2009), "The Open Method of Coordination – Effectively Preventing Welfare State Retrenchment?", in S. Kröger (editor) *What we have learnt: Advances, pitfalls and remaining questions in OMC Research*, European Integration online Papers (EIoP), Special Issue 1, Vol. 13, Art. 11. Available at: http://eiop.or.at/eiop/texte/2009-011a.htm.

Büchs, M. (2008), "The Open Method of Coordination as a 'Two-Level Game'", *Policy & Politics*, Vol. 36, 2: 21-37.

Büchs, M. and Friedrich, D. (2005), "Surface Integration. The National Action Plans for Employment and Social Inclusion in Germany", in J. Zeitlin *et al.* (editors) *The Open Method of Coordination in Action: The European Employment and Social Inclusion Strategies*, Brussels: PIE-Peter Lang: 249-86.

Cantillon, B. (2010), "Disambiguating Lisbon. Growth, Employment and Social Inclusion in the Investment State", CSB Working Paper No. 10/07, October.

Dawson, M. (2009), "EU law 'transformed'? Evaluating accountability and subsidiarity in the 'streamlined' OMC for Social Inclusion and Social Protection", in S. Kröger (editor) *What we have learnt: Advances, pitfalls and remaining questions in OMC research*, European Integration online Papers

(EIoP), Special Issue 1, Vol. 13, Art. 8. Available at: http://eiop.or.at/eiop/texte/2009-008a.htm.

de la Porte, C. (2008), "The European Level Development and National Level Influence of the Open Method of Coordination: The Cases of Employment and Social Inclusion". *Unpublished PhD thesis*, Department of Social and Political Studies, European University Institute, Florence.

de la Porte, C. (2007), "Good Governance via the OMC: the cases of employment and social inclusion", *European Journal of Legal Studies*, Vol. 1, No. 1.

de la Rosa, S. (2007), *La méthode ouverte de coordination dans le système juridique communautaire*, Brussels: Bruylant.

de la Porte, C. and Nanz, P. (2004), "The OMC – A Deliberative-Democratic Mode of Governance? The Cases of Employment and Pensions", in The Open Method of Coordination in the European Union, Special issue of *Journal of European Public Policy*, Vol. 11, 2: 267-288.

EAPN (2008), *Building Security, Giving Hope. EAPN Assessment of the National Strategic Reports on Social Protection and Social Inclusion (2008-10)*, November.

Eckardt, M. (2005), "The open method of coordination on pensions: an economic analysis of its effects on pension reforms", *Journal of European Social Policy*, Vol. 15, 3: 247-267.

ESN (2009), "Perspectives from practice". *Review of the National Reports on Strategies for Social Protection and Social Inclusion* 2008-10, January.

European Centre for Social Welfare Policy and Research *et al.* (2008), "Quality in and equality of access to healthcare services".

European Parliament (2007), *Draft Report on institutional and legal implications of the use of 'soft law' instruments*, Doc 2007/2028(INI) of 15 March 2007.

FEANTSA (2007), *Untapped Potential: Using the Full Potential of the OMC to Address Poverty in Europe*, Brussels.

Featherstone, K. (2005), "'Soft' Coordination Meets 'Hard' Politics: The European Union and Pension Reform in Greece", *Journal of European Public Policy*, Vol. 12, 4: 733-50.

Ferrera, M. (2009), "The JCMS Annual Lecture: National Welfare States and European Integration: In Search of a 'Virtuous Nesting'", *JCMS: Journal of Common Market Studies*, Vol. 47, 2: 219-233.

Flear, M. (2009), "The Open Method of Coordination on Health Care after the Lisbon Strategy II: Towards a Neoliberal Framing?", in S. Kröger (editor) *What we have Learnt: Advances, pitfalls and remaining questions in OMC Research*, European Integration online Papers (EIoP), Special Issue 1, Vol. 13, Art. 12. Available at: http://eiop.or.at/eiop/texte/2009-012a.htm.

Frazer, H. and Marlier, E. (2009), *Assessment of the extent of synergies between growth and jobs policies and social inclusion policies across the EU as evidenced by the 2008-2010 National Reform Programmes: Key lessons*, Brussels: European Commission.

Frazer, H. and Marlier, E. (2008), *Building a stronger EU Social Inclusion Process: Analysis and recommendations of the EU Network of independent national experts on social inclusion, prepared on behalf of the European Commission*, Brussels: European Commission.

Friedrich, D. (2006), "Policy Process, Governance and Democracy in the EU: The Case of the Open Method of Coordination on Social Inclusion", *Policy & Politics*, Vol. 34, 2: 367-383.

Greer, S. and Vanhercke, B. (2010), "Governing Health Care through EU Soft Law", in: E. Mossialos, T. Hervey, R. Baeten (editors) *Health System Governance in Europe: The Role of EU Law and Policy*, Cambridge: Cambridge University Press: 186-230.

Hamel, M.-P. and Vanhercke, B. (2009), "The Open Method of Coordination and Domestic Social Policy Making in Belgium and France: Window Dressing, One-Way Impact, or Reciprocal Influence?", in M. Heidenreich and J. Zeitlin (editors) *Changing European Employment and Welfare Regimes: The Influence of the Open Method of Coordination on National Reforms*, London: Routledge: 84-111.

Héritier, A. and Lehmkuhl, D. (2008), "Introduction. The Shadow of Hierarchy and New Modes of Governance", *Journal of Public Policy* (2008), 28: 1-17.

Hervey, T. (2010), "Adjudicating in the Shadow of the Informal Settlement?: The European Court of Justice, 'new governance' and social welfare", Submitted to *Current Legal Problems*, January.

Hervey, T. (2008), "The European Union's Governance of Health Care and the Welfare Modernization Agenda", *Regulation & Governance*, Vol. 2, No. 1: 103-120.

Hervey, T. and Vanhercke, B. (2010), "Health care and the EU: the law and policy patchwork", in: E. Mossialos, T. Hervey and R. Baeten (editors) *Health System Governance in Europe: The Role of EU Law and Policy*, Cambridge: Cambridge University Press: 84-133.

Horvath, A. (2007), "Committee Governance after the Enlargement of the EU: Institutionalisation of Cooperation within the Social Protection Committee", *European Political Economy Review*, 6: 53-73.

INBAS GmbH, and ENGENDER (2009), Study on Stakeholders' Involvement in the Implementation of the Open Method of Coordination (OMC) in Social Protection and Social Inclusion, Draft Interim Report: Country Reports & Case Studies, August, Brussels: European Commission, Directorate-General Employment, Social affairs and Equal opportunities.

Jacobsson, K. (2005), "Trying to Reform the 'Best Pupils in the Class'? The Open Method of Coordination in Sweden and Denmark", in J. Zeitlin *et al.* (editors), *The Open Method of Coordination in Action: The European Employment and Social Inclusion Strategies*, Brussels: PIE-Peter Lang: 107-36.

Jacobsson, K., and Johansson, H. (2009), "The Micro-Politics of the Open Method of Coordination: NGOs and the Social Inclusion Process in Sweden", in M. Heidenreich and J. Zeitlin (editors) *Changing European Employment and Welfare Regimes: The Influence of the Open Method of Coordination on National Reforms*, London: Routledge: 173-91.

Kröger, S. (2009), "The Open Method of Coordination: Underconceptualisation, Overdetermination, De-politicisation and Beyond", in S. Kröger (editor) *What have we learnt: Advances, pitfalls and remaining questions in OMC research*, European Integration online Papers (EIoP), Special Issue 1, Vol. 13, Art. 5. Available at: http://eiop.or.at/eiop/texte/2009-005a.htm.

Kröger, S. (2008), Soft Governance in Hard Politics: European Coordination of Anti-Poverty Policies in France and Germany, Wiesbaden: VS Verlag für Sozialwissenschaften.

Letzner, P. and Schmitt, V. (2007), "La mise en œuvre de la méthode ouverte de coordination dans le secteur de l'assurance vieillesse en Allemagne: un processus d'harmonisation", *Retraite et Société*, 50: 234-242.

Lodge, M. (2007), "Comparing Non-Hierarchical Governance in Action: the Open Method of Coordination in Pensions and Information Society", *Journal of Common Market Studies*, Vol. 45, 2: 343-365.

Marlier, E., Atkinson, A.B., Cantillon, B. and Nolan, B. (2007), "The EU and Social Inclusion: Facing the challenges", Bristol: The Policy Press.

Morissens, A., Nicaise, I. and Ory, G. (2007), "Belgium, Tackling child poverty and promoting the social inclusion of children. A study of national policies", HIVA KU.Leuven, Peer Review and Assessment in Social Inclusion. Available at: http://ec.europa.eu/employment_social/social_inclusion/docs/experts_reports/belgium_1_2007_en.pdf.

Natali, D. (2009), "The Open Method of Coordination on Pensions: Does it de-politicize pensions policy?" in: *WEST EUROPEAN POLITICS* (4/2009): Special Issue "Managing conflicts of interest in EU regulatory processes", editors: Deborah Mabbett, Waltraud Schelkle.

Norris, J. (2007), *Searching for Synergy: Governance, Welfare, and Law in Two EU Member States*, unpublished Ph.D. thesis, Department of Sociology, University of Wisconsin-Madison.

O'Donnell, R. and Moss, B. (2005), "Ireland: The Very Idea of an Open Method of Coordination", in J. Zeitlin *et al.* (editors) *The Open Method of Coordination in Action: The European Employment and Social Inclusion Strategies*, Brussels: PIE-Peter Lang: 311-50.

OSB Consulting (2006), *Final Technical Report: Peer Review and Assessment in Social Inclusion*, prepared in cooperation with CEPS/INSTEAD and IES.

Pochet, P. and Natali, D. (2005), "Réseaux européens relatifs aux pensions: la participation d'intérêts organisés au processus décisionnel de l'UE", *Revue belge de sécurité sociale*, No. 2: 307-38.

Preunkert, J. and Zirra, S. (2009), "Europeanization of Domestic Employment and Welfare Regimes: The German, French, and Italian Experiences", in M. Heidenreich and J. Zeitlin (editors), *Changing European Employment and Welfare Regimes: The Influence of the Open Method of Coordination on National Reforms*, London: Routledge: 192-213.

Radulova, E. (2007), "Variations on Soft EU Governance: the Open Method(s) of Coordination". In D. De Bievre and C. Neuhold (editors), *Dynamics and Obstacles of European Governance*, Cheltenham: Edward Elgar: 3-27.

Sacchi, S. (2006), "Il metodo aperto di coordinamento", *URGE, Working Paper*, No. 8. Available at: http://www.urge.it/files/papers/22wpurge82006. pdf.

Sirovátka, T. and Rákoczyová, M. (2009), "The Impact of the EU Social Inclusion Strategy: the Czech case", in A. Cerami and P. Vanhuysse (editors), *Post-Communist Welfare Pathways. Theorizing Social Policy Transformations in Central and Europe*, Palgrave/Macmillan.

Social Inclusion Unit (2004) "Evaluation: the Social Inclusion Initiative Big Picture – Roundtables", Background Discussion Paper Two, *Social Inclusion Initiative Indicators*, Adelaide South Australia: Department of the Premier and Cabinet.

Social Protection Committee (2009), *Growth, Jobs and Social Progress in the EU: A Contribution to the Evaluation of the Social Dimension of the Lisbon Strategy*, Brussels: European Commission. Available at: http://ec.europa.eu/ social/BlobServlet?docId=3898&langId=en.

Social Protection Committee (2008), *Child Poverty and Well-being in the EU – Current Status and Way Forward*, Luxembourg: OPOCE. Available at: http://ec.europa.eu/social/main.jsp?catId=751&langId=en&pubId=74&type=2 &furtherPubs=yes.

The Tavistock Institute (2006), *Evaluation of the EU Programme to Promote Member State Cooperation to Combat Social Exclusion and Poverty*, Final Synthesis of the Main Report, Engender and ECWS.

Vandenbroucke, F. (2002), "The EU and Social Protection: What Should the European Convention Propose?", MPIfG Working Paper 02/6, Max-Planck-Institut für Gesellschaftsforschung, June 2002.

Vandenbroucke, F. (2001), "Open Coordination on Pensions and the Future of Europe's Social Model", Closing speech at the Conference *Towards a new architecture for social protection?*, Leuven, 19-20 October, 2001.

Vandenbroucke, F. and Vleminckx (2011/forthcoming), "Disappointing poverty trends: is the social investment state to blame? An exercise in soul-searching for policy-makers", *Journal of European Social Policy*.

Vanhercke, B. (2010), *An Analytic Overview of Evaluation Results of the Social OMC*. Deliverable 2 of the Study "Assessing the Effectiveness and the Impact of the Social OMC in Preparation of the New Cycle", PROGRESS, Brussels: European Commission.

Vanhercke, B. (2009), "Against the odds. The Open Method of Coordination as a selective amplifier for reforming Belgian pension policies", in S. Kröger (editor) *What we have learnt: Advances, pitfalls and remaining questions in OMC research*, European Integration online Papers (EIoP), Special Issue 1, Vol. 13, Art. 16. Available at: http://eiop.or.at/eiop/texte/2009-016a.htm.

Vanhercke, B. (2009a), *Hoezo, ver van ons bed? Over de wisselwerking tussen het Belgische en Europese armoedebeleid*, in J. Vranken, G. Campaert, D.

Dierckx en A. Van Haarlem (editors) *Arm Europa. Over armoede en armoedebestrijding op het Europese niveau*, Leuven: Acco, 79-100.

Vanhercke, B. (2007), "Is the OMC growing teeth? The governance turn in EU social policy coordination", *Unpublished 'Second year' paper*, University of Amsterdam.

Vanhercke, B. and Campaert, G., (2009), "Lokaal Sociaal Beleid Onder de Radar. Activerende Sociale Insluiting via het Europees Sociaal Fonds", in Vranken, J., Campaert, G., Dierckx, D. And Van Haarlem, A. (editors.), *Arm Europa. Over armoede en armoedebestrijding op het Europese niveau*, Leuven: Acco, pp. 65-77.

Vanhercke, B., Cincinnato, S. and Nicaise, I. (2008), *Belgium – The Social Inclusion Strand of the EU Social Protection and Social Inclusion Process – Awareness and perception of the process, strengths and weaknesses, suggestions for the enhancement of its impact*, HIVA, K.U. Leuven, on behalf of the European Commission Directorate-General Employment, Social affairs and Equal opportunities.

Verschraegen, G., Vanhercke, B., Verpoorten, R. (2011) "The European Social Fund and Domestic Activation Policies: Europeanization Mechanisms, Journal of European Social Policy, Vol. 21(1): 1-18.

Zeitlin, J. (2009), "The Open Method of Coordination and National Social and Employment Policy Reforms: Influences, Mechanisms, Effects", in M. Heidenreich and J. Zeitlin (editors) *Changing European Employment and Welfare Regimes: The Influence of the Open Method of Coordination on National Reforms*, London: Routledge: 214-45.

Zeitlin, J. (2008), "The Open Method of Coordination and the Governance of the Lisbon Strategy", *Journal of Common Market Studies*, Vol. 46, 2: 437-46.

Zeitlin, J. (2005), "Conclusion: The Open Method of Coordination in Action: Theoretical Promise, Empirical Realities, Reform Strategy", in J. Zeitlin *et al.* (editors), *The Open Method of Coordination in Action: The European Employment and Social Inclusion Strategies*, Brussels: PIE-Peter Lang: 441-98.

6. Assessing the EU Approach to Combating Poverty and Social Exclusion in the Last Decade

Mary DALY[1]

6.1 Introduction

One of the most significant achievements of the Lisbon European Council in March 2000 was to place social issues firmly on the EU policy agenda, reinvigorating EU social policy which had been in the doldrums since the heady days of the Delors era in the late 1980s and early 1990s. Poverty and social exclusion have been central to the new momentum – the first decade of the new century was a time when the EU made one of the most concerted attempts anywhere in recent history to engage with poverty and social exclusion. There was nothing foretold about this – the EU is primarily a project oriented to markets and economic efficiency. It has placed its faith in a market-led strategy for growth rather than, for example, redistributive policies aiming for social justice and equality. Moreover, the EU's space for manoeuvre in social policy was and is limited: the principle of subsidiarity (which grants Member States autonomy in social policy) as well as the resulting weak legal competence and lacking funds for redistribution seriously restrict the EU's role in social policy. Against this background, the aim of this piece is to outline and assess the anti-poverty/social exclusion activities of the EU in the last decade. The Lisbon process offers a unique opportunity to study: a) the evolution of poverty and social exclusion as concepts for policy and analysis in contemporary times; and b) the extent and coherence of the EU's latest social policy activities.

The aim of the piece is to offer a critical analysis of the ideas and substantive policy models underlying the Open Method of Coordination on Social Protection and Social Inclusion (the so-called "Social OMC"). Governance is not the focus here (see chapters by Frazer and Marlier, by Vanhercke and by Zeitlin in the present volume). Rather, the relevant

---

[1]   I would like to thank Eric Marlier for his detailed comments on parts of an earlier draft. I am indebted also to both Dave Gordon and Ruth Levitas for very helpful feedback. Address for correspondence: m.daly@qub.ac.uk.

social policy statements, activities and agreements are analysed and assessed for how they conceptualise and understand poverty and social exclusion. Focused on the Social OMC, the piece proceeds in four parts. Section 6.2 is devoted to a short historical tracing of the two concepts in EU activities prior to Lisbon. We move on from this to analyse how poverty and social exclusion were framed in terms of objectives and policy orientations under Lisbon and empirically as objects of measurement and indicator development (Sections 6.3 and 6.4). A short conclusion brings the piece to a close (Section 6.5).

6.2 The Background to Poverty and Social Exclusion in the EU Repertoire

Neither poverty nor social exclusion was a newcomer to the EU stage in 2000. Indeed, the two concepts have a rather long and intertwined history within the EU.

Poverty is the elder of the two concepts. EU policy interest in poverty dates back at least to the early 1970s when the first anti-poverty programme was introduced. This programme, like its two successors in the 1980s, mainly consisted of term-limited projects that undertook research, information exchange and evaluation. The word "programme" is something of a misnomer, however, especially if we understand it in terms set by the national welfare state template wherein anti-poverty measures usually take the form of minimum income provisions – redistribution is their *métier*. The EU, as always with social policy, is different. The first poverty programme (subsequent ones also) consisted of a relatively small number of local projects in Member States which were focused on experimental actions around information, research and anti-poverty activity. Building up a credible information base about social and economic problems in Europe and how they could be counteracted was a key goal of these programmes. Following the first programme in the 1970s, there were two more which ran in the 1980s and early 1990s. The Commission's plans for a fourth poverty programme in the mid-1990s were scuppered – mainly by Germany and the UK which opposed a role for the EU in the area of poverty other than in the capacity of research coordination. Some say that it was the attention focused on the politically contentious concept of poverty that was unpopular with Member States (Berghman, 1995). Since then, a different approach has been adopted and the concept of "social exclusion" has increasingly accompanied that of poverty.

In fact, the EU has been one of social exclusion's main advocates and sponsors, since the concept first appeared in French social policy discourse in 1974 (Silver, 1994; Levitas, 1998). As it established itself over the course of the 1980s and 1990s, the "social problem" orientation of the social exclusion approach was highlighted – that is, it focused on a range of social ills such as unemployment, marginalisation or homelessness. However, social exclusion is a concept with a more wide-ranging set of references than individual social problems. At the micro or individual level, it is meant to pick up on the cumulation of numerous conditions of disadvantage such as low income, poor health, low education and skills and social isolation. People are seen to be cut off from the mainstream, cast adrift by the disempowering and immobilising effects of various disadvantages. At a more macro level, the concept proffers two types of structural critique. On the one hand, economic change, in particular the decline occasioned by de-industrialisation and jobless growth, have distanced many people from the labour market. In its second structural register, social exclusion points to problems in and of society. The failure here is one of social integration – the capacity of existing structures and arrangements to enable people to be active participants in social life, to engage in supportive social relations and to give their loyalty to a common moral and social order. With such a broad-ranging set of references, social exclusion is one of those chameleon-like concepts whose meaning can be stretched in numerous, even conflicting, directions.[2] It is for this and other reasons a controversial concept – academic scholarship is far more critical of it than social policy practice (Levitas, 1998; Daly and Saraceno, 2002). In the EU's usages, the meaning has varied as a short overview of the concept in EU discourse prior to Lisbon demonstrates.

Social exclusion made its first official appearance on the EU stage in 1989 – *The Community Charter of Fundamental Social Rights for Workers* (the Social Charter as it is known) was one of the first high-level EU policy documents to refer to social exclusion. The context here was the run-up to the Single European Market. The *Resolution of the Council of Ministers for Social Affairs on Combating Social Exclusion*, issued in 1989, was the concept's birth certificate, however (Council, 1989). In this document, social exclusion was differentiated from poverty and emphasis was laid on structural factors and in particular (reduced) access to the labour market. The solution proposed was to improve opportunities and access to services such as education, employment, housing, community services and medical care. In late 1992, the Commission issued a Communication with the title *Towards a Europe of Solidarity – Intensifying the Fight against Social Exclusion, Fostering Integration* (European Commission, 1992). This was the high watermark of EU discursive engagement with social exclusion prior to

---

[2]   Social cohesion is another such concept.

Lisbon. A visionary document, the Communication developed a horizontal understanding of social exclusion, pointing out that social exclusion involves not just disparity between the top and the bottom of the socio-economic scale but also between those comfortably placed within society and people on the margins. The White Paper on social policy, issued in July 1994, while very focused on labour-market related measures and with an undertone of what would later become known as "activation", made a case for EU action in the field of poverty and social exclusion, especially in terms of the integration of those excluded from the labour market (European Commission, 1994). At this stage unemployment, employability, labour force adaptation and job creation were monopolising policy attention in Europe. Conceiving of these as European phenomena or problems, the extraordinary European Council held in Luxembourg in November 1997 gave the EU competence in employment policy. However, in a considerably less-heralded development, it also inserted social exclusion into the Amsterdam Treaty (which entered into force in 1999), adding a new Article (137(2) TEC) authorising measures to facilitate cooperation among Member States in order to combat social exclusion. Although if judged against the yardstick of legal regulation it might be seen as weak in that "knowledge exchange" is hardly a substitute for strong EU competence, the new Treaty provision was to provide a legal basis for a specific EU-wide process in this area in 2000.

Obviously then, social exclusion had a considerable history in EU social policy deliberations prior to the March 2000 Lisbon European Council. One has to ask why the preference for social exclusion though? There are a number of reasons. First, with poverty out of political favour, social exclusion had numerous benefits in an EU context, not least the fact that as a "diagnosis" and set of solutions it seemed to fit the rapidly changing times and capture the emergence of new forms of deprivation. Second, social exclusion is a concept with a strong orientation to change and so could easily provide the basis for a discourse about updating the European social model. A normative concept such as this could help to identify the common values underlying the European social model (which has always been an element of EU activity). Third, there was also the concept's "newness". This meant that it was not associated with any of the existing welfare state models in the Union and so an EU stamp could be imprinted on it (Daly, 2006). Bauer (2002) has suggested that the Commission had to generate a new discourse (that is, social exclusion) in order to legitimate the EU as a social policy actor (given the subsidiarity principle). Other factors were causal also, not least the need to develop an approach that spoke to the concerns of a range of Member States. Social exclusion's wide analytic lens and chameleon-like character meant that the concept could be manipulated and stretched to fit very different kinds of settings. This is almost *de rigueur* in an EU social policy context given that the Member States have very different social policy traditions. So social exclusion, for example, captures something core to the Continental European welfare states where social policy serves a social integration function in the sense of creating a harmonious society and managing the contestation that emanates from social class inequalities. In the more liberal-oriented states such as the UK and Ireland, social exclusion's references to lack of involvement in the labour market strikes a chord as does its interest in minimum income for these are countries oriented to poverty alleviation. Hence, the double use of poverty and social exclusion in the Lisbon programme has to be attributed to these origins also. When set in this complex background, it is little wonder that the EU's usage of social exclusion has varied in meaning and application over time – rather than an accident this was almost a condition of its usage. The next section focuses on how poverty, social exclusion and more broadly social protection have been conceived in the Lisbon process.

6.3 Social Policy Emphases in Lisbon

The agreement reached at Lisbon in March 2000 by the EU Heads of State and Government ushered in a period when social exclusion was foregrounded for the purposes of EU policy cooperation and coordination. For the first five years of Lisbon anyway, social cohesion (which was interpreted in terms of reducing social exclusion and poverty) sat alongside job creation and economic growth as objectives of this new phase of EU development. Given the simultaneous focus on all three, one could say that the EU went beyond the market-building project to develop a positive social policy project (Jacobsson, 2009). As is now well known, the fields in which EU processes were initiated included employment, social exclusion, pensions and healthcare, in the overall goal of achieving a balanced pursuit of economic, employment and social progress (Dieckhoff and Gallie, 2007, page 481). From the perspective of social policy, the initial Lisbon agreement brought two core developments: a) an agreement that Member States would coordinate policy on employment, poverty and social exclusion; and b) the application and development of the OMC to these domains. This very innovative governance mechanism consisted of common objective setting and regular progress reporting and review of progress at both national and EU levels. The open method was introduced first for employment in 1997, then in poverty and social exclusion in 2000, pensions in 2001 and healthcare and long-term care in 2004. (For a detailed historical account, see Marlier *et al.*, 2007, Chapter 2.)

147

It would be wrong to treat Lisbon as if it were a single development or phase. In fact, there have been two social Lisbons. The first lasted until March 2005, the second from then until June 2010 when the Lisbon Strategy and all agreements and plans relating to it were replaced by the Europe 2020 Strategy. Dissatisfaction with "results" and the pace of achievement of the original objectives especially in relation to economic growth and job creation led to a review of the process in 2003 (European Communities, 2004). Against the wishes of some actors in the process – especially the economically-oriented actors[3] – social Lisbon survived. A new cycle of governance, begun in 2005 with the relaunch of Lisbon in March of that year, saw the integration of the employment and economic policy processes into a single "national reform" process (focused on "growth and employment making for social cohesion"). The social inclusion OMC was kept separate, although there was to be greater synergy and "conversation" (in the sense of each being expected to feed into the other) between its strategic goals and those of the national reform process as well as greater synchronisation of timing. The social process itself also underwent reform, mainly in that the heretofore separate processes of social inclusion, pensions and healthcare and long-term care were integrated ("streamlined" in the EU's inimitable language) from 2006 on in an attempt to rationalise and strengthen them. "Social protection and social inclusion" was the umbrella term applied to this integrated set of social policies. The objectives also changed; Table 6.1 shows how.

Table 6.1: Dominant emphases of the common objectives relating to poverty and social exclusion in the EU under Lisbon

2000-2004*	2005 – 2010**
Facilitate participation in employment and access by all to resources, rights, goods and services	Guarantee access for all to the basic resources, rights and social services Address extreme forms of exclusion
Help the most vulnerable	Inclusion in employment Fight poverty and exclusion among the most marginalised groups
Prevention of the risks of social exclusion	
Mobilisation of all relevant bodies	Ensure good policy coordination and involvement of all relevant actors, including people experiencing poverty

* European Council (2000). **As expressed in European Commission (2005) and (2008).

---

[3]   These are centred around the European Commission's Directorate-General "Economic and Financial Affairs" (DG ECFIN), the ECOFIN Council, and the EU Economic Policy Committee.

Comparing the emphases over the different periods, Table 6.1 shows that between 2000 and 2005, EU social policy had a blueprint for a relatively radical attack on social exclusion. It covered a range of bases: access to resources, rights, goods and services, helping the most vulnerable, preventing social exclusion, and mobilising those affected. The orientation was more social democratic than anything else: the desired European model was one that emphasises social rights and understands the "community" as one in which people are or should be economically, socially and politically included. However, this "strong vision" did not survive the changes in 2005 and by 2005 the blueprint had altered significantly. There were three main changes. First, as mentioned, "making a decisive impact on the eradication of poverty and social inclusion" became one of three strands of a "streamlined" social process (along with pensions and healthcare and long-term care) rather than the prime focus as previously. The second change was in the understanding of how social inclusion (now dominant as a term) would be brought about. This was seen to follow from success in achieving targets on economic growth and jobs and the reform ("modernisation") of the European social model rather than, as previously, the result of concerted actions. In effect, the social goals were "downgraded" in the sense that they were to follow from economic priorities rather than to be aimed for directly. This set the scene for the third set of changes – the objectives themselves became narrower and more focused on particular domains and sub-groups (compare the two columns in Table 6.1). In the poverty and social exclusion strand, labour market participation came to be more heavily emphasised as did the "extreme" forms of exclusion. Furthermore, the efficiency of policies and coordination replaced "mobilisation". "Involvement" was the new term used; it was framed in terms of policy coordination and governance rather than as formerly political engagement. While it would be an exaggeration to say that the re-launched Lisbon switched to a different paradigm – moving from social development in its own right to social development as trickle down from economic growth – the second phase of Lisbon was much more neo-liberal in orientation than the first.

In terms of social policy substance, over the course of the ten years of Lisbon, four substantive social policy issues have emerged to the front of the social process (apart from pensions and healthcare) (see also chapter by Frazer and Marlier in the present volume). The first is *active inclusion*, especially of those furthest from the labour market. This was developed especially in a European Commission Recommendation on active inclusion which sets out the principles and practical guidelines on a comprehensive strategy based around three pillars: adequate income support, inclusive labour markets and access to quality services (European Commission, 2008a). The second strong focus has been *child poverty and child well-being*. As well as being highlighted throughout the process, this was activated by a thematic year on the subject in 2007 and the adoption of a report on the subject by the Social Protection Committee (2008), which Frazer and Marlier (2010) suggest is the first EU-wide benchmarking exercise based almost exclusively on the commonly-agreed indicators. Thirdly, *homelessness and housing exclusion* have been prominent in the Social OMC process and these too were the subject of a thematic year (2009). Fourthly, underpinning all of these – and also more generally in the EU's approach as developed through Lisbon – is a recognition of the *importance of the availability of a range of social services*. All can be traced to a social exclusion perspective (although they are rooted in other concerns and concepts as well). As mentioned, social exclusion has a core concern with labour market issues and so the EU's focus on those furthest from the labour market evokes a particular interpretation of social exclusion; the concern with child poverty reflects an understanding of the long-term effects and inter-generational transmission of poverty and social deprivation; the emphasis on homelessness picks up on the "extreme marginalised" references in the concept; access to housing and other services is under-pinned by a recognition that income on its own is an insufficient cause of and response to exclusion. If Lisbon has a distinctive identity as a social policy project, it is in the emergence/acceptance of these by the Council and the Commission (although not necessarily by the Member States) as common social policy concerns and important objects of policy attention. It is hard to see a distinctive social policy model here although some have claimed it as a social investment approach (Palme, 2009). In my view, it is too incomplete, too fragmented and the process has been too fluid to depict social policy under Lisbon as a distinct social policy model.

As well as putting substance on a social policy programme around poverty, social exclusion and social protection, the Lisbon process has also devoted considerable resources to defining and empirically measuring the phenomena and problems involved.

6.4 Poverty and Social Exclusion in Empirical Terms

One of the key elements of the Social OMC and of the EU's engagement with poverty and social exclusion is that it set in train a series of data and measurement-related resources, discourses and activities. In fact, over time these have assumed increasing importance. A new pan-European data survey – the EU Statistics on Income and Living Conditions (EU-SILC) – was implemented progressively as from 2003; it now covers all 27 EU countries as well as a growing number of non-EU European countries (for example, Croatia, Iceland, Norway, Switzerland, Turkey). EU-SILC replaced the European Community Household Panel Survey (ECHP). It is based on the idea of a common "framework" and no longer a common "survey" as was the case for the ECHP. The common framework defines the harmonised lists of target primary (annual) and secondary (every four years or less frequently) variables to be transmitted to Eurostat; common guidelines and procedures; common concepts (household and income) and classifications aimed at maximising comparability of the information produced. EU-SILC mainly focuses on income – detailed income components are collected mainly at personal level although a few income components are included in the household part. In addition, information is collected on material deprivation, housing conditions, labour-related activities, education and health.

The process has also generated a considerable degree of activity around the production of a set of cross-national statistical tools and benchmarks to inform and improve policy monitoring in the domain of poverty and social exclusion (as well as pensions and healthcare and long-term care, which are not addressed here). This has been a primary task of the EU Social Protection Committee (SPC), the EU body consisting of officials from each Member State as well as representatives of the European Commission which serves as a vehicle for cooperative exchange between the European Commission and the Member States in regard to modernising and improving social protection systems and their indicators. In 2001 the Committee established an Indicators Sub-Group to work on the development of indicators and statistics in support of its tasks.

The result is both an ongoing discourse about the measurement of poverty and social exclusion and an agreed set of common indicators that have been continually updated over time.[4] At the 2001 Laeken European Council, 18 indicators for social inclusion were adopted (Table 6.2, column 2). These have been further developed and reworked. In 2009, the SPC adopted a revised set of indicators covering all three strands of the Social OMC, with major additions to the EU social inclusion portfolio which now also covers housing (on the indicators agenda since 2001) and material deprivation. Indicators and data are of deep significance – they help to define a common set of phenomena and obviously to measure it. Marlier *et al.* (2007, page 146) suggest that the investment in both the EU-SILC and the development of common indicators have the potential to transform the basis for social

---

[4]   The SPC Indicators Sub-Group also develops indicators in the other two strands of the Social OMC (i.e. pensions as well as healthcare and long-term care), which we do not discuss in the present chapter.

reporting in the EU. They qualify the statement because the indicators are not used as well as they might be, either in terms of being adopted by Member States for their own analysis and policy development or being applied by Member States or the EU in systematic, forensic-type analyses which detail the "problem" and the causes.

Table 6.2: Commonly agreed indicators of poverty and social exclusion (in "social inclusion" and/or "overarching" EU portfolios)

Dimensions	2001	2006*	2009**	2010 – target indicators
Income poverty and inequality	At-risk-of-poverty rate	At-risk-of-poverty rate	At-risk-of-poverty rate	At-risk-of-poverty rate
	Relative median at-risk-of-poverty gap	Relative median at-risk-of-poverty gap	Relative median at-risk-of-poverty gap	
	Persistent at-risk-of-poverty rate	Persistent at-risk-of-poverty rate	Persistent at-risk-of-poverty rate	
	S80/S20 (income quintile ratio)	S80/S20 (income quintile ratio)	S80/S20 (income quintile ratio)	
Economic activity	Long-term unemployment rate	Long-term unemployment rate		
	Persons living in jobless house-holds (0-17 and 18-59)	Persons living in jobless house-holds (revised definitions; 0-17 and 18-59)	Persons living in jobless house-holds (revised definitions; 0-17 and 18-59)	Persons aged 0-59 who live in households with very low work attachment (threshold 0.2)
		Employment gap of immigrants		
	Coefficient of variation of unemployment rates at regional level	Coefficient of variation of employment rates at regional level	Coefficient of variation of employment rates at regional level	
Educational disadvantage	Early school leavers	Early school leavers	Early school leavers	
Health	Life expectancy at birth Self-defined health status by income level	Healthy life expectancy Self-reported unmet need for healthcare	Healthy life expectancy Self-reported unmet need for healthcare	

Dimensions	2001	2006*	2009**	2010 – target indicators
Material deprivation			Share of population living in households lacking at least 3 items among the following 9: i) unexpected expenses, ii) one week annual holiday away from home, iii) pay for arrears (mortgage or rent, utility bills or hire purchase instalments), iv) a meal with meat, chicken or fish every second day, v) keep home adequately warm, or could not afford (even if wanted to, i.e. "enforced lack") vi) a washing machine, vii) a colour TV, viii) a telephone, ix) a personal car	Share of population living in households lacking at least 4 of the 9 deprivation items agreed in 2009
Child well-being		To be developed	In process	
Housing	Housing costs, housing quality and homelessness explicitly identified as important priority for indicator development	To be developed	2 secondary indicators and 2 context statistics adopted, but further work, including further improvement of the quality of the data is needed before a primary housing indicator can be identified. There are still no EU indicators on homelessness	

* As in the streamlined social inclusion "Laeken" portfolio of primary indicators as agreed by the SPC on May 22nd 2006. ** European Commission (2009).

It will be obvious from Table 6.2, which shows only the primary EU indicators for social inclusion, that the discourse and practice as regards indicators is becoming more differentiated and complex over time. From the outset, primary indicators were differentiated from secondary indicators, then revision in 2006 added another layer of context indicators and made a useful distinction between "national" and "EU" indicators. The latter differentiation has been instrumental in allowing flexibility and responsiveness to emerging issues and local context (Marlier *et al.*, 2010). Now, since June 2010, there has been a further elaboration which will be discussed later.

Table 6.2 shows the evolution of the primary indicators over the four iterations. Looking at the left-most column, we can see that from the outset, poverty and social exclusion were conceptualised in terms of four domains: income (level and inequality), economic activity (unemployment, joblessness and "regional cohesion" measured by regional variation in employment rates), educational disadvantage, and health status. Of these, income predominated until 2009; since then, the portfolio has become more balanced across the different dimensions. In 2006, the indicators were reviewed, especially to reflect the streamlining of the social protection and social inclusion processes. A glance at the appropriate column in Table 6.2 shows the inclusion of a new domain in relation to employment gap of immigrants. A slot for one or more indicators of child well-being has been foreseen since 2006 and work on these is in progress since 2007. EU material deprivation indicators, added in 2009, focus on financial stress, consumption deprivation and household facilities – a threshold of lacking any three is designated as indicating deprivation (for the Europe 2020 social inclusion target, the threshold has been raised to four items). This move to a standardised measure of disadvantage has been in the pipeline for a considerable period and the agreement to have an indicator on it is significant in an EU context given strong resistance among some Member States. It is also controversial since setting out a threshold for the standard and style of living has many political implications and is considerably adrift of how many Member States conceptualise and measure poverty and deprivation.

Taking an overview, we see that income poverty has been to the fore, especially in the early period, and that there are a number of different income poverty measures in the EU list:

- At-risk-of-poverty rates at different thresholds (40%, 50%, 60% and 70% of the national median equivalised household income);
- An at-risk-of-poverty gap to measure the "intensity" of poverty;
- An at-risk-of-poverty rate "anchored" at a point in time;
- A persistent at-risk-of-poverty rate.

While the underlying thrust is to be as precise as possible about the measurement and what is being measured, one outcome of this now common practice of giving multiple definitions and indicators is to open up income poverty as a matter of interpretation. Contributing also to a possible destabilisation of the meaning of poverty is a linguistic change – instead of poverty the EU speaks in terms of "at-risk-of-poverty". While this is a more accurate term from a definitional perspective, it does tend to change poverty from a condition to a risk and, overall, it destabilises the meaning of poverty and renders it a function of measurement rather than a condition that exists for real people in real life.

We see also that indicator development has extended considerably beyond income poverty and income inequality, so much so that the indicator list has now a much stronger claim to multi-dimensionality. In fact, the indicators have a stronger claim to multi-dimensionality than the policy substance. This suggests some disjunction between the objective setting and the indicator setting/ monitoring, as does the absence of a set of indicators for the fourth objective (of mobilisation and/or policy coordination – see last row of Table 6.1).

The breaking news in relation to the Social OMC is the agreement by the June 2010 European Council on a social inclusion/ poverty reduction target of 20 million by 2020. This is a major development. Targets in the social domain have always proved controversial and no EU-wide poverty reduction target was agreed over the 10 years of the Lisbon process – in fact this is the first such target ever in the EU and it has major implications (see chapter by Walker in the present volume). In the social field in particular, it represents something of a different tack. The last column in Table 6.2 gives an idea of how the target is to be operationalised. In effect, there are three possible indicators: at-risk-of-poverty rate (based on the 60% median threshold); deprivation (the indicator used for the target is measured by a less lenient threshold as compared with the standard EU indicators of lacking at least four of the nine listed items); and the proportion of people in households with a low work attachment.

The latter is new and is effectively a measure of so-called "work intensity".[5] Using a combined measure[6] a household is defined as poor if any of the three conditions hold true:

- Low income (60% median threshold)
- AND/OR materially deprived
- AND/OR in a jobless household.

---

[5] In July 2010, the SPC and its Indicators Sub-Group agreed to set the threshold for this work intensity indicator at 0.20 primarily because above this limit the rates of poverty and material deprivation start decreasing rapidly. The definition used for the "targeted indicator" is quite different from that used for the standard indicator of jobless households; the data source is also different (EU-SILC in the case of the target and the Labour Force Survey in the case of the standard EU indicator of joblessness).

[6] In line with the principle of subsidiarity, Member States may choose to use any of the three, two, or all three. In fact, they may even choose an indicator of their own preference, although they must (in theory at least) make an evidence-based case for their choice of indicator if they move away from the EU-specified indicators.

On the basis of the figures for 2008, this definition gives an EU population of 120 million "poor or socially excluded" people which is the population level from which progress towards the 20 million target will be measured.

While much is unknown about how the target as a global or national target will be reached, there are both opportunities and risks in it. The opportunities lie in a firmer commitment and normative framework around poverty and social exclusion. The risks are that it might propel a move back to a more uni-dimensional approach (rather than the multidimensionality implied by social exclusion), that there is too much "individuality" allowed to Member States in defining their conception of the target, and that the resulting actions will leave untouched those most mired in poverty and deprivation (what Robert Walker in his chapter terms "creaming"; see also chapter by Frazer and Marlier).

6.5 Conclusion and Overview

The Lisbon process constitutes one of the most significant attempts anywhere to come to terms with the complexity and multidimensionality of poverty and social exclusion, especially from a technical, measurement point of view, and to author a social policy approach which rests centrally on these two concepts. While there is much debate and discussion over whether the Lisbon process has been a success or not and it is still too early to come to a definitive conclusion in this regard, it is possible to identify a range of achievements.

1. Poverty has been put on the EU political agenda and the still new concept of social exclusion has been elaborated as an approach to social policy. The EU approach has a number of hallmark features:

   - a multi-dimensional understanding of disadvantage is offered which merges incomes with a wider perspective but stays close to exclusion from the labour market as the guiding frame;

   - participation by the disadvantaged themselves is raised as an objective of policy (although is not operationalised from the perspective of measurement and its significance in the EU programme declined over the 10 years of Lisbon);

   - agreement has been reached on the use of an innovative and highly complex set of indicators to measure the nature of the "problems" and progress towards addressing them.

2. Although it offers a broad interpretation, the Social OMC has focused on emerging risks and target groups. While these are very worthy of emphasis, there is a critical point to be made that the selective approach risks fragmentation. This is true at two levels. First, it is evident in the focus on three strands of social policy:

poverty/social exclusion, pensions and healthcare and long-term care. These make for a rather hollow and incomplete social policy programme. Second, within each of these strands, the Lisbon process has picked up on particular policy areas. In the poverty and social exclusion strand for example, there have been four major thematic areas: active inclusion, child poverty and child well-being, homelessness and housing exclusion, access to services. The result is that the EU tends to follow a fragmented or selective approach which could be said to be "patchwork" in nature.

At the time of writing (July-October 2010), the details of the post Lisbon scenario are not yet clear. Apart from the poverty target, two other developments are known. First, a guideline on poverty and social inclusion (Guideline 10), which sets out the policies to reach the proposed target and which will probably form an important part of the future social objectives (though not the sole basis as other guidelines also include major social elements), has been included under the ten Europe 2020 Integrated Guidelines for growth and jobs adopted by the Council (see opening chapter). This guideline, the only one with an explicit social inclusion focus, is one of four employment guidelines. For those sceptics who have always seen the EU interest in poverty and social exclusion as at root a liberal-oriented, labour market-related project, the location and relative "loneliness" of the poverty guideline are proof positive of this. However, in its content the guideline is quite broad and emphasises the importance of access to high quality, affordable and sustainable services and the key role of social protection systems (including pensions and access to health care). It therefore restates some of the fundamental principles established to date and as Ferrera points out in his chapter has a social rights' orientation. The second known element of the new programme or project is that it will comprise a European Platform against Poverty (EPAP), one of seven so-called "flagship initiatives". No details are available at the time of writing on what will be the focus and content of this initiative.

As we look forward and take account of what happened under Lisbon, a number of lessons from the first ten years merit emphasis.

1. It is important to stabilise and consolidate the meaning and focus of the poverty/social exclusion approach. There are two issues here. First, the ink was hardly dry on the very ambitious objectives agreed at the Nice European Council in December 2000 when they were changed in the relaunched Lisbon Strategy in 2005. Secondly, for this and other reasons, there has been instability in how the EU has understood the problems that the Social OMC is meant to address and the causal processes involved. One can identify several competing visions during the ten years of Lisbon: one focusing

primarily on low income and access to minimum income or social assistance; another focusing on activation and labour market exclusion as the primary cause of social exclusion; a more inclusive, society-based analysis alongside a narrower, extreme cases type of focus or, in other words, shifting emphasis on the social conditions of all to those of the poor and marginalised. No social policy project can be sustained with such diverse interpretations of what the core problem is. A longer-term perspective and clarity in the understanding about the core challenges are therefore essential preconditions as we go forward.

2. There is also the matter of closer linkages between the three strands of the Social OMC: pensions, healthcare and long-term care, and poverty/social exclusion. These have, to date anyway, proceeded more or less along separate tracks, in many ways reflecting policy-making patterns at Member State level where these are typically covered by different ministries or departments. The linkages between them have to be much more clearly explicated for a "streamlined" process to take root.

3. As well as greater coherence in the focus of the social policy goals and objectives, it is also vital to clarify the place of social policy in the larger economic project. As we saw, social cohesion was effectively downgraded during the course of Lisbon's ten years: from a stand-alone position at the outset of the process it was transformed into something that would follow from economic and employment growth. There is leeway and potential in the Europe 2020 framing to upgrade social exclusion and poverty, making them a fourth pillar (along with economic development, employment and environmental factors).

4. The two levels focused on in this piece (policy focus and indicator development/empirical measurement) have proceeded along parallel tracks rather than as an integrated whole. They need to be brought much closer together and in fact can be used in a complementary fashion, not least in that the data and use of indicators can help to provide a more grounded and causal analysis and lend policy development a stronger evidence base. If used to best effect, the developments in conceptualisation and measurement would allow a more penetrating analysis of the strengths and weaknesses of existing approaches within and across Member States and also at EU level. They would also facilitate an understanding of the more structural references in the concept of social exclusion rather than the descriptive approaches that have predominated to date. The processes that lead to exclusion and poverty would be the focus rather than those affected by the processes (which is the

strong tendency in the current emphases on the long-term unemployed, children and the homeless).

The foregoing analysis provides a basis on which to conjecture about the possible form and contribution of the EPAP. In my view, the EPAP should be seen as complementary or value-added to the Social OMC. It should have more than a single objective or focus and should operate at a number of levels. In terms of roles, one function could be to identify innovative linkages among social policies and between social, employment and economic policies for example, treating this as a matter of policy design, policy implementation and policy monitoring. Another way in which it could have a forward-looking perspective is in terms of forecasting and identification of emerging issues and possible solutions. A third possible role would be to achieve a presence for and raise the visibility of the Social OMC at national level. As a national-level set of activities, this could encompass awareness-raising and knowledge-diffusing actions around poverty and social exclusion. The hope would be that this would help to raise political commitment in the Member States to prioritising social issues. A related function would be to improve or sustain high stakeholder engagement. Of course, awareness- and commitment-raising and stakeholder-binding activities are also necessary at EU level for the Social OMC has had relatively little visibility at this level also. A fourth possible role or function is around monitoring and impact assessment. As shown in this chapter, much energy has been devoted under the Social OMC to developing a set of indicators. The next step is to apply these in a systematic fashion to enable not just stocktaking but monitoring of impact. We need to know much more about how different policy programmes operate and their impact in response to the problems they are meant to address in different contexts (see chapter by Kühnemund in the present volume).

Finally, all of this has to be set within the new opportunities opened up by the new Lisbon Treaty and Article 9 in particular (the so-called "Horizontal Social Clause"; see opening chapter). As Ferrera shows in his chapter in this volume, the Treaty provides the justification for EU action on a broader range of social issues than heretofore (including a high level of education, training and protection of human health and a reduction of inequality). Given that there is now a stronger legal base, EU action on poverty and social exclusion among other domains need no longer to depend on a "community of the willing" (a phrase used by Jacobsson (2009: 127)). What the analysis of the development of poverty and social exclusion under Lisbon suggests, though, is that every step on this ground will be hard fought and highly contested and that political commitment (at a range of levels) has to be carefully nurtured.

References

Bauer, M.V. (2002), "Limitations to agency control in European Union policy-making: The Commission and the poverty programmes", *Journal of Common Market Studies*, 40, 3: 381-400.

Berghman, J. (1995), "Social exclusion in Europe: Policy context and analytical framework", in G. Room (editor) *Beyond the threshold*, Bristol: Policy Press, 10-28.

Council of the European Communities (1989), *Resolution of the Council of Ministers for Social Affairs on Combating Social Exclusion* (89/C277/01) (Luxembourg: Official Journal, C277).

Daly, M. (2006), *Social Exclusion as Concept and Policy Template in the European Union*, Cambridge, MA: Minda de Gunzburg Center for European Studies, Harvard University, Working Paper No. 135.

Daly, M. and Saraceno, C. (2002), "Social exclusion and gender relations", in B. Hobson, J. Lewis and B. Siim (editors) *Contested concepts in gender and social politics*, Cheltenham: Edward Elgar, 84-104.

Dieckhoff. M. and Gallie, D. (2007), "The renewed Lisbon Strategy and social exclusion policy", *Industrial Relations Journal*, 38, 6: 480-502.

European Commission (2009), *Portfolio of indicators for the monitoring of the European Strategy for Social Protection and Social Inclusion – 2009 update*, Brussels: European Commission. Available at: http://ec.europa.eu/social/main.jsp?catId=756&langId=en.

European Commission (2008), *A renewed commitment to Social Europe: Reinforcing the Open Method of Coordination for Social Protection and Social Inclusion*, Communication COM(2008) 418 final, Brussels: European Commission.

European Commission (2008a), *Commission Recommendation on the active inclusion of people excluded from the labour market*, Communication COM(2008) 639 final, Brussels: European Commission.

European Commission (2005), *Working together, working better: A new framework for the Open Coordination of Social Protection and Inclusion Policies in the European Union*, Communication COM(2005) 706 final, Brussels: European Commission.

European Commission (1994), *Social policy – A way forward for the Union – A White Paper*, Communication COM(94) 333, Brussels: European Commission.

European Commission (1992), *Towards a Europe of solidarity – Intensifying the fight against social exclusion, fostering integration*, Communication COM(92) 542, Brussels: European Commission.

European Communities (2004), *Facing the challenge. The Lisbon Strategy for Growth and Employment*, Luxembourg: Official Publications of the European Communities.

European Council (2000), *Presidency Conclusions Nice European Council 7, 8 and 9 December*, Brussels: European Council. Available at: http://ue. eu.int/ueDocs/cms_Data/docs/pressData/en/ec/00400-r1.%20ann.en0.htm.

Frazer, H. and Marlier, E. (2010), "The EU's approach to combating poverty and social exclusion: Ensuring a stronger approach in the future by learning from the strengths and weaknesses of the current approach", *Kurswechsel*, 3: 34-51.

Jacobsson, K. (2009), "Achievements and non-achievements of the European Employment Strategy", in N. Morel, B. Palier and J. Palme (editors) *What future for social investment?*, Stockholm: Institute for Future Studies, 119-130.

Levitas, R. (1998), *The inclusive society? Social exclusion and new labour*, Basingstoke: Palgrave Macmillan.

Marlier, E., Cantillon, B., Nolan, B., Van den Bosch K. and Van Rie, T. (2010), "Developing and learning from measures of social inclusion in the European Union", in D.J. Besharov and K.A. Couch (editors) *International policy exchange series*, New York: Oxford University Press.

Marlier, E., Atkinson, A.B., Cantillon, B. and Nolan, B. (2007), *The EU and social inclusion: Facing the challenges*, Bristol: Policy Press.

Palme, J. (2009), "The quest for sustainable social policies in the EU: The crisis and beyond", in N. Morel, B. Palier and J. Palme (editors) *What future for social investment?* Stockholm: Institute for Future Studies, 177-193.

Silver, H. (1994), "Social exclusion and social solidarity: Three paradigms", *International Labour Review* 133, 5/6: 531-578.

Social Protection Committee (2008), *Child Poverty and Well-Being in the EU: Current status and way forward*, Luxembourg: OPOCE. Available at: http://ec.europa.eu/social/main.jsp?catId=751&langId=en&pubId=74&type=2 &furtherPubs=yes.

7. A *Territorialised* Social Agenda to Guide Europe 2020 and the Future EU Cohesion Policy

Marjorie JOUEN[1]

7.1 Introduction

In April 2009, the European Commission published an independent report written by Fabrizio Barca, entitled "An agenda for a reformed cohesion policy" (Barca, 2009). The report developed an in-depth analysis of what makes cohesion policy exemplary, and what should be preserved or deepened, highlighting the excesses and false interpretations that need to be eliminated or re-framed. It included many proposals that aim to give cohesion policy a key role in the dynamics of European integration once more. The key concept that was supposed to give coherence to the new regional policy was the "*territorialised* social agenda".

In this post-crisis period, this report should act as a point of reference within the wider debate on the policy model associated with the European socio-economic model of development. The Europe 2020 Strategy certainly makes more room for the social dimension than the 2005 refocused Lisbon agenda (which considered only growth and jobs issues), by promoting smart, sustainable and inclusive growth on an equal footing. Yet it did not establish any clear relationship between the territorial dimension and the EU targets (in the field of social inclusion, employment and education; see opening chapter) on the one hand, and the flagship initiatives on the other (i.e. the agenda for new skills and jobs, the European Platform against Poverty, and Youth on the Move) associated to a greater or lesser extent with this third pillar. Worse still, there were worrying signs that the Commission appeared to be consider-

[1] I wish to thank Fabrizio Barca for his helpful comments and suggestions on an earlier version of this paper even if I take of course full responsibility for its content. Address for correspondence: mjouen@notre-europe.eu.

ing the option of separating the European Social Fund (ESF) from the Structural Funds[2] after 2013.

As we approach the start of the official negotiations on the future of the EU's cohesion policy and as the Member States begin to bring their policies into line with the Europe 2020 priorities, it is time to examine the Barca report's proposals so that we can make best use of them. Some of its ideas should be developed and detailed in the form of concrete measures and legal provisions, with a view to transforming the territorialised social agenda into a road-map for EU action in the coming months.

To this end, the present paper begins by returning to the main messages set out in the Barca report. It then proceeds to discuss the various methods and tools that could be used to "socialise" cohesion policy, and ultimately to "territorialise" the EU social objectives.

7.2 The Barca Report: An Inspiring Blueprint for Addressing Social Issues from a Territorial Perspective

7.2.1 Cohesion policy as an EU integration tool

In his report, Barca first explains that the EU's legitimacy hinges on its capacity to have a decisive impact on the lives of EU citizens – without interfering in national or local practices, but rather by marking out the contours of a common vision. He then considers that the territorial dimension of cohesion policy represents a cornerstone around which the policies of EU development should be built. In so doing, he is expanding further on Jacques Delors' initial vision, i.e. "competition that stimulates, cooperation that strengthens, solidarity that unites", which underpinned the Single Act along with its two principal achievements, the single market and regional policy.

In short, from 1988 to 2007, EU action in the field of cohesion policy increased dramatically from 10% to more than 40% of the EU budget. During the first 10-15 years, the Structural Funds comprised five funds: ESF, ERDF (European Regional Development Fund), Cohesion Fund, EFF (European Fishery Fund) and EAFRD (European Agricultural Fund for Rural Development). These funds were closely integrated into regional or area-based development programmes, according to specific "objectives" (e.g. less-developed regions, declining rural areas, industrial restructuring areas, etc.). Since 2000, the "integration

---

[2]   Currently, the Structural Funds are the European Social Fund (ESF), the European Regional Development Fund (ERDF) and the Cohesion Fund.

rule" has weakened progressively and the "sectoral" funds for rural and coastal areas have been managed separately.

Barca highlights a succession of weaknesses that have hampered cohesion policy over the past ten years:

- a gradual shift in semantics and ideas that has led to cohesion policy being seen as a form of redistribution or an instrument of approximate convergence by increases in GDP *per capita*;
- the process of "Lisbonisation", which as from 2005 emphasises competitiveness to the detriment of solidarity and which impoverishes the role of multi-level governance in cohesion policy;
- the idea that the social dimension is "the price we have to pay" for achieving unity in our markets and currency, rather than as an end in itself.

On this particular issue, Barca believes that, in fact, the reverse is true: the economic element of the EU project is not the main objective, but rather a means of achieving prosperity and peace in the Union.

Barca believes that cohesion policy has played a major role in the "paradigm shift" at national, regional and local levels in the conduct of policies to support growth, investment, human resource development and day-to-day democracy. This policy was not however capable of creating a broad EU consensus, giving visibility to the most efficient methods, or of stimulating sustained innovation on the ground.

He criticises the excesses that neo-liberal thinking have brought about through "the intellectual complacency of a majority of the 'economics profession' (quoting D. Acemoglu) over what markets can achieve". For him, the division of labour between, on the one hand, a Union that is preoccupied with markets and liberalisation, and, on the other, Member States which guarantee social protection and well-being leads to a dead-end. Instead, he believes that the progress of EU integration assumes an allocation of responsibilities and multi-level cooperation mechanisms guided by high-level political compromise. This compromise, similar to the Rousseauian idea of a "social contract", is vital for today's enlarged Union. To achieve a "re-founding" status, this compromise should encompass not only the economic dimension of the European project but its political and democratic dimensions as well.

7.2.2 Major assets of a place-based development policy

A large part of the Barca report is dedicated to the debate between cohesion policy (i.e. a place-based policy) and the sectoral policies (i.e. place-blind policies). Barca devotes much attention to the debate which is currently raging among the world's development policy gurus (notably, World Bank 2008 and OECD 2008). Some of these analysts, who have distanced themselves from the Washington consensus but who are still uncertain as to the institutional capacities at decentralised levels, seem to consider geographic inequalities as an inevitable product of growth. As a result, they call for policies that encourage mobility, along with "spatially blind" measures, preferably managed at national level.

Barca positions himself firmly in the opposing camp. He uses the comparison with the United States to cast aside any thought of replacing cohesion policy with sectoral policies. He urges the introduction of a place-based policy, which he considers to be:

- a long-term development strategy aimed at fighting both the under-exploitation of full potential and the persistent social inequalities in a given place;
- centred on the integrated production of public goods and services, determined in accordance with local preferences and knowledge, through participatory political institutions;
- supported by a system of multi-level governance which includes financial transfers subject to strong conditionality.

For him, the place-based paradigm is infinitely superior simply because it is more effective. It makes it possible to identify and take account of people's preferences and knowledge. Moreover, it avoids the "one-size-fits-all" syndrome, by allowing public goods and institutions to be tailored to local needs. It is particularly suitable to Europe, where as a result of various interdependencies and legacies, most challenges to globalisation and the Single Market concern places rather than sectors. It is also the only feasible solution since, unlike the sectoral paradigm, it is compatible with the EU's limited democratic legitimacy. What is more, sectoral top-down interventions are not consistent with the role of the Member States in the area of social and economic development. On the contrary, place-based interventions combine the EU's responsibility for setting goals and guidelines with the national, regional or local actors' responsibility for implementing policy according to contexts.

In Barca's view, cohesion policy has been constricted by the perpetual tensions between subsidiarity (giving freer rein to lower-level authorities, following the rationale that they are closer to the ground and therefore better able to choose suitable measures) and conditionality (obliging lower-level authorities to follow rules, in line with the imperative to make the ensemble coherent). It has suffered from a prevalence of poor political reasoning, such as the argument about a fair "net return", hiding the weaknesses of internal governance, the monopolisation of European funds by local elites, favouritism, etc. In a context where academic discourse is discrediting public intervention, this tension has resulted in a gradual erosion of the consensus around the added value contributed by the EU.

As a consequence, the cohesion policy's territorial dimension has been gradually limited to local development (with the LEADER programme in rural areas and the URBAN programme in towns) and territorial cooperation, rather than occupying a place at the heart of the policy. Priority has been given to support for sectoral economic policy (tourism, research, support for SMEs etc.) and social policy, effectively endangering the effectiveness of cohesion policy.

Barca backs his position with reference to current academic knowledge about development dynamics, and the theories of new economic geography about the role of agglomerations, market forces, institutions, etc. This analysis allows him to ensure that his plea for external public intervention directed towards supporting local potential is based on solid economic arguments. He explains that the endogenous political-economic-social process cannot eradicate certain cases of inefficiency and social exclusion for three main reasons: local elites may lack the capacity to innovate, they may not be willing to do so and they may not be sufficient for innovation.

For Barca, all regions must be eligible for cohesion policy, to the extent that the two problems identified – under-exploited local potential, and social exclusion – may very well manifest themselves at sub-regional levels. It is for the national or regional authorities to determine the appropriate geographic perimeter where such problems are present and where public interventions have a chance of success.

His final argument against sectoral policies consists of a rejection of the Open Method of Coordination (OMC) as a possible alternative path for affluent regions that could no longer benefit from the Structural Funds. For him, this should be seen as a step backwards, because cohesion policy represents a somewhat more advanced approach. It uses the right methods to handle different levels of governance and to integrate various sectors within a comprehensive policy. Today, the OMC targets only national policies within a sectoral logic. In addition, its capacity to involve sub-national levels has proved disappointing, despite the willingness of these actors to play an active role.

7.2.3 Territorialised social agenda: a comprehensive concept

Barca calls for a fundamental change in the policy's direction, based on five general principles gleaned from past experience: the concentration of resources; orientation of subsidies towards results; mobilisation and learning; strengthening of the Commission; reinforcement of a high-level system of checks and balances. He considers that these proposals cannot be implemented gradually, but instead must be introduced immediately. Hence, a general agreement needs to be reached, which assumes the simultaneous conclusion of three types of negotiations – concerning resources, governance and goals. He explains that the EU would not be withdrawing competences from the Member States in the welfare sector, but rather accepting the consequences of economic transformation (globalisation, single market, etc.) and existing policies (Lisbon Treaty, Stability and Growth Pact).

He sums up his proposals as follows: "Re-launching cohesion policy requires both the adoption of a strong political concept and reform of the priorities and governance. It also requires building a new political compromise, linked to an appropriate negotiation calendar."

The so-called political concept is a *territorialised* social agenda, i.e. a development policy which aims to achieve both efficiency and social inclusion – in other words, "a policy aimed at giving all places the opportunity to make use of their potential (efficiency) and all people the opportunity to be socially included independently of where they live (social inclusion)."

Barca insists that cohesion policy should rely on two key concepts: efficiency and equity. He defines territorial efficiency as "the capacity of a territory to make the most of its resources". In fact, the full exploitation of local potential is determined not by the given technological conditions, but by the interaction of institutions and decisions – both private and public, economic and political. As for equity, Barca essentially refers to the recent advances made by the OECD, the World Bank and the EU itself, acknowledging the multi-dimensional character of social exclusion and the added value of social-inclusion policies which work against factors beyond the control of individuals. These advances today open up a little-contested field of possibilities for a territorialised approach to social exclusion.

Barca considers that these two concepts deserve equal attention. Even if there are occasionally synergies between efficiency and equity, the link is not automatic: social exclusion does affect the overall efficiency of a locality, but improving local efficiency does not necessarily guarantee social inclusion. As an example, he explains that territorialisation should not be seen as a synonym for immobility and that the EU should bear the extra costs of maintaining populations within its territory and also allow individuals to choose whether or not to move. By the same token, it would be misleading to consider that affluent regions should be exempted from concerns about social inclusion, since pockets of poverty are sometimes highly local in nature and inequalities exist between individuals.

The priorities that should be the focus of cohesion policy may be defined based on the notion of the "European public good" (a good which benefits all EU citizens, one of which no one can or should be deprived) and three criteria – the EU character of the problem (EU-wide relevance); the suitability of solving it through the adoption of a territorial approach (place-based nature); and the possibility of conclusively checking the effectiveness of the policy (verifiability). Then, six priorities may be envisaged and opened up for discussion: in the area of territorial efficiency (innovation and climate change); in the area of social inclusion (migration and children); and, with equal importance, skills and ageing.

7.2.4 Reforming governance

For Barca, the reason for the failure of the Lisbon agenda is crystal clear: defective governance, not to mention defective multi-level governance. This diagnosis, even if expressed in a more nuanced manner, is also shared by several social policy analysts (see for example chapters by Natali and by Frazer and Marlier in the present volume). Conversely, however, this very aspect is one of cohesion policy's biggest assets (Bache, 2008). Thus, the strong political compromise that must form the basis of a European socio-economic development model can be established by drawing up a European strategic development framework – this should take place prior to budgetary negotiations and be detailed at national and regional levels.

The proposed system aims to restore a balance between the different levels of governance, and thus, in a certain sense, to "put national authorities in their place" – authorities which have never been slow to weaken European action – even if this means losing powerful support. Conscious of the fact that it is not possible to circumvent the national level entirely, yet equally aware that this level often represents a problem or obstacle to European cohesion, Barca imagines a system which makes the national level accountable to higher (European) and lower (regional or local) levels. The formula proposed is "a new contractual relationship between the Commission and Member States (or sometimes regions), which focuses much more on performance and – in terms of central priorities – provides room for adapting institutional changes to specific contexts". These contracts would be specific to each country and would take shape according to the results of a strategic national debate on priorities and objectives.

Barca acknowledges the policy's role in spreading a culture of assessment – previously unfamiliar to most countries – at national level, and especially at regional and local levels. However, he regrets that it has not really enabled any growth in knowledge as to the effectiveness of development policy. In general, Barca believes that the weakness of micro-economic assessments results from the responsibility given to Member States – in the absence of an impact assessment strategy and in the presence of a strong tropism in terms of criteria and procedures.

Thus, to make the action of multi-level governance effective, Barca advocates reinforced conditionality within the framework of these "contracts". In his view, they represent the only technique that might be capable of combining conditionality and subsidiarity. However, he is not naïve as regards the risks of by-passing or blockages that may threaten tests of conditionality (verification of additionality, performance conditions, etc.). What is more, he has no illusions about the unwieldy nature of the various controls. He therefore proposes a reversal of current practice: clauses affecting administrative procedures should be strictly adhered to, whereas those targeting results and impact should benefit from a degree of tolerance.

Barca does not underestimate the challenge of transforming the current national strategic reference frameworks (NSRF) into agreements on aims and means, to which Member States and regions will commit themselves. He therefore foresees a somewhat complex arrangement which would leave Member States and regions significant room for manoeuvre regarding the exact targets of subsidies – on condition that the strategic justifications are defined from the start, the objectives identified and the criteria for the impact assessment are incontestable. The Commission's role would be substantially changed as a result: it would intervene to carry out concrete assessments of the implementation capacity of national or regional authorities. The monitoring of contracts would allow for annual reports by Member States, presentation of the results obtained and their relation to the initial objectives and targets – and would serve as a basis for more thorough discussion among the Member States.

In addition, various measures are envisaged to improve the quality of the assessments and collective learning. Although Barca retains the current system's principle of co-financing, he advocates improving coherence between cohesion policy and the Stability and Growth Pact and puts various proposals on the table. To rebuild the cohesion policy's capacity for innovation, he imagines a dual system, with specific budgetary obligations for Member States and a specific budget to enable the Commission to approve the most interesting experiments and to conduct its own experimentation.

7.3 Europe 2020: an Opportunity to "Socialise" the Cohesion Policy

7.3.1 Opening up a new field of action for local and regional authorities

Unquestionably, the Europe 2020 Strategy marks a turning point in relation to the policy pursued since the end of the 1990s, for it must not be forgotten that some of the premises of the Lisbon Strategy were already present in the European Employment Strategy launched in 1997 and that the Agenda 2000, which served as a basis for the 2000-2006 programmes, was devised in 1998. From the viewpoint of local and regional authorities and cohesion policy, this change involves both governance and the stated goals.

As regards governance, while the lack of ownership by the general public in the Lisbon process was constantly deplored (Committee of the Regions (CoR), 2009; Fabry and Fernandes, 2010), some experts and stakeholders have stressed the interaction between the Structural Funds and the Social OMC as one of the good practices (Metis, 2009; Eichhorst *et al.*, 2010). Drawing on these lessons, the European Commission states that "all national, regional and local authorities should implement the partnership, closely associating parliaments, as well as social partners and representatives of civil society, contributing to the elaboration of national reform programmes as well as to its implementation" (European Commission, 2010). In return, the Structural Funds and the cohesion policy are called on to help by participating in achieving the Europe 2020 Strategy objectives.

This new situation seems to have been relatively well perceived by local and regional authorities, who see here a potentially well-balanced opportunity to strengthen their involvement in the decision-making process, rather than comply with constraints which are inappropriate and ultimately inoperable (Association of European Regions, 2010; CoR, 2010 and 2010b). After having stressed the specific nature of cohesion policy and its objectives derived from the Treaties, the Committee of the Regions has transformed the overall offer of partnership into a campaign encouraging the conclusion of "Territorial pacts between national governments and regional and local authorities to achieve the Europe 2020 objectives" (CoR, 2010a). These pacts would aim at establishing common agreement on quantified targets and policies adapted to the specific conditions of individual countries in order to feed into national reform programmes. They would also touch upon the conditions for policy implementation, given that in some fields and in some Member States, in particular the most decentralised ones, implementation is almost exclusively the preserve of the regions.

The Committee of the Regions has also announced its intention to produce an annual monitoring report on the overall participatory process and, more particularly for the flagship initiatives, to evaluate the results achieved according to the level of governance and the methods used.

7.3.2 A possible "socialisation" of cohesion policy

As regards aligning cohesion policy more closely with the Europe 2020 priorities, not least social inclusion, this requirement can be considered to correspond to the need for EU measures to be more effective, as has been indicated earlier (Frazer and Marlier, 2009). Moreover, a better integration of different policy tools and policy coordination, on the one hand, and the Structural Funds on the other, seems the most obvious step towards a more effective influence on national reforms (see chapter by Natali in the present volume).

From the point of view of policy content, this represents an ideal opportunity to put into effect Barca's recommendations (see chapter by Ferrera in the present volume). Whilst talking about a "territorialised social agenda", Barca drew attention, above all, to the existence of a new challenge for cohesion policy and argued in favour of taking greater account of the social cohesion objective. He came to the conclusion that there was a need to introduce criteria concerning individuals, in addition to criteria for local and regional authorities, in order to determine the allocation of Structural Funds. Thus he was interested in finding the best way of giving cohesion policy a social dimension. This appears to be the very challenge referred to in the June 2010 European Council's conclusions, which state that neither cohesion policy nor the common agricultural policy must be sidelined.

It seems possible to reintroduce Barca's six-point agenda (innovation, climate change, migration, children, skills and ageing) on the basis of which each region will be able to make its own choices, according to its economic and social circumstances, strengths and weaknesses, provided that the three strands (smart, sustainable and inclusive) of Europe 2020 are present. Balancing these three strands will probably also have to be adapted to the needs of each region.

Faced with the tendency towards an excessive willingness to focus action, it will probably be important to remember the often-used argument that social inclusion should not be a separate policy objective since it is naturally correlated with growth. However, empirical evidence shows that no correlation exists and, in reality, the balance between the two is an empirical matter. This suggests that social inclusion and efficiency objectives must be kept distinct from each other, and the contracts promoted by Barca may offer a suitable framework for them. This means too that the use of the ESF and ERDF should be closely integrated within regional development programmes. Such an approach now seems to be supported by the European Commission (see the Commission's Communication of 9 November 2010; European Commission, 2010d).

This broad approach obviously fed into the Communication on the EU budget review (European Commission, 2010c) which states that, in the poorest regions, cohesion policy support is important to tackle issues such as social exclusion or environmental degradation, for example in urban areas. It also details the content of the "menu" of thematic priorities "directly linked to the Integrated Guidelines and flagship projects of Europe 2020" which will be offered to Member States and regions for concentrating EU and national resources. In practice, the European Commission intends to adopt a Common Strategic Framework which "would encompass the action covered today by the Cohesion Fund, the ERDF, the ESF, the EFF and the EAFRD" and would "also identify linkages and coordination mechanisms with other EU instruments such as programmes for research, innovation, lifelong learning, and networks".

7.3.3 Performance criteria which can be used immediately

As regards the other major failing highlighted by Barca, namely the predominance of financial controls and focus on absorption capacity to the detriment of the evaluation of practical results, the June 2010 European Council's decision to set a social inclusion/poverty reduction target (see opening chapter) may help considerably. The target and the indicators on which it is based, together with the other commonly agreed EU social indicators, should also make it easier to carry out the monitoring and the analysis needed to establish an appropriate development strategy at national, regional and local level (see chapters by Frazer and Marlier, by Walker and by Zeitlin in the present volume). In addition, the commonly agreed indicators should be used diagnostically to understand why some Member States may be performing worse than others against their respective national targets (Marlier *et al.*, 2007).

In practice, for small countries with national programmes, these indicators would have a direct impact on the strategy associated with the Structural Funds, since they would fix the targets to be achieved. For large and medium-sized countries where programming is done at regional level (NUTS II[3]), the problem of the availability of indicators at an appropriate level is far from being resolved. True, exploratory work has begun under the auspices of ESPON (European Observation Network for Territorial Development and Cohesion)[4], as part of the 2007-2013 objective of territorial cooperation, but it will be some years before this work is complete.

On the eve of the opening of negotiations on the post-2013 financial perspectives, this obstacle must not be underestimated: it is not only technical, but also political. Changing the criteria would have major consequences (including budgetary ones), which to date have not been fully contained.

To unlock the situation – for in the course of recent months the prospect of the introduction of greater conditionality on results achieved has gained considerable recognition – EU regions are considering the possibility of reversing the process by starting at the end. In other words, rather than set long-term objectives to be achieved in 2020, the regions could start to select some indicators already in use to describe their past situation and shed light on their track record to date (CoR, 2010c). This would enable them to carry out an individual qualitative evaluation over an average period before making a comparison with the others. Each region could thus gradually prepare to produce evidence on results obtained, as regards social inclusion. This would make it easier for them to set precise tailor-made objectives when the new European budgetary programming gets under way in 2014. Technical support from the European Commission and Eurostat would, of course, be necessary.

The choice of appropriate indicators should respect the following two conditions:

- allow strong ownership by combining simplicity, verifiability and potential for communication to European citizens;
- achieve a consensus among regions, whose social inclusion priorities tend to differ.

7.4 "Territorialising" the EU Social Objectives

That is not to say that the avenue opened up by the idea of a territorialised social agenda is not worth pursuing. The fact is that it was not treated as such by Barca, as it was not part of his mandate, which was limited to cohesion policy. Nor was it really explored by the March

---

[3]   For more information on "NUTS", see: http://epp.eurostat.ec.europa.eu/portal/page/portal/nuts_nomenclature/introduction.

[4]   Notably the INTERCO project (see http://www.espon.eu).

2010 Commission Communication (2010), which confined itself to presenting reinforced territorial cohesion as an almost automatic consequence of growth or access to employment for all. It would consist of firmly bringing the EU social objectives closer to cohesion policy; in other words, exploring the implications of the new territorial cohesion objective (introduced by the Lisbon Treaty) in the next programming regulations, ensuring that the EU cohesion policy fully takes on board the EU social objectives and also incorporating the territorial approach into EU coordination and cooperation in the social field.

7.4.1 Social and territorial inclusion, a new objective

Incorporating territorial cohesion into endeavours to achieve more inclusive growth would, in effect, territorialise those benefitting from the social inclusion initiatives. This approach is clearly underpinned by the issues raised by the debate on the 2008 Green Paper on Territorial Cohesion (European Commission, 2008a; Jouen 2008): differences in regions' exposure to the challenges of globalisation, climate change, demographic ageing and energy poverty. Conventionally, cohesion policy uses a rather "top down" programming process, although the top (i.e. the regional and local authorities) is not very far from the bottom in this case. However, when Barca talks about the need for external intervention to overcome the limits of local elite groups, he is thinking more of empowerment of local communities and their inhabitants and greater powers for civil society organisations. He refers to the integrated local development approach, pointing out moreover that cohesion policy has evolved in such a way as to reduce it to relative insignificance. This approach consists essentially of creating a push-pull mechanism, to encourage local authorities to make room for local projects and support them (pull) and to support them with advice and technical and methodological assistance (push).

The first areas targeted could be those identified by the Lisbon Treaty (Article 174): rural areas, areas affected by industrial transition, and regions which suffer from severe and permanent natural or demographic handicaps such as the northernmost regions with very low population density and island, cross-border and mountain regions. Urban districts in difficulties would also be included.

The second category could be areas which have experienced internal social deterioration compared to other regions. Marlier *et al.* (2007) suggest that the EU portfolio of social indicators could be complemented with a "background statistic" based on a common income threshold of 60% of the EU-wide median, which could be an important way of addressing the key issue of social cohesion/ convergence across the Union. Introducing an indicator of this kind could cause scepticism, given the already major disparities in *per capita* GDP between EU regions. However, greater comparability can be introduced by making use of purchasing power parity. Nevertheless, as Marlier *et al.* highlight by referring to the word "convergence", the value of this indicator lies not so much in its actual level but rather in its evolution over time.

We will, in effect, see – as we already know thanks to the *per capita* GDP – that over 10 years the situation of certain old-style industrial regions has not improved, and has even deteriorated. However, it will also be possible to ascertain whether this relative impoverishment has exacerbated inequalities, in other words whether the situation of the poorest people has deteriorated.

Thus, if we apply this EU-wide approach and calculate on this basis regional poverty risk estimates (rather than national estimates) and if we look at the evolution of these regional estimates over time, this might make it easier to identify those regions which have succeeded in preserving a certain level of social cohesion, where others have not. On the basis of this neutral observation of "territorialised social de-cohesion" the causes can be established. In effect, a rise in the number of people in a situation of poverty or a fall in the income of the poorest people can be the result of social policy becoming less effective at local level or a failure of social policy to react to a new situation, or can even result from other policies or public services becoming generally less effective.

This approach would make it possible to address the areas covered by the EU social objectives from a territorial perspective, which would be completely new despite the fact that the importance of places as factors in the effectiveness of social action has already long been acknowledged. It would build substantially on the progress made by recognising the multi-dimensional nature of social exclusion.

7.4.2 Incorporating the territorial dimension into EU coordination and cooperation in the social field

Similarly, the territorial dimension should be mainstreamed into all socially-related policies in the broad sense: policy to combat social exclusion; employment policy; training policy; equal opportunities and anti-discrimination policies, etc.

In any event, the most effective route would be to take the opportunity afforded by the European Council's work to revamp governance of the different processes related to Europe 2020, in this instance in respect of EU coordination and cooperation in the social field.

From a territorial point of view, the governance of EU coordination and cooperation in the social field is currently unsatisfactory. It is too focused on regulation and the design of policies, and not concerned enough with the implementation of these policies, i.e. how to ensure funding, and who does what (Rubio, 2009). A shift in focus would immediately reveal the important role played by local and regional authorities in delivering and coordinating social provisions. In fact, when it comes to employment policies, legislation is usually a national function, although it can also be regional in federal states. In the social inclusion policy field, there is a variety of legal arrangements and coordination provisions with local and regional authorities, the social partners, other stakeholders and special interest groups in terms of policy implementation through a large variety of methods. Local and regional authorities are involved in virtually all policy stages, but there is a real "reporting gap", as they are in general rarely mentioned in official national reports (Metis, 2009).

This is a request coming not only from local and regional authorities, but also from the major social policy stakeholders (EAPN 2009, 2010 and 2010a; ESN 2010). For example, the Commission suggested that the "European Platform against Poverty" (EPAP) could ensure "social and territorial cohesion such that the benefits of growth and jobs are widely shared and people experiencing poverty and social exclusion are enabled to live in dignity and take an active part in society" (European Commission, 2010).

Institutional arrangements for involving local and regional authorities are a vital step towards enhancing the capacity of EU coordination and cooperation in the social field to promote horizontal and bottom-up forms of learning (see chapter by Zeitlin in the present volume). In practice, from an institutional perspective this could mean involving the Committee of the Regions. From an operational perspective, it might also be useful to take on board specialised networks or associations, both in the partnership process put in place in the context of EU coordination and cooperation in the social field and in implementing the three flagship initiatives concerned. "Territorialisation", i.e. active participation of local and regional actors, should be ensured in every coordination process in the social field.

7.5 Conclusion

In this chapter, we have tried to explain why a *territorialised* social agenda might be useful to guide Europe 2020 and the future EU cohesion policy. It would consist of firmly bringing the EU social objectives closer to cohesion policy. Or, more concretely, it would consist of exploring the implications of the new territorial cohesion objective in the next programming regulations, ensuring that the EU cohesion policy fully takes on board the EU social objectives and also incorporating a territorial approach as element in EU coordination and cooperation in the social field.

References

Association of European Regions (2010), The Presidents of European regional and local organisations meet President Barroso and advocate for a bottom-up approach to the Europe 2020 Strategy, Available at: http://www.aer.eu/en/news/2010/2010062901.html.

Bache, I. (2008), Europeanization and Multi-level Governance: Cohesion Policy in the European Union and Britain, Lanham/New York: Rowman and Littlefield.

Barca, F. (2009), *An agenda for a reformed cohesion policy: A place-based approach to meeting European Union challenges and expectations*, Independent Report prepared at the request of Danuta Hübner, Commissioner for Regional Policy, Brussels: European Commission. http://ec.europa.eu/regional_policy/policy/future/pdf/report_barca_v0306.pdf.

Barroso, J.M. (2009), *Political Guidelines for the Next Commission*, Brussels: European Commission.

Committee of the Regions (2010), *Consultation: Your Voice on Europe 2020: Final Report*, Brussels: Committee of the Regions. Available at: http://portal.cor.europa.eu/europe2020/news/Documents/Your%20Voice%20on%20Europe%202020%20Final%20Report.pdf.

Committee of the Regions (2010a), *Territorial Pacts to achieve the objectives of the Europe 2020 Strategy*, Brussels: Committee of the Regions. Available at: http://portal.cor.europa.eu/europe2020/news/Pages/CoROctoberBureau2010.aspx.

Committee of the Regions (2010b), *Contribution of cohesion policy to the Europe 2020 Strategy*. Available at: http://coropinions.cor.europa.eu/CORopinionDocument.aspx?identifier=cdr\coter-v\dossiers\coter-v-008\cdr223-2010_fin_ac.doc&language=EN.

Committee of the Regions (2010c), *Measuring progress – GDP and beyond*. Available at: http://coropinions.cor.europa.eu/CORopinionDocument.aspx?identifier=cdr\enve-v\dossiers\enve-v-002\cdr163-2010_fin_ac.doc&language=EN.

Committee of the Regions (2009), *Consultation of European Regions and Cities on a New Strategy for Sustainable Growth: A New Lisbon Strategy after 2010*, Brussels: Committee of the Regions.

Eichhorst, W. *et al.* (2010), *Analysis of the Social Agendas*, Project financed by the European Parliament. Available at: http://www.iza.org/en/webcontent/publications/reports/report_pdfs/iza_report_24.pdf.

European Anti-Poverty Network Ireland and European Anti-Poverty Network (EAPN) (2010), *Building Social Europe*, Dublin: EAPN Ireland. Available at: http://www.eapn.ie/eapn/wp-content/uploads/2010/06/EAPN-Ireland-February-Conference-Report.pdf.

European Anti-Poverty Network (2010a), *EAPN proposals on the 'European Platform against Poverty'*, Brussels: EAPN. Available at: http://www.eapn. org/images/stories/docs/EAPN-position-papers-and-reports/eapn-flagship-platform-against-poverty-proposals-en.pdf.

European Anti-Poverty Network (EAPN) (2009), *A Europe we can trust: Proposals on a new EU post-2010 strategy*, Brussels: EAPN.

European Commission (2010), *Europe 2020: A strategy for smart, sustainable and inclusive growth*, Communication COM(2010) 2020, Brussels: European Commission. Available at: http://ec.europa.eu/eu2020/pdf/COMPLET%20 EN%20BARROSO%20%20%20007%20-%20Europe%202020%20-%20 EN%20version.pdf.

European Commission (2010a), *Proposal for a Council Decision on guidelines for the employment policies of the Member States: Part II of the Europe 2020 Integrated Guidelines*, Communication COM(2010) 193/3, European Commission, Brussels: European Commission. Available at: http://ec.europa. eu/eu2020/pdf/proposition_en.pdf.

European Commission (2010b), *Governance, Tools and Policy Cycle of Europe 2020*, Brussels: European Commission Secretariat-General, 13 June.

European Commission (2010c), *The EU budget review*, Communication COM(2010) 700, Brussels: European Commission. Available at: http://ec.europa.eu/budget/reform/library/com_2010_700_en.pdf.

European Commission (2010d), *Conclusions of the fifth report on economic, social and territorial cohesion: the future of cohesion policy*, Communication COM(2010) 642 final [SEC(2010) 1348 final], Brussels: European Commission. Available at: http://ec.europa.eu/regional_policy/sources/ docoffic/official/ reports/cohesion5/pdf/conclu_5cr_part1_en.pdf.

European Commission (2008), *Renewed Social Agenda: Opportunities, Access and Solidarity in 21st Century Europe*, Communication COM(2008) 412 final, Brussels.

European Commission (2008a), *Green Paper on Territorial Cohesion: Turning territorial diversity into strength*, Communication COM(2008) 616 final, Brussels. Available at: http://ec.europa.eu/regional_policy/consultation/ terco/paper_terco_en.pdf.

European Council (2010), *European Council 17 June 2010: Conclusions*, Brussels: European Council.

European Social Network (2010), *EU2020: Building a more Caring and Inclusive Europe. A contribution to the debate on the future of the social OMC beyond 2010*, Brighton: European Social Network. Available at: http://www.esn-eu.org/publications-and-statements/index.htm.

Fabry, E. and Fernandes S. (2010) *Europe 2020: l'urgence d'impliquer les porteurs de stratégie*, Paris: Notre Europe. Available at: http://www.notre-europe.eu/uploads/tx_publication/Bref17-EF-SF_01.pdf.

Frazer, H. and Marlier, E. (2009), *Assessment of the extent of synergies between growth and jobs policies and social inclusion policies across the EU as evidenced by the 2008-2010 National Reform Programmes: Key lessons*, EU

Network of Independent Experts on Social Inclusion, Brussels: European Commission. Available at: http://www.peer-review-social-inclusion.eu/ network-of-independent-experts/2008/second-semester-2008.

Jouen, M. (2008), *Territorial cohesion: from theory to practice*, Paris: Notre Europe. Available at: http://www.notre-europe.eu/uploads/tx_publication/ Policypaper35-MJouen-TerritorialCohesion-en.pdf.

Marlier, E., Atkinson, A.B., Cantillon, B. and Nolan, B. (2007), *The EU and Social Inclusion: Facing the Challenges*, Bristol: Policy Press.

METIS (2009), *Investing in people and modernising labour markets*, Study for the Committee of the Regions. Available at: http://portal.cor.europa.eu/ europe 2020/Library/Documents/Rapport%20final%20lot%20III%20après%20relect ure%20sans%20track%20changes%20pour%20impression-EN.pdf.

OECD (2008), "Making the most of regional development policy through multi-level governance" in *Source OECD Urban, Rural and Regional Development*, Vol. 2008, No. 11: 206-291.

Rubio, E. (2009), *Social Europe and the crisis: defining a new agenda*, Paris: Notre Europe. Available at: http://www.notre-europe.eu/uploads/tx_ publication/Policypaper36-en-agenda.pdf.

World Bank (2008), *Reshaping Economic Geography: World Development Report 2009*.

8. Social Impact Assessment as a Tool for Mainstreaming Social Protection and Inclusion Concerns in Public Policy

Martin KÜHNEMUND[1]

8.1 Introduction

This chapter summarises the main results of a study commissioned by the European Commission (Directorate-General "Employment, Social affairs, Equal opportunities" (DG EMPL))[2] to support mutual learning on social impact assessment within the Open Method of Coordination on Social Protection and Social Inclusion (Social OMC). The overall objective was to describe, compare and analyse the different ways in which social impact assessment is currently carried out in the European Union (EU) Member States, and to identify recommendations for the implementation of effective social impact assessment systems and for effective social impact analysis.

Social impact assessment (IA) is linked with the principle of "good governance", which is firmly integrated in the common objectives of the Social OMC that were agreed by all EU Member States. On this basis, a consensus has developed over the years around the idea that if they are to be effective, social protection and social inclusion policies need to be integrated (i.e. there is a need for a strategic approach and for mainstreaming social inclusion and social protection objectives into other policy areas; integration with growth and jobs policies and with sustainable development policies is particularly important). They also need to be based on facts (evidence-based policies, policy evaluation) and to involve stakeholders (transparency and stakeholder involvement in the design, implementation and monitoring of policies).

---

[1] I would like to thank Lorna Schrefler for her valuable contribution to the study and Peter Lelie for his helpful suggestions and constructive criticisms. Address for correspondence: martin.kuehnemund@evaluationpartnership.com.

[2] The study was carried out by The Evaluation Partnership (TEP) and the Centre for European Policy Studies (CEPS) between 2008 and 2010. The full results are available from the following DG EMPL website: http://ec.europa.eu/social/main.jsp?langId=nl&catId=89&newsId=935&furtherNews=yes.

Since the start of the OMC, Member States have been reporting on their efforts to make progress in this respect. In this context, *ex ante* social IA has increasingly come to the fore. Several Member States are currently experimenting with such arrangements and the European Commission has established a system of integrated impact assessment. The increased interest in social IA is also reflected in recent EU policy documents such as the 2008 and 2010 Joint Reports on Social Protection and Social Inclusion (European Commission, 2008 and 2010). For instance, the 2010 Joint Report emphasises that social IA becomes even more relevant in the current economic and budgetary circumstances (European Commission, 2010, page 140): "Given that pressure aimed at limiting public expenditures is to be expected in most of the Member States in the coming years, the development of an adequate *ex ante* social impact assessment capacity in the context of integrated impact assessment arrangements should be encouraged. Strengthening such "social" component can contribute to more effective and efficient social policy measures. Applied to non social policy measures, it can contribute to avoiding unintended negative social impacts and to better exploiting possibilities for positive synergies (mainstreaming). In this respect, the Social OMC can be used as a forum for exchanging know how between the Member States and between the Member States and the European Commission."

Since 2008, a number of initiatives have been developed to support Member States that want to put in place social IA at the national and sub-national levels. In November 2008, a peer review on the subject was organised in Bratislava.[3] Eight Member States and two EU stakeholder networks discussed how to develop and successfully implement social IA.

The Lisbon Treaty, which came into force on 1 December 2009, gives an increased status to social issues. Of particular significance is Article 9, which states that "In defining and implementing its policies and activities, the Union shall take into account requirements linked to the promotion of a high level of employment, the guarantee of adequate social protection, the fight against social exclusion, and a high level of education, training and protection of human health" (European Union, 2009). As put by Frazer and Marlier in their contribution to the present volume, "a major political and legal challenge will now be to give a concrete meaning to this new social clause". In the first instance, this clause should provide "a more solid basis for requiring the EU, that is *both* the European Commission and EU Member States, to mainstream

---

[3] See: http://www.peer-review-social-inclusion.eu/peer-reviews/2008/social-impact-assessment.

the EU's social objectives into policy-making and, for this to be effective, to systematically carry out social IAs of all relevant policies."

For the purpose of this study, "impact assessment" (IA) is understood as a tool and process to estimate the likely future impacts of policy proposals. Its ultimate objective is to lead to better informed and more evidence-based political decisions. As far as "social impacts" are concerned, the study took the definition of social impacts used in the Commission's IA guidance[4] as a starting point, and then developed its own working definition for analytical purposes.

The study consisted of three main stages. First, a general overview (mapping) of the social IA arrangements in the EU at the national and, where applicable, regional level. Then, a comparative analysis of ten well developed or particularly interesting social IA systems. And finally, a comparative analysis of a sample of 30 concrete examples of social IAs carried out in the framework of the selected social IA systems.

8.2 Social IA in Europe: Key Findings

Social IA in the EU Member States takes two main forms. It is either undertaken as one part of an integrated IA that considers all relevant impacts of a proposal, be they economic, environmental, or social; or through a specific impact test that only covers one specific type of social impact (e.g. gender equality or health impacts). The specific impact tests are usually a reflection of government priorities or even specific events or situations, such as the paedophilia cases in Flanders in the late 1990s (→ youth IA), the tensions between religious communities in Northern Ireland (→ equality IA), a report that uncovered institutional racism in the police in the UK (→ race equality IA), or the Irish 1997 National Anti-Poverty Strategy (→ poverty IA).

As of early 2009, 21 of the 27 Member States had some form of integrated IA system in place. Several of those systems were only created relatively recently, or had only recently been revamped. A few others were about to be reviewed. Most of the integrated IA systems that were examined were launched as part of a drive for better regulation (some-

---

[4] The list of possible social impacts considered here cover 9 aspects: a) Employment and labour markets; b) Standards and rights related to job quality; c) Social inclusion and protection of particular groups; d) Gender equality, equality treatment and opportunities, non-discrimination; e) Individuals, private and family life, personnel data; f) Governance, participation, good administration, access to justice, media and ethics; g) Public health and safety; h) Crime, Terrorism and security; and i) Access to and effects on social protection, health and educational systems. In the meantime, this list has been complemented with two more impacts (Culture and Social impacts in third countries). See European Commission (2009), pages 35-36.

times instigated or reinforced by international organisations such as the OECD or the EU), usually with a strong focus on minimising unnecessary administrative and/or compliance burdens. Social considerations usually did not play a key role in the conception of these systems, although one can observe a recent trend towards more "integrated" systems that take into account the three pillars of sustainable development (economic, environmental, social).

Most of the Member States that do not have an integrated IA system in place nonetheless have other arrangements to undertake ex ante reviews of the likely effects of new policies or laws, albeit often on a less systematic and more ad hoc basis. Some were also planning to introduce a formal integrated IA system in the near future. All in all, some kind of mechanism to assess the likely social impacts of new proposals (be it through an integrated IA system, specific impact tests, or other tools or processes) exists in 25 of the 27 Member States, as well as in several regions. The specificities of those systems and mechanisms vary widely in terms of aspects such as the kinds of social impacts that are considered, the rules and procedures that have to be followed and the involvement of different actors. Crucially, the amount of guidance and orientation provided regarding which types of social impacts (if any) should be considered varies considerably, as does the extent to which certain impacts always have to be checked for. Some systems (such as Finland; see Ministry of Justice, 2008) provide a detailed list of social impact categories that should be checked; others remain quite vague (such as the UK; see Department for Business, Innovation and Skills, 2010). Those systems that do provide categories sometimes use a different approach: some define *types* of impacts such as employment or health (e.g. Poland; see Ministry of Economy, 2006), while others focus on the affected *groups* that should be considered, such as those at risk of poverty (e.g. Ireland; see Office for Social Inclusion, 2008, and Department of the Taoiseach, 2009).

It is also important to note that in many (if not most) Member States, there is a significant implementation gap between formal IA rules and requirements, and what actually happens in practice. This is partly due to the relatively recent introduction or revision of many IA systems. As regards specifically social IA, the extent to which social impacts are actually analysed in practice, and the depth and scope of the analysis, varies considerably from case to case. Generally speaking, the comprehensive and consistent assessment of all likely social impacts of proposals represents a challenge that has not been fully overcome in any of the systems that were examined (see Section 8.3 below). The comparative analysis of integrated IAs revealed that the consideration of different types of social impacts is driven primarily by two factors: the nature of the policy in question and the specific social goals it pursues, and (where applicable) the impacts that are obligatory to assess. In other words, IAs were most likely to undertake an in-depth assessment of (1) the specific social benefits of policies (where these could be used to justify the proposal), and (2) the likely social costs and/or benefits in areas where the assessment is mandatory (such as employment in Poland or equality in the UK). Other social impacts were frequently mentioned, but rarely analysed in any amount of detail.

Nonetheless, the IAs that were reviewed contain a number of interesting examples of both qualitative and quantitative techniques and tools for social IA (including multi-criteria analysis to compare hard-to-quantify impacts, different approaches to "monetise" (i.e. analyse in terms of monetary value) the benefits of increased employment and skills, micro-simulation models that can be used to estimate the distributional effect of measures on the income of different population subgroups, and a method to determine impacts on disadvantaged areas). In social IA practice, such relatively sophisticated methods co-exist with purely narrative, sometimes very brief, mentions of what social impacts are likely to occur, frequently without any evidence to substantiate this or allow for an understanding of the order of magnitude of the impacts.

Relevant examples of specific impact tests include equality IA (in Ireland, the UK and Northern Ireland), poverty IA (in Ireland), child IA (in Flanders), and income effects tests (in the Netherlands). Each of these tools shows clear potential to produce an in-depth assessment of a specific type of social impact, and several of the examples that were reviewed provided highly useful and relevant results. However, the number of times such specific impact tests are used in practice tends to remain low (unless they are made mandatory for all proposals), and their usefulness depends to a considerable degree on how relevant the specific impact is for the proposal in question. Where this is not the case, such tests can be perceived as excessively rigid, tedious and burdensome, and lead to results whose usefulness is doubtful.

Summing up, it is clear that social IA is still in its infancy in most European countries. While most of the IA systems that were examined do (in theory at least) consider the social dimension in order to arrive at an integrated, balanced assessment of all likely impacts of new policies, in practice the assessment of social impacts is often less well developed than the assessment of economic or financial impacts, and sometimes even entirely missing. Examples of IAs that contain an in-depth analysis of social impacts are few and far between; where they do exist, they are most often conducted on policies with a specific social rationale.

This is not to say that social impacts are systematically and intentionally neglected in the IA systems that were examined. Rather, it is primarily a consequence of one or more (depending on the IA system in question) of the following key factors:

- The IA tool is notoriously difficult to reconcile and effectively integrate with previously existing policy development processes. Many of the IA systems examined are in a relatively early stage of their development; to a greater or lesser extent, they all suffer from systemic flaws and shortcomings (not least among them time and resource constraints and the fact that political pressure limits the room for evidence based policy-making) that can impede a thorough and detailed assessment of all likely impacts.

- Social impacts can be particularly difficult to assess. The term "social impacts" includes a very diverse set of fundamentally different impact categories that can be difficult to fully grasp, identify and analyse for a non-specialist. Furthermore, most social impacts do not lend themselves well to quantification or monetisation.

- Some IA systems do place the main emphasis on economic impacts (either explicitly or implicitly). While none of the IA systems examined categorically exclude social impacts from the analysis, there are those that dedicate a considerably larger amount of effort to analysing aspects such as business impacts (incl. administrative burdens) or impacts on public budgets.

Nonetheless, effective social IA is possible. There are pockets and/or isolated examples of good practice in all of the systems that were assessed. Because the circumstances (political, cultural, temporal, personal, etc.) of each system, IA tool and specific case vary so much, and how well rules or systems work usually depends greatly on the specific policy proposals in question and the mindset and qualifications of the individuals or departments preparing them, it is very difficult to draw general conclusions as to the effectiveness of social IA "systems" or "tools" as a whole.

However, there are a number of common challenges that apply, to a greater or lesser extent, to social IA across most jurisdictions and circumstances. Any Member State looking to set up an effective system for social IA, or to improve their current systems, will have to be aware of and address these challenges (although the preferred responses will inevitably vary depending on the priorities, capacities and constraints of each Member State).

8.3 Common Challenges for Social IA in the EU Member States

This section outlines the ten main common challenges to social IA that have been identified, and discusses why they should be addressed in order to facilitate effective social IA systems and practice. Some of these challenges are not specific to *social* IA only, but are common to all dimensions of integrated IA. Section 8.4 expands on the key issues that are specific to the social dimension of IA, and illustrates some of the possible approaches to tackling these challenges, and the trade-offs that they imply.

8.3.1 Acceptance of IA and buy-in

An indispensable prerequisite for effective IA (including social IA) is the existence of a general policy-making culture among both policy officers and managers that does not only see IA as an additional administrative burden, but accepts it as a tool and a process that adds value to policy-making. If this is lacking, IA can easily turn into a mere tick-box exercise. When this happens, the analysis of social impacts is often one of the first victims (as producers focus only on those elements that are strictly defined and required).

Such an "IA culture" takes time to evolve, and it is influenced by a number of factors including the political and administrative system and culture, and the tradition (or lack thereof) of policy analysis and evidence-based policy-making. In some countries, such as the UK, the environment is clearly more favourable for IA, and this tends to translate into a higher acceptance, and consequently a more effective use, of IA tools and processes.

In countries and regions where IA is not yet as firmly integrated in the policy-making culture, a conscious effort is required to convince civil servants and politicians of its usefulness. It is also important to give IA a chance to gain a foothold in public administrations by not introducing overly complex and burdensome IA systems in environments that are not ready for them. This includes complex social IA mechanisms and tools: it can be more effective to be less ambitious initially, and gradually expand the IA toolkit once officials have become used to it.

8.3.2 IA process and timing

Leading on from the point above, the usefulness of IA is reduced significantly if it is understood only as another *document* that accompanies policy or legislative proposals. Such IA reports may help to enhance transparency, but they are very unlikely to have any influence on the proposals (in the sense of helping to choose the most favourable option, maximising positive impacts and minimising costs and unintended consequences). For IA to play this role, it needs to be understood as a *process* that runs alongside and informs the entire policy development process.

One of the main challenges in this respect is the timing of that process. To be fully effective, IA needs to start early enough in the process to be able to affect the policy proposal it accompanies (rather than only justify it ex post). This is especially true for social impacts: unless any potentially adverse social effects are identified sufficiently early for the drafting officials to attempt to mitigate them by adapting the proposal, there is a high risk that they will be ignored or suppressed at a later stage. In the case of several of the examples that were reviewed, the IA was produced very late and only to comply with the formal requirement. But numerous IAs from across many IA systems were also examined, which began early enough to help to explore options, frame the policy, gather input from various relevant actors, and (in some cases) improve the proposal that was eventually tabled. In terms of a system design that facilitates and encourages the use of IA as an iterative process, it is worth highlighting the UK. The fact that an early version of the IA has to be published for consultation means a late start is usually not an option. Furthermore, it means that early IAs tend to consider different options and their likely impacts in an exploratory way, and allows the final IA to only focus on the preferred option, and undertake an in-depth assessment of its costs and benefits.

With regard to the IA process, it should be noted that the different political and administrative environments in Europe represent specific challenges and opportunities for IA, and in some cases have lead to variations from the Anglo-Saxon "prototype" in the way IA is implemented. For example, some countries (such as the Netherlands and many Nordic countries) run a more de-centralised IA system, where IA is used flexibly by the ministries as they prepare legislation, but the results of IA are not necessarily made public or widely disseminated. In other systems, such as Poland or the Czech Republic, stakeholder consultation is primarily carried out through committees (rather than through open public consultations). Furthermore, there can be differences between single-party and coalition governments, with the latter posing a particular challenge to effective IA (since important decisions are often subject to negotiation among coalition partners, reducing the potential influence of IA).

Such factors are important to keep in mind when designing a realistic IA system; some adaptations of "standard" IA rules and processes may be required, but such deviations do tend to come with their respective risks. The transparency and openness of the IA process in particular can be a key factor for effective IA; although different IA systems take different approaches to the publicity of the results, there are indications that whether or not IAs are publicly accessible can make a big difference to how seriously they are taken.

8.3.3 Commitment to consider social impacts

The primary focus of the majority of integrated IA systems continues to be on the economic impacts. While there are some systems where social impacts are not included within the scope of IA to begin with, the de facto focus on the economic dimension also applies to many systems that in principle attach equal importance to all three pillars of sustainable development (economic, environmental and social). The challenge therefore is for MS to: 1) decide (or, where applicable, revisit) whether social impacts should be embedded within their respective IA systems, and (if the answer to 1 is yes) 2) ensure that this commitment is clearly communicated and enforced in practice.

In the context of integrated IA, it is interesting to note that there are several examples of IA systems that start out by focusing on economic impacts, but eventually move towards an integrated assessment (sometimes by merging previously fragmented IA tools). However, the fact that the IA guidance documents place similar weight on the different "pillars" often does not filter through to the reality. To some extent, this might be due to integrated guidance (such as that recently adopted in Finland, which emphasises social impacts) having come into force only recently. However, it also seems that merely emphasising the importance of the social dimension in the written guidance is not enough. In order for social impacts to be assessed seriously, IA producers need to be under the impression that this coincides with the expectations of potential IA users and will be enforced systematically.

Specific impact tests such as equality IA or poverty IA can be a useful way of assessing certain types of social impacts. However, it seems that such tests are more suited to facilitating an analysis of certain impacts than to ensuring they are consistently mainstreamed into policymaking. In other words, such tests represent an opportunity to explore specific social impacts in more depth for proposals for which this is deemed relevant, but they are usually not mandatory and therefore implementation does not tend to be very widespread. There is a recent trend to increasingly link such tests with integrated IA in an attempt to achieve greater consistency and more equal coverage, but the examination of a number of examples suggests that the level of effort and methodological rigour invested in such tests often drops if they are carried out purely to comply with a legal obligation.

8.3.4 Definition of social impacts

Another key challenge to effective social IA is the fact that the term "social impact" is potentially so broad that it tends to mean very little to most non-specialists. Unlike the category of environmental impacts, which immediately evokes certain images, social impacts can be quite baffling for some. The category as it is generally understood includes a mix of quite different types of impacts. Some of these are clearly different from the other main impact categories (e.g. impacts on fundamental rights, safety and security, etc.), but the category of social impacts can also include impacts that can be perceived as economic or even environmental, if and when they apply to specific segments of society (especially disadvantaged or vulnerable groups). Furthermore, some social impact categories, such as on social inclusion, are not widely understood by civil servants who work in other policy areas.

The integrated IA guidance documents in different countries/ regions take quite different approaches to the issue of what constitutes a social impact that should be considered. None of them actually provides a clear definition of social impacts. As to different types of social impacts, at one extreme, the Finnish IA guidelines provide a comprehensive list and explanation of all potentially relevant impact types, as well as a checklist with concrete sub-questions under each of the seven headings. At the other extreme, some countries simply state that social impacts should be assessed, but provide no further guidance as to what and how.

There does not seem to be a direct correlation between the level of guidance and the diversity of social impacts that were assessed under the different systems, so it is not possible to determine what the optimal level of detail is. However, it does seem clear that some orientation is helpful to guide IA producers towards considering relevant social impacts, whereas overly complex or lengthy lists or descriptions risk being ignored in practice. In the absence of useful and realistic basic guidance, the risk is that the assessment of social impacts is undertaken (if it is undertaken at all) more with the specific objectives of the proposal in mind, and limited to the direct and easy to identify social *benefits*. However, social *costs* of proposals are less frequently identified, and it is here that guidance is especially useful to help IA producers think through any unintended consequences that proposals may have on certain groups in society.

8.3.5 Proportionate level of analysis

Leading on from the challenge of defining/ categorising potential social impact types, the question then becomes: which impacts should be analysed in each case, and in what level of detail? This is a crucial area: if the choice is left entirely to the discretion of the drafting officials, there is a risk that significant impacts may be neglected. However, if the consideration of certain impacts is mandatory, the assessment can easily turn into a tick-box exercise. In any case, it is a generally accepted principle in IA that the depth and scope of the assessment should be proportionate to the significance of the likely impacts, so that scarce resources are not wasted on analysing irrelevant impacts.

Defining the proportionate level of analysis ex ante is very difficult, given all the different factors that may come into play (including the type and content of the proposal, point in the policy process, significance thresholds for different impacts, etc.). Several IA systems therefore follow what is essentially a two-step approach, consisting of a series of screening questions about different types of social impacts which civil servants should work through. If a significant impact in a certain area appears likely, a more detailed assessment (sometimes in the form of a specific impact test) should be undertaken. Such tools can be useful to provide orientation and get officials to think systematically about potential social impacts, but their effectiveness depends on several factors, primarily whether the procedure and prescribed format appears relevant to the specific case in question and is not excessively burdensome. This varies to some extent in all of the systems, depending on the concrete case in question. Generally speaking, if the framework is mandatory and very rigid, there is a risk of merely formal compliance without significant added value.

8.3.6 Analytical methods, tools and data sources

One of the challenges mentioned most frequently by IA producers across nearly all countries and regions is the lack of appropriate tools, models and/or data sources to assess social impacts *quantitatively*. Cost-benefit analysis (i.e. an estimation of the likely costs and benefits of proposals expressed in monetary terms) is a core feature of most integrated IA systems, but social impacts can be very hard to reconcile with this analytical model because they are often difficult to monetise. The main exception to this are impacts on employment and impacts on household income levels, which can be quantified via more or less sophisticated models.

Therefore, most social IA remains purely qualitative. This in itself does not have to be a major problem, given that most systems acknowledge that quantitative analysis has its limitations, and encourage IA producers to also specify impacts that cannot be monetised. But in spite of this, there is a fairly widespread feeling among IA producers and users that quantitative analysis is necessarily more robust, and qualitative elements largely subjective. Sometimes producers admitted to not taking into account social impacts that could not be quantified because this would not have fitted with the overall analytical approach taken by the IA.

A related challenge is that when a qualitative "analysis" of social impacts is carried out, the examples examined suggest that this most often takes the form of a simple mention that a certain impact (e.g. improved health or reduction of inequality) will occur. Depending on the significance of the respective impacts, this can be entirely appropriate (see the principle of proportionate analysis above). However, if and when impacts are likely to be significant, even a qualitative assessment should be based on evidence, including a thorough analysis of the baseline situation and the likelihood and scope of the impact, drawing on relevant information (which can include existing studies on the effects of similar policies or stakeholder consultation results). A few of the IAs examined provide a blueprint for how this can be done. Thus, there is room for improvement concerning both quantitative and qualitative methods for social IA, as well as the related data sources such methods could draw on. Ideally, an explicit strategy should be developed to identify and address specific data gaps for social IAs.

8.3.7 Capacity and expertise

As noted previously, high quality social IA requires officials to have a solid understanding not only of how the IA process works, but also of what different types of social impacts might be applicable and how these can be identified and (where relevant) analysed. A lack of capacity and expertise among officials who do not regularly deal with social policy is a frequently cited barrier to more effective social IA. While high quality guidance documents are undoubtedly important, this barrier cannot be overcome solely with detailed written material. Most civil servants use the IA guidelines to obtain an initial overview of the process, but they do not necessarily work through the documents in a systematic way. The often large gap between the rules in the written guidance and the actual practice of (social) IA corroborates this finding.

Therefore, written guidelines should ideally be complemented by other methods. Training is one way of achieving this, but the numbers of civil servants that require IA training is high, and very significant time and resources would have to be invested to train them all. Also, training on integrated IA normally has to cover a broad range of approaches, cases and eventualities, meaning that the amount of attention that can be paid to assessing specific types of social impacts will always be limited.

It therefore seems indispensable to make available ad hoc support and guidance to officials who have to produce IAs if and when required.

The available evidence suggests that this is best delivered from within ministries, as is the case with the Better Regulation Units (for integrated IA) and Diversity and Equality Units (for equality IA) in individual UK government departments, or with the IA support functions in European Commission's Directorate-Generals. Such units or functions can best play the role of a "critical friend" that provides assistance in a constructive way and, where necessary, points officials to relevant sources of information or expertise. However, for this to be effective for social IA, there needs to be a consistent understanding among all ministries that social impacts are an important part of IA, and that IA reports will be scrutinised accordingly (see also point 8.3.3 above and point 8.3.10 below).

8.3.8 Stakeholder consultation

Input from stakeholders and interested parties is conducive to high quality IA for at least two main reasons: stakeholder input can be an important source of data and information for the assessment of impacts; and the scrutiny and challenge by stakeholders constitutes an additional quality control mechanism. In the IA systems where stakeholders are extensively involved, their scrutiny tends to be one of the key drivers for the quality, comprehensiveness and balance of IAs. The role of stakeholders is particularly crucial as concerns social impacts, since (in the absence of quantitative data or models) their input can provide key evidence for the qualitative assessment. The experience and expertise present in civil society concerning societal issues and problems is invaluable to ensure relevant social impacts are identified and assessed adequately.

The examination of a number of examples showed that some form of consultation (public or targeted) was undertaken for the vast majority of IAs. Depending on the prevalent political and administrative culture, this can take different forms, ranging from formal public consultations in the Anglo-Saxon countries to the frequent use of existing committees or other fora or bodies to gather stakeholder input (e.g. in Poland or Finland). Nearly all stakeholders who were interviewed showed a keen interest in social IA, but emphasised that consultation is only really useful if the results are actually taken into account when finalising the IA and the proposal it accompanies. Several concerns with consultation methods were also raised, including inappropriate timing, channels and targeting.

Perhaps even more fundamentally, it is important to emphasise that – although consultation generally forms part of the policy-making process (and therefore also the IA process) in most cases – seen across Europe, the publication of draft IA reports for consultation is the exception rather than the norm. In most jurisdictions, consultation results may feed into and inform the final IA report, but stakeholders are not actually able to view or comment on the results of the early stages of IA. This is lamentable considering that early publication of draft IAs (which is mandatory in the UK) helps to ensure a sufficiently early start of the IA process (see also point 8.3.2 above), and means that stakeholder input can still have an influence on fundamental decisions such as the choice of options or the types of impacts that should be taken into account.

8.3.9 IA as an aid to political decision-making

One of the main objectives of most IA systems (in addition to leading to better, more balanced and less costly policy proposals to come out of government departments) is to inform the political decision-making process, mainly in the legislative branch of governments. In general terms, the users of IA who were interviewed (i.e. high-ranking government officials, MPs and their research staff) tended to agree with the usefulness of IA in principle, but also emphasised that their actual use as an aide to political decision-making should not be over-estimated. According to many interviewees, IAs are primarily useful as an additional source of background information on what the government's thinking behind a proposal is and to give an indication of likely costs and benefits. However, there was also widespread agreement that other factors, such as evidence provided by relevant stakeholders, tend to be at least as important as IAs as a source of background information.

From the examination of a selection of examples of social IAs, it is clear that the extent to which IAs are taken into account by political decision makers varies significantly. Although there are some common trends across countries and regions, the actual use made of IAs seems to depend primarily on the specific IA and proposal in question. Some of the examples that were found to be most useful by the interviewees were precisely the ones that presented a solid evidence base and were still relatively succinct. Very long IAs, or IAs that were perceived as highly subjective, were found much less useful.

In terms of the specific social dimension of IA, the views of users varied considerably, partly based on their own areas of expertise and political affiliation. Many of the senior government officials and MPs who were interviewed were in favour of a stronger consideration of social impacts, and shared the view that this is currently a weakness of many IAs. However, not all potential users viewed the social dimension as a key element of IA, and some interviewees saw a risk that if IAs consider in detail elements that do not lend themselves to monetisation (including wider social impacts), they might become too discursive, broad and lose much of their focus and value. This point links in with the challenges outlined under point 8.3.6 above; while there are concerns about subjectivity, there is also clearly a (potential) demand for methodologically robust social IA.

8.3.10 Quality control and system oversight

The way in which IA system oversight and quality control is provided varies from system to system. Often there are several layers of quality control, including both internal (within the ministries or departments that produce the IAs) and external elements (in other ministries or departments, and in some cases via scrutiny by stakeholders, MPs, and the public at large). However, effective and comprehensive *external* quality control is a challenge given both resource constraints (a systematic check of all IAs is often not possible) and political considerations (ministries are often reluctant to impose additional duties upon each other). As a result, in many IA systems the central unit or function's role is largely limited to coordination and the development of guidance, rather than actual quality assurance of individual IAs.

The available evidence suggests that, given these realities, internal quality control may be the more promising and realistic option, at least in the short to medium term. One mechanism that is quite effective is the sign-off by both the chief economist (who is normally supported by a team of analysts) and the responsible minister that has recently been introduced in the UK. Coupled with the external scrutiny, this provides a strong incentive for producers to ensure that their IAs are thorough and comprehensive. The cases reviewed suggest that mostly, both ministers and chief economists do take their role quite seriously, and often ask for additional information or clarification, and sometimes even comment on draft IAs in the earlier stages.

Concerning the social dimension, this is not normally represented strongly in central oversight functions (except for bodies that oversee the application of specific social impact tests). It may be worth considering how the expertise of ministries dealing with social affairs can best be leveraged for quality control. An example of where this has happened can be found at the European Commission level, where a DG EMPL director provides social impact expertise to the IA Board.

8.4. Solutions for Effective Social IA

Many of the challenges outlined in the previous section relate to factors that are broader than social IA, i.e. they have an effect on social IA because they concern IA in general. It is important to highlight these insofar as they need to be addressed in order to facilitate effective social IA. However, the main purpose of this paper is not to reiterate what is considered to be good practice with regard to general IA processes, rules, timing etc.; other studies (such as the EU-commissioned EVIA project) as well as reports by organisations such as the OECD have already dedicated many pages to this.

Instead, the focus in the following pages is on the elements that are specific to social IA. Even the systems that perform relatively well regarding the more general IA practices and processes (such as the UK) have not necessarily found adequate responses to some of the specific challenges of social IA, including how to facilitate a consistent understanding of social impacts, how to ensure they are seriously considered, and how to analyse them in depth. Potential solutions to the specific challenges in the social domain can be summarised under the following three key questions.

8.4.1 How can Member States ensure a common understanding of what constitutes a relevant social impact?

In order to overcome the lack of a consistent understanding among IA producers (as well as managers and users) of what constitutes a social impact that should be considered as part of the IA process, some form of guidance is required. Some countries and regions have developed lists of types of social impacts, but these tend to be rather lengthy and complex, and often include grey areas, duplications and/or overlaps. However, the vast majority of social impacts can be summarised under a relatively limited list of impact types, namely:

- Employment (including labour market standards and rights)
- Income
- Access to services (including education, social services, etc.)
- Respect for fundamental rights (including equality)
- Public health and safety

This list covers a very large part of the impacts considered in IAs. Crucially, some social impact categories or assessment types that are not included in the list above are actually covered through the combination of the five parameters with specific population groups. For example, social inclusion is normally understood as the result of a combination of most or all of the factors listed above, when applied to those groups that are at risk of social exclusion. It is therefore recommended that Member States examine their respective IA systems (be they integrated systems or specific impact tests) through the lens of these five broad categories of social impacts, with a view to identifying overlaps and gaps, and eventually devising simpler and clearer guidance for social IA.

8.4.2 How can Member States ensure that relevant social impacts are considered and identified, particularly in the early stages of the IA process?

Given the focus on economic impacts that is prevalent in many IA systems, Member States should clarify whether social IA should indeed form part of integrated IA, and how this fits and can be reconciled with the (perceived or real) need to conduct a cost-benefit analysis. If social IA is seen as a key part of IA, this should be expressed clearly in the written guidance as well as in IA training sessions. In addition, the social dimension should ideally be represented in both IA system oversight and in ad hoc assistance (e.g. through the creation of networks of experts).

Table 8.1: Possible basic format for a screening tool

Is the proposal likely to have an impact on individuals' or groups of individuals'...	Likely positive impact?	Likely negative impact?	Affected group(s)	Likely scale of impact
Employment status or opportunities	(Y/N)	(Y/N)		
Disposable income				
Access to services[5]				
Respect for fundamental rights[6]				
Health and safety				
Other social impacts				

On a more practical level, there have to be appropriate screening mechanisms or tools to enable and encourage civil servants to actually consider social impacts seriously when producing IAs. Such tools already exist in several systems, but they are sometimes not designed very well. A basic screening framework for social impacts needs to be reasonably easy to understand and concise, as well as a means of guiding IA producers' thought processes in a clear way. Such a framework could be structured around the five basic impact categories listed above, and require producers to specify which groups are likely to be affected

---

[5] "Access to services" refers primarily to citizens' access to key public services, including services provided by the social protection, health and educational systems.

[6] The exact fundamental rights to be covered would depend on those granted by the constitution of each country. They would typically include freedom (of expression, association, movement etc.), equality or equal treatment, privacy, property, etc.

under each impact type. A possible basic format for a screening tool is shown in Table 8.1.

8.4.3 What approaches, methods, tools and data sources should be used to assess relevant social impacts?

The tension between the quantitative ambitions of most IA systems and the qualitative reality of most social IAs was one of the prominent themes of the study. Developing and disseminating knowledge about tools, methods and data sources to measure social impacts quantitatively should certainly be one priority. As regards monetised methods, the focus should be on widening the awareness and use of existing models (primarily for employment and income effects; see also Ecorys, 2010), and on further developing these models and others to make them applicable to a wider set of geographical and policy situations. Improved quantitative (non-monetised) assessment would require (but also facilitate) the use and development of relevant data sources and indicators.

However, it is also important to set realistic expectations as to which kinds of social impacts can more easily be quantified, and which will have to remain (primarily) qualitative. For the latter, facilitating *thorough* and *robust* qualitative social IA should be a priority. This could be done inter alia through providing clearer guidance as to what constitutes qualitative "analysis" (as opposed to just a cursory mention), but also by widening the available evidence base through wider and better use of stakeholder consultation. Strengthening the link between ex post evaluation and ex ante IA is another key area to enhance social IA and learn from past experiences.

8.5. Conclusions

Social impact assessment is a potentially very powerful process and tool for both the European Commission and Member States to mainstream the EU's social objectives into policy-making. But although most Member States have an integrated IA system in place that could be used for this purpose, and several have also begun to experiment with other tools to assess specific types of social impacts, effective social IA remains a challenge. Seen across Europe, the in-depth analysis of the likely social impacts of policies (in particular policies that do not pursue explicitly social objectives) is the exception rather than the norm.

This is partly the result of shortcomings with the application and implementation of IA in general (and not only its social dimension). IA is still a relatively new process and tool in most Member States and the concept of evidence-based policy-making can be difficult to reconcile and integrate with previously existing policy processes. For any kind of ex ante IA to be fully effective, there needs to be a shift in the policy-making culture and officials need to have sufficient time, knowledge, skills and support to make it work. However, it is also true that social IA is often even less well developed than the other dimensions of IA. This can be the result of specific methodological difficulties (often related to the challenge of quantifying social impacts), but it is also often due to more mundane reasons, including a basic lack of understanding among many civil servants and policy-makers of what exactly is meant by the term "social impacts", and the fact that economic impacts are often (explicitly or implicitly) prioritised over social impacts in IAs.

These challenges and shortcomings should not obscure the fact that examples of effective social IA do exist and have become more numerous in recent years. The fact that several Member States have begun to review and revise their IA systems to facilitate a better consideration of social impacts is encouraging. In order to make further progress, all Member States should carefully consider their respective responses to the key challenges for effective social IA that are listed in this chapter, in particular how they can foster an IA culture in general, and enable and incentivise their government officials to understand, seriously consider, identify and (where appropriate) analyse in depth the different relevant types of social impacts.

The European Commission and the Social OMC are in a unique position to support the efforts of Member States to facilitate more effective social IA. On a strategic level, centralised monitoring coupled with a system of incentives at the EU level can facilitate the adoption and, most importantly, the implementation of social IA across Europe. In this context, clarifying the linkages between the priority areas of the Europe 2020 Strategy and social IA, as well as with strategic indicators developed in the context of the European Employment Strategy (regarded by Member States as a useful forum for mutual learning; see Begg, Erhel and Mortensen, 2010) and/or the assessment of EU structural policies, can help to raise the profile of social IA.

On a more practical level, the Commission and Member States can use the Social OMC to foster the exchange of experiences and mutual learning on current social IA practice, inter alia by holding regular workshops, training and/or benchmarking exercises, with a view to developing a "learning network" and fostering a wider usage of existing approaches and tools which are not widespread or only used in a limited number of countries. Developing dedicated online tools for social IA, including a library of examples of social IAs, could form part of this process. Resources should also be pooled at the EU level to address the problem of assessing social impacts quantitatively, in particular by supporting the expansion of existing (and the development of new) pan-

European datasets and sophisticated statistical and modelling instruments for social IA (in particular micro-simulation models).

References

Begg, I., Erhel, C. and J. Mortensen (2010), *Medium-Term Employment Challenges*, special CEPS report for the Directorate-General of Employment, Social Affairs and Equal Opportunities, Brussels: Centre for European Policy Studies.

Ecorys (2010), *Review of Methodologies Applied for the Assessment of Employment and Social Impacts*, final report, Rotterdam/Brussels: Ecorys.

European Commission (2010), *Joint Report on Social Protection and Social Inclusion 2008*, Brussels: European Commission. Available at: http://ec.europa.eu/social/BlobServlet?docId=5503&langId=en.

European Commission (2009), *Impact Assessment Guidelines*. Available at: http://ec.europa.eu/governance/impact/commission_guidelines/docs/iag_2009_en.pdf.

European Commission (2008), *Joint Report on Social Protection and Social Inclusion 2008*, Brussels: European Commission. Available at: http://ec.europa.eu/social/BlobServlet?docId=2386&langId=en.

European Union (2009), *Consolidated Version of the Treaty of Lisbon*, Brussels: European Union. Available at: http://www.consilium.europa.eu/ showPage.aspx?id=1296&lang=en.

Finland, Ministry of Justice (2008), *Impact Assessment in Legislative Drafting – Guidelines*. Publication 2008:4. Available at: http://www.om.fi/en/Etusivu/Parempisaantely/Vaikutustenarviointi.

Ireland, Department of the Taoiseach (2009), Revised *RIA Guidelines – How to conduct a Regulatory Impact Analysis*, June 2009. Available at: http://www.betterregulation.ie/eng/.

Ireland, Office for Social Inclusion (2008), *Guidelines for Poverty Impact Assessment*, March 2008. Available at: http://www.socialinclusion.ie/pia.html.

Poland, Ministry of Economy (2006), *Wytyczne do Oceny Skutkow Regulacji (OSR)*, October 2006. Available at: http://www.mg.gov.pl/NR/rdonlyres/49F92D8B-5D7B-4D1E-AB62-F9E12365DFB9/56421/Wytycznedoocenyskutkowregulacji1.pdf.

United Kingdom, Department for Business, Innovation and Skills (2010), *Impact Assessment Guidance*, April 2010. Available at: http://www.berr.gov.uk/assets/biscore/better-regulation/docs/10-898-impact-assessment-guidance.pdf.

9. The Potential of Eurotargets:

Reflecting on French Experience

Robert WALKER[1]

9.1 Introduction

Decisions taken by the European Union (EU) Heads of State and Government at their meeting on 17th June 2010 arguably marked a new phase in the story of EU policy-making. Most notable was the adoption of five EU headline targets to be achieved by 2020 (see opening chapter). They include quantifiable targets for reducing by 20 million the number at risk of poverty and social exclusion, increasing education attainment (reducing school drop-out rates to less than 10% and increasing the share of 30-34 year olds with tertiary education to at least 40%), and raising the employment rate (to 75% for persons aged 20-64). Targets not only establish goals but encourage and facilitate the measurement of progress. They increase accountability and, by doing so, ratchet up the pressure on politicians and policy-makers to deliver against the targets, thereby stimulating public debate and engagement and adding momentum to the policy-making process. Member States are obliged to act to implement these policy priorities and "in close dialogue with the Commission, rapidly [to] finalise their national targets, taking account of their relative starting positions and national circumstances" (European Council, 2010, page 3).

The introduction of targets is a logical but not inevitable development of the approach to policy-making triggered by the Lisbon Strategy and epitomised by the Social Open Method of Coordination (OMC). The OMC is characterised by experimentation and knowledge creation and by participation of the social partners and civil society more generally, thereby giving credibility and legitimacy to a process that could otherwise be seen as light on democratic input. It makes a virtue of decentralised policy-making that, in turn, accommodates a wide diversity of normative perspectives and policy mechanisms. At the same time, peer review and friendly competition is intended to propel national

---

[1] Address for correspondence: robert.walker@socres.ox.ac.uk.

policies forward in ways that are consistent with EU goals. The introduction of targets can exploit the same mechanisms but might, in theory at least, shift the change dynamic from achievements to performance. Whereas the beauty competition that is the OMC, with Member States placed alongside each other, is intended to stimulate admiration and emulation, the introduction of targets means that Member States can be ranked by performance, thereby potentially creating the pressures and policy adrenalin that characterise a race.

Targets are not new in policy-making at the level of Member States. Moreover, it is at least arguable that the Social OMC and associated peer reviews have been important in the adoption of policy targets across the EU. To take the example of poverty, Ireland introduced a quantitative poverty reduction target in 1997. Initial success encouraged the Irish government to make the target more ambitious and, with adoption of EU-SILC as the mechanism for monitoring performance, to target the elimination of "consistent" poverty (defined as combination of income poverty and material deprivation) by 2016. Various countries, including Belgium, Greece, Portugal and Spain, have since established quantitative targets to reduce general poverty under the Social OMC, while the United Kingdom introduced a child poverty target in 1999 and gave it legislative authority by including it in the Child Poverty Act 2010. The French government is committed to reducing poverty by a third between 2007 and 2012 and, in May 2009, introduced a set of indicators – the "*Tableau de bord*" or "Scoreboard" – against which to assess progress and which formed the topic of an EU peer review held in Paris in December 2009 (Walker, 2010). As from June 2010, all Member States are required to adopt national social inclusion/ poverty reduction targets consistent with that adopted by the June 2010 European Council at EU level. The EU target is defined in terms of the number of persons who are at risk-of-poverty and victims of social exclusion according to three indicators (at-risk-of poverty; material deprivation; and belonging to a "jobless" household). Member States are at liberty "to set their national targets on the basis of the most appropriate indicators, taking into account their national circumstances and priorities" (European Council, 2010, page 12) raising obvious issues about the relationship between national and EU targets.

The new EU policy rubric agreed by EU Heads of State and Government in June 2010 establishes a style of governance powered by targets, albeit they apply, as yet, to only five areas. If the new Europe 2020 Strategy is perceived to be successful it seems improbable that targets will not be applied more widely. Hence, the rubric might be viewed as a pilot, a further element in the experimentation and knowledge building that has characterised EU policy-making since the Lisbon

Treaty (see chapter by Zeitlin in the present volume). The aim of this contribution is to draw selectively on the experience gained from the use of targets at national level to begin reflection on the challenges that will need to be overcome if targets are to drive rather than obstruct progressive EU policy-making. No claim is made to the comprehensiveness of the review; rather recent French experience with the "Scoreboard" is taken as a case-study to illustrate particular issues. The chapter therefore begins with a brief account of the French Scoreboard and the political strategy that underpins it before addressing four issues: the politics of targets; criteria for setting targets; the risk of policy distortion; and the symbiosis with policy design. In each case the issues are first discussed in a French context before considering the implications for the EU strategy. The chapter ends with interim conclusions.

9.2 The French Poverty Target and "Scoreboard"

When, on 17 October 2007, Nicolas Sarkozy, President of France, announced the intention of the French government to reduce poverty by a third within five years, he also made clear the point of introducing a target, namely to galvanise political forces for change: "I want to see this long neglected social issue become a political issue. I set this target to force us to deliver. It will force us to unearth the mechanisms that spawn poverty and to set up the ones that will eradicate it." (French Presidency of the European Union, 2008.)

Table 9.1: Thematic objectives of the French "scoreboard"

To fight	*To promote access to*
1. Poverty and inequality; 2. The accumulation of difficulties in living conditions; 3. Child poverty; 4. Youth poverty; 5. Poverty in old age; 6. Poverty of people who have a job;	7. Employment; 8. Housing and maintaining housing; 9. Education and training;
To support access to	*To fight*
10. Care;	11. Financial (banking) exclusion.

Source: Walker (2009)

In order to monitor performance against this target the French government, through a process of extensive consultation, developed a set of indicators – the *"tableau de bord"* or "Scoreboard" – comprising some 38 indicators organised within 11 thematic policy objectives (Table 9.1). The number of specific indices within each theme varies but in each case includes one or more quantified targets – 18 in total that are required to be met within five years, the clock having been set running at October 2007. The "central" index, required to fall by a third, is an "anchored in time" measure of income poverty defined with respect to a threshold of 60% of median. This measure reflects living standards at the beginning of the monitoring period, maintains the value of the threshold in terms of what can be purchased but is not adjusted to take account of rises (or falls) in general French living standards.

Multiple indicators are included in the Scoreboard in order to compensate for the limitations of a single measure of poverty, to better reflect the multi-dimensional nature of poverty and to recognise the contribution required from the whole of government for the poverty reduction target to be met. Relative poverty rates, with thresholds set at 40, 50 and 60% of median income, are included specifically to ensure that the reduction in poverty achieved is not associated with increased inequality and social exclusion.

Comparison of the French Scoreboard with the latest incarnation of the Laeken indicators used to monitor the risk of poverty and social exclusion at EU level is instructive (European Commission, 2009). The Scoreboard gives much greater prominence to "anchored in time" measures of income poverty than do the Laeken indicators where such measures only appear as contextual ones. Two primary level Laeken indicators are not included in the Scoreboard: the difference between the employment rates of immigrants and non-immigrants, (possibly a reflection of the nature of French assimilation policies) and the rate of long-term unemployment. The Scoreboard includes some poverty and social exclusion dimensions that were not yet in the Laeken indicators list at the time of implementation, but were included in the list as from 2009 (though with slightly different definitions); and others that are still not on the Laeken list (and which, therefore, may be of particular interest to other Member States and to the European Commission). Measures in the first group include material deprivation and housing, while financial (or banking) exclusion features in the second; the latter is a dimension of poverty not yet considered for inclusion in the Laeken indicators but one shown to be a considerable problem for people living on low incomes (Carbo *et al.*, 2007; Collard *et al.*, 2001). The Social Protection Committee and its Indicators Sub-Group should explore this important aspect on the basis of the module on "Over-indebtedness and financial exclusion" that was included in the 2008 wave of the EU Statistics on Income and Living Conditions (EU-SILC). Finally, while the Scoreboard employs measures of relative poverty to capture inequality, omitting direct indices of income inequality such as the Gini coefficient and the S80/S20 income quintile ratio, it includes substantive indicators that nevertheless also reflect inequality. There are two indicators that both directly measure class-based aspects of inequality (namely in dental treatment received by young people and access to continuing education) and two measures that indirectly reference inequality. The latter, relative health expenditures by persons in the lowest income decile, and the rate of non-negotiable (*Préengagées*) expenditure among persons in the lowest income quintile, refer indirectly to inequality through focusing on one section of the income distribution and thereby calling into question the relative circumstances of persons with different levels of income.

The intent of the French leadership is that the poverty target should simultaneously fulfil three functions: to stimulate interest in poverty and social exclusion; to build support for reform, and to pressurise all parts of government to deliver reform and policy outcomes. The "Scoreboard" is the stimulus through which these goals are to be achieved – a mechanism of accountability that is to take two forms: the political equivalent of the victor's podium when targets are seen to have been met and the counterpart of medieval punishment stocks, with public humiliation and opprobrium, when they were missed. Moreover, in the same way that the poverty target is enshrined in legislation through the law of 1 December 2008, so, too, is the Scorecard. The same law referred specification of the measurement of poverty to a decree to be issued by the *Conseil d'Etat* (Council of State) which, when published on 21st May 2009, specified that a monitoring scorecard, annexed to the Decree, should be used.

With the target and scorecard intended to create an institutionalised momentum for change, the policy package was completed by the introduction of "active inclusion", a mechanism based on the premise, to cite President Sarkozy, that it is necessary; "to consistently reward work as opposed to government benefits, and to ensure that work invariably provides a door out of, and protection from, poverty" (French Presidency of the EU, 2008, page 1). In the French version, "active inclusion" is based on "three complementary and inseparable principles": a guaranteed adequate minimum income; policies promoting labour-market integration; and access to quality social services. Among the most important of the reforms introduced in 2007 were: the replacement of *"Revenu Minimum d'Insertion"* (RMI) and certain other benefits by the *"Revenu de Solidarité Active"* (RSA) which was piloted in 34 *départements* prior to full implementation on 1 June 2009; the *Grenelles de l'insertion* (Round-Table on Inclusion) which sought to gather ideas from stakeholders and produced a set of shared guidelines and priority projects in 2008; and a call for innovative policy ideas to be tested by social experiment.

The poverty target and the associated Scoreboard are not simply a technical exercise. Rather they are central elements in a larger strategy designed to make poverty more visible, to stimulate public debate, to mobilise policy intent and to incentivise effective policy delivery designed to reduce poverty. The Scoreboard is viewed as an instrument of observation, evaluation and partnership: it will record trends and suggest whether policy changes are having the desired effect. It is intended to stimulate interaction within government and beyond in developing sensitive indicators and in implementing policies likely to be effective given the multi-faceted nature of poverty.

9.3 Strategy and Politics

Where used, targets frequently become a natural part of the policy process, essential for establishing attainable policy objectives and useful for incentivising and monitoring performance. However, there is rarely much that is natural or neutral about the introduction of targets. They symbolise proactive policy-making, dissatisfaction with the status quo and a deliberate initiative to shake up policy by doing things differently.

This was clearly the case in France where targets and the Scoreboard were part of bold, not to say audacious, attempt to shift the terms of debate premised on the belief that there was currently insufficient support both inside and outside government to do more to tackle poverty. The idea was that targets, their publication and discussion about them build support and public interest that can further motivate and increase pressure for reform.

It is a little premature to assess the extent to which these premises hold in France since only one set of results have been published (in October 2009; "Haut-Commissaire aux Solidarités Actives Contre la Pauvreté" (HCSACP) [2009]). There is evidence that targets in Ireland and the UK built sustained political support. The Irish Anti-Poverty Strategy remained in place for over 12 years, while in the UK, the Child Poverty Act, giving a legal basis to the target and the establishment of a Commission to monitor it, was passed in the last days of the 2004-10 Labour government without objection from the opposition parties subsequently elected into power. Moreover, in the UK the political risks of failing to meet anti-poverty targets have proved to be less than those in the case of health, possibly because the targets are recognised to be ambitious and because comparatively few people perceive themselves to be personally affected by the outcome (Child Poverty Action Group (CPAG), 2008).

On the other hand, there is limited evidence that targets stimulate popular support; rather they empower non-governmental organisations

(NGOs) and pressure groups to lobby and engage with government (Bamfield, 2005). Voters typically underestimate the chances of ever suffering from poverty and attach greater importance to quality health care, good education services and sustained employment (European Commission, 2009a). The evidence is that public support divides on ideological lines (O'Kelly, 2007; Castell and Thompson, 2007). Therefore to ensure ongoing debate, the British government explicitly encouraged civil society organisations to lobby to keep child poverty on the agenda and funded them to do so. In Ireland, the Combat Poverty Agency fulfilled a similar pressurising function until its absorption by the Office for Social Inclusion, a move some commentators feared would remove a powerful irritant for change. The French government engaged extensively with NGOs in drawing up the content of the Scoreboard. Then, following the onset of the 2008 recession with the need to develop real-time monitoring of the changing circumstances of low income families, it similarly consulted the largest associations concerned with the fight against poverty, involving them in the collection of data on trends in the number of applicants for services such as food aid, housing assistance, clothing assistance and job search, and information on the nature of problems being encountered.

Experience suggests that there is a need to have powerful and sustained support from the very top of government and a strong champion to lead, incentivise (possibly financially) and cajole government departments and agencies to take ownership of the anti-poverty targets. This is perhaps particularly the case when progress falters or other demands become pressing. The French presidential language emphasises that the French poverty reduction target is "a goal for the government as a whole" and a "goal for every minister" and, insofar as the Scoreboard is the product of an inter-ministerial committee, it reflects this across government perspective. Moreover, when announcing the poverty target, the French President gave very public backing to the High Commissioner charged to champion delivery of the targets. Nevertheless, it may yet prove to be a considerable challenge for a junior minister to break the mould of ministerial policy-making. In Britain, under Labour governments, this formal responsibility changed hands between senior ministers but the personal interest of Gordon Brown, as Chancellor of the Exchequer and subsequently Prime Minister, is generally viewed to have been the critical motivator. Indeed, under his auspices, the poverty targets were incorporated as Public Sector Agreements (PSAs) between HM Treasury and individual government ministries and underpinned by the possibility of financial sanction. Where sustained championing is not forthcoming, poverty targets easily fall into disuse much as commitments to mainstreaming social inclusion have been shown to be very vulnerable in the face of political neglect. (O'Kelly, 2007)

In the EU context, championing is likely to be required at both EU and Member State levels. The inclusion of social policy goals as EU wide targets is a landmark development bringing social policy issues more centre stage and creating new interdependencies both between the Commission and Member States and between Member States themselves. Nevertheless, ongoing concerns about both the global and domestic economies could easily cause politicians and policy-makers to neglect issues of poverty, inclusion and social cohesion. Not every government will be equally committed to the Euro-target and there is the ever-present risk that national political realities will dominate over EU concerns.

The Euro-targets leave open the contribution expected to be made by each Member State to the overall EU goal. Will some Member States be expected to make a larger contribution to meeting the target than others or will an equal proportionate contribution be demanded from each Member State even if this is not necessarily the most cost effective way of attaining the EU anti-poverty/social inclusion target? It is certainly important that the EU targets and the national ones to be agreed are mutually supportive and that the connecting logic is both transparent and comprehensive. Getting an effective logic agreed is likely to require persuasive champions as will sustaining commitment if progress slips and some Member States prove to be less successful than others.

There is clearly a role, therefore, for the European Commission, no doubt with the aid of civil society organisations, to champion the contributions made by individual Member States to achieving the EU goal. The Social Protection Committee (SPC), which coordinates the Social OMC, might reasonably be charged with this task although historically it has often wielded limited influence on key decisions and initiatives. Perhaps, therefore, the President of the European Council (or that of the European Commission?), or a special envoy reporting directly to the President, might prove more effective in delivering the targets.

Champions will also be required at Member State level who could find the leverage of needing to report directly to the President useful if the brief of the EU champion were to be appropriately drawn. At national level the demands of competing policy goals are, if anything, more severe than at EU level and are often reinforced by the power of economic ministries, the impermeability of departmental boundaries and the difficulty of coordinating the cross-governmental action necessary to tackle poverty and social exclusion that are both multi-causal in nature. Experience in France, the UK and elsewhere suggests that anything less than the public and continuing commitment of a president or prime minister is insufficient. Championing of Social OMC has generally been at lower level with senior ministers more engaged in the newer Member States where EU support is seen as essential to enhance basic provisions. Often National Strategy Reports on Social Protection and Social Inclusion have been seen as addenda to the real process of national policy-making and relegated to the responsibility of comparatively junior officials in relatively peripheral ministries. While a missed target ready to be scooped by an investigative journalist might pose a greater political threat than the off centre critique offered by peer review, it remains critical that national targets reflect national policy objectives and are integral in the delivery and monitoring of policy nationally. Achieving this is perhaps made more difficult by the narrowly focussed Euro-targets.

In the absence of strong political champions at national level, representative organisations of civil society have tended to perform the roles of appraiser, auditor and critic and may well need to continue to do so in the new age of Euro-targets (McKendrick *et al.*, 2008). An important bi-product of the preparation of National Reports and National Action Plans under the Social OMC has been a strengthening of the capacity of civil society in many Member States to engage in policy debate. This may well have aided the French government in its consultations on the Scorecard. However, interpretation of statistical trends and the impact of policies are inherently complex and technical matters that require specialist skills. It is highly probable, therefore, that the monitoring and interpretation of indicators is going to require sustained investment in the analytical capacity of civil society. For many years, the Irish government supported the Combat Poverty Agency to undertake analyses of poverty and to promote critical discussion.

Targets, therefore, are not a simple addition to Social OMC provisions. For targets to be successful, to generate policy outcomes different from those that would have occurred anyway, they need to create a new dynamic that generates additional incentives for relevant stakeholders or added pressures on them. As they are intended to work in France, targets increase the transparency and accountability of all levels of government, between each level and to the public and hence strengthen democracy. For targets to work well at EU level, similar developments are likely to be necessary.

9.4 Setting Targets

Targets should be set to stretch organisations but need to be realistic and attainable. Ideally they should also be simple, understandable and as few in number as is appropriate given the policy goals and the nature of the implementation logic. Targets must also accurately reflect both the policy objectives and the priorities among them so that policy distortion is prevented and the scope for creaming and gaming is curtailed[2]. The metrics in which the targets are expressed, for example, the indices of poverty, employment and educational attainment, need to be statistically robust, capture the essence of the problem, and be responsive to policy intervention while not being amenable to manipulation (European Commission, 2009).

Targets need to be realistic to maintain the credibility of the process and evidence of some measurable success appears to be important in keeping the continued involvement of stakeholders; this occurred in both Ireland and the United Kingdom but not in Lithuania where targets quite rapidly fell into disuse (Jones, 2009; Walker, 2009). However, judgements about what is attainable are not straightforward and depend on context. They need to be informed, but not entirely constrained, by prior experience including knowledge of local institutions, analysis of the policy problem and studies of recent trends and policy outcomes. They should take account of the implementation logic by means of which it is anticipated policies will have purchase on the targets and meaningful assessments of the likely effectiveness of new policies. Step changes of enormous proportions are unlikely to be attainable and certain policies cannot achieve particular results. However, the rationale for setting targets is to encourage changes that make it more likely that policy objectives will be reached. This may require a change of policy, the reorganisation of institutions and/or working practices and/or an alteration in the nature and level of funding.

Engaging stakeholders in the design of measures and building a shared understanding of the scale and nature of the challenge of reducing poverty and increasing social inclusion, as the French government has done, may lessen criticism if progress proves not to be as anticipated. The British experience demonstrates this to be true such that the political costs of missing targets do not have to be excessive. Moreover, it is probable that a common understanding of the nature and scale of the problem enables politicians and policy-makers to take chances that may support policy innovation and advance. Whether involving civil society directly in setting targets would further lessen the political costs of missing targets is unclear but is at least a possibility. Nevertheless, the policy logic for targets and public accountability requires some external critique to maintain a pressure on governments to deliver as promised; while consultation is essential, taking it to the point of captur-

---

[2] Creaming refers to the process of targeting individuals and resources explicitly to maximise measured outcomes, for example by focussing help on those just beneath the poverty threshold. Gaming refers to the adoption of practices that deliberately serve to overstate actual success.

ing civil society within the inner policy family is likely to prove counterproductive. Some judicious balance of engagement and independence is required.

Above all, of course, what is attainable is determined by the available volume, quality and use of resources – financial, institutional, managerial and staffing.

It is not clear how the French government determined the level and timing of the core poverty reduction target and the resources that it is prepared to invest in ensuring that the target is met. However, as Table 9.2 shows, to reach the target will require a considerable step-change over past performance. Nevertheless, the simulated results for 2007-2009 presented in the first annual report on the French Scoreboard look very promising with respect to both the anchored in time indicator and the relative measure, and it will be interesting to learn how closely these projections match with the actual figures when they become available. (See Table 9.3 and HCSACP, 2009.)

To the outsider, it is similarly not immediately evident how the Euro-targets were chosen and therefore the extent to which the above considerations played on the minds of decision takers. The core poverty and social exclusion target implies a reduction in the number of poor or socially excluded of a sixth (17%) over the next decade. There is no long-term statistical series that is directly comparable that can indicate how reasonable this target might be. However, poverty and social exclusion on this core measure fell by 0.84% between 2007 and 2008, or 8.4% extrapolated over a decade which, even discounting the effects of the recession, is a rate of improvement that falls far short of the target requirement. The more straightforward risk of income poverty measure (with the threshold set at 60% of equivalised median income) fluctuated between 15 and 16.2% in the decade to 2008 and was higher at the end of the decade than at the beginning. This again underlines the ambition of the EU social inclusion target.

The employment target is possibly even more vulnerable to external economic shocks than the poverty rate. The aspiration is to increase to employment rate among 20 to 64 year olds from its current (2009) level of 69.1% to 75%, which represents a rate of improvement over twice that which was achieved between 2000 and 2009 (2.5%). In fact, the EU employment rate peaked at 70.5% in 2008 which means that in a single year the recession wiped out more than a third of the gross improvement accomplished during the decade. Only Denmark, The Netherlands, Finland and Cyprus bettered the EU target in 2009.

Table 9.2: French scoreboard:
selected income based measures and targets

	Latest value	Latest trend	Target (5 years)
Poverty rate anchored in time (initial threshold at 60% of equivalent median income)	12.5% (2007)	-4% (2002-5) -5% (2006-7)	-33%
Rate of income poverty threshold at 60% of median equivalent income	13.4% (2007)	Stable (2002-5) +2% (2006-7)	-15%
Poverty intensity/Severity	18.2% (2007)	+12% (2002-5) +1% (2006-7)	Stability
Poverty persistence rate	9% (2000)	Stable (1997-2000)	Stability
Rate of non-negotiable (Préen-gagées) expenditure for individuals in the lowest income quintile	53 (2005)	+18% (2002-5)	Stability

Source: HCSACP (2009)

Table 9.3: French scoreboard: selected simulation results
for income based measures 2007-2009

2007-2009	Population	Change in % points	Change in %
Poverty rate anchored in time (2006)	Total population All workers	-1.6 -1.3	-14 -19
Rate of income poverty threshold at 60% of median equivalent income	Total population All workers	-0.7 -0.8	-5.5 -10.4
Poverty intensity/ severity	Total population	-0.8	-4.5

Source: HCSACP (2009)

The educational attainment target to increase participation in tertiary education from 32% to 40% is, by contrast, only a little more challenging in statistical terms than extrapolating the achievements of the preceding decade during which rates rose from 22.4 to 32.3%. Moreover, the 2020 target is already exceeded by 10 of the 27 Member States. That said, one would expect each marginal gain in educational attainment to be increasingly difficult to deliver. The easy gains, the "hanging fruit", will already have been taken and further progress will require substantial improvements in the quality of primary and secondary education so as to qualify students for tertiary education rather than merely to provide it for already qualified students. While some countries fall a long way short of the EU-wide target (Italy, Romania, Slovakia and the

Czech Republic would all need to double their provision) and therefore might be expected to contribute quickly to the Euro-target, many others may be faced with very high marginal costs of improvement.

At face value, therefore, it seems likely that for these Euro-targets to be attained there needs to be a step change in the aspirations and political ambition of Member States. Whether the targets are attainable is a moot point but it is imperative, if they are to retain their motivational purpose, that they are not considered to be purely aspirational, rhetorical window dressing separate from the real world of policy-making. For this to happen, for politicians and civil society to remain engaged to create the stimulus of public accountability, waypoint targets should be clearly established to mark progress towards the global goal (Atkinson and Marlier, 2010). In the light of actual developments it might even be appropriate to modify the targets to keep them attainable. This could mean lowering the targets or, if progress is unexpectedly fast, increasing them as happened in Ireland when economic growth eased the task of reducing poverty.

9.5 Targets and Distortion

A longstanding criticism of targets used in public policy is that their very success in directing energies leads to distortion, causing the bigger picture of strategic objectives to be lost with administrations focusing, instead, on meeting targets rather than delivering the full range of services most cost effectively.

It is too soon to say whether application of the French Scoreboard, let alone the EU targets, will have unintended consequences but the potential is there. The choice of an "anchored in time" poverty measure as the prime target in the French Scoreboard creates the incentive to focus on economic growth rather than income redistribution as the principal policy driver, thereby probably stimulating inequality and, possibly, reducing social cohesion. The French government is sensitive to this latter possibility, including measures of relative poverty to capture this effect. However, relative poverty measures necessarily focus on low incomes and will miss the global changes in income distribution and attenuation resulting from increased higher incomes that direct measures of income inequality would detect. With a generic poverty target in place, the policy inducement is to focus on those social groups that are most easy to lift above the poverty threshold at the expense of others that are more difficult to help. On the other hand, those most difficult to help are likely, during their lifetimes, to spend a disproportionately large number of years in poverty thereby contributing to high poverty rates in the longer term while also increasing measures of the severity and persistence of poverty.

The Scoreboard was explicitly designed to shift media interest away from an exclusive focus on income poverty, but it nevertheless retains a heavy emphasis on quantitative measures of income poverty omitting qualitative aspects of the poverty experience and many dimensions of the broader concept of social exclusion. There are no measures, for example, of the sense of personal failure, worthlessness, alienation, powerlessness and lack of choice associated with poverty, all features that people with direct experience of poverty tend to prioritise (Castell and Thompson, 2007; Walker *et al.*, 2009). Similarly, there are few indicators in the Scoreboard that relate to social capital or to the political, cultural and ethnic exclusion associated with poverty. Measures of victimisation, exploitation, gender inequality and discrimination, of security, substance abuse and crime, and of isolation, homelessness, poor infrastructure, physical dilapidation and access to energy are all largely omitted (Jones, 2009).

While some of these omissions are no doubt explicable in terms of a lack of available data as well as policy intent, they ensure that the Scoreboard is, at best, partial and, at worst, biased as a measure of poverty and social exclusion. This difficulty is exacerbated by the fact that, with one exception, namely the priority given to the anchored in time measure, equal weight is assigned to each indicator. This effectively means that the importance attached to an aspect of poverty is determined by the number of measures included. Moreover, while it might be argued that criticism concerning a lack of weighting is misplaced because no attempt is being made to provide a single cumulative poverty index, the emphasis given in the cut and thrust of political debate is likely to be determined by what measures are included and their number.

The EU poverty/social inclusion target measures (at-risk-of poverty, material deprivation, jobless households) avoid the trap of relying on "anchored in time" measures of poverty that make targets easier to meet but prioritise growth while ignoring any associated increase in income inequalities that might prove corrosive to social cohesion. However, the at-risk-of poverty measure is prone to a number of distortions. It can be unstable when incomes are clustered around the poverty threshold (which can occur if benefit levels rates keep people close to the poverty line). It takes no account of the severity of poverty and ignores both improvements and deterioration in the circumstances of the very poorest families. It is also prone to record counterintuitive falls in poverty in good economic times and increases during bad ones on account of the sensitivity of median incomes to growth-associated inequality. This last problem is, in part, countered by inclusion of material deprivation which is more stable, though it is sensitive to the choice of measures of depri-

vation included and vulnerable to becoming outdated due to technological advance and market penetration (e.g. mobile phones replacing
landlines and becoming universal rather an element of deprivation[3]).
Adding the third measure, workless households, draws attention to the
possible need to accommodate trade-offs between competing targets;
reducing the number of workless households through the supply of low
waged employment could increase income poverty if persons find
themselves to be worse off in work than on benefits. While basing the
target on a combination of just three measures could be justified on
grounds of parsimony and as a means of focussing administrative
energies, it also increases the risk of distortion and the ease of gaming.
It would seem to be essential, therefore, to follow the French example
and to continue to monitor a wide range of Laeken-style indicators to
guard against both possibilities. In addition, the commonly agreed
indicators should be used diagnostically to understand why some Member States may be performing worse than others against their respective
national targets (Atkinson and Marlier, 2010).

The EU social inclusion target is based on a simple additive measure
that takes no account of the trade-offs between the three chosen dimensions of poverty and social exclusion. It counts the number of people
who are at risk-of-poverty and/or materially deprived and/or living in
households with very low work intensity. It generates higher estimates
of poverty than the combined measures used nationally in Britain and in
Ireland because it counts as poor or socially excluded any person who
scores on one or more dimensions rather than on all three. Equally, it
does not acknowledge the possibility that persons who suffer from two
or all three problems considered might warrant higher policy priority
with the result that policy success in effectively targeting this group
would not be appropriately rewarded. Indeed, no account is taken to the
multi-dimensional and cumulative nature of poverty and social exclusion which means that there are many different aspects (experiential and
behavioural) that need to be tackled by different packages of policies
(Tomlinson and Walker, 2009). Furthermore, equal weight is implicitly
given to each of the three dimensions of poverty and social exclusion.
This clearly allows for different national priorities but both ignores

---

[3] The EU measure does not distinguish mobile telephones from landlines. The measure
of "material deprivation" covers indicators relating to economic strain, durables,
housing and environment of the dwelling. Severely materially deprived persons, according to the definition used in the EU target, have living conditions severely constrained by a lack of resources; they experience at least 4 out of the 9 following dep-
rivations items: cannot afford i) to pay rent or utility bills, ii) keep home adequately
warm, iii) face unexpected expenses, iv) eat meat, fish or a protein equivalent every
second day, v) a week holiday away from home, vi) a car, vii) a washing machine,
viii) a colour TV, or ix) a telephone.

debates about the relative merits of each dimension as an index of disadvantage and permits countries to choose the easiest route to reducing measured poverty and social exclusion which might result in creaming and short-termism.

The failure to prioritise among the poverty and social exclusion indicators on which the EU target is based, instead assigning them equal weight and ignoring trade-offs between them, is repeated with the five headline targets. It is neither self evident that there are no trade-offs between the headline targets, at least in the short term, nor clear that targets on energy intensity and "greenhouse gas" emissions, for example, are necessarily compatible with increased employment or lower poverty rates, especially given the perspective of tight public finances. What is presumed depends on the theory of change that is employed. The lack of priorities can be seen as evidence of the determination to leave Member States in the driving seat of policy reform or, again, one could argue that the choice of just five targets demonstrates a great deal of prioritisation. Either way, a lack of prioritisation between policy targets and the various indices used for monitoring progress has been found, at national level, to lessen the effectiveness of targets in stimulating fundamental institutional reform. It remains to be seen whether the same is true of supra-national policy targets.

9.6 Targets and Policy Design

As already noted, policy targets should be fully compatible with the underlying policy logic or theory of change. Insofar as they are, targets provide scholars with evidence of the ideological underpinnings of policy while providing policy-makers with information as to the effectiveness or otherwise of policy and evidence of any need for reform.

In the French case, the ideology and policy logic were made clear by the President of the Republic (French Presidency of the EU, 2008, page 1) when he stated that the welfare system (*minima sociaux*) had to be reformed: "In order to consistently reward work as opposed to government benefits, and to ensure that work invariably provides a door out of, and protection from, poverty".

The Scoreboard includes certain intermediate indicators, such as in-work poverty, jobless households and access to training, that are consistent with the important role assigned to employment as a defence against poverty. A priori, these would seem to fulfil the Laeken criterion for effective indicators, namely being responsive to policy interventions but not readily subject to manipulation. However, other important measures are omitted including, for example, unemployment rates, unemployment duration, benefit replacement rates, wage rates and wage dispersion, security of employment and job quality, employment retention and progression, labour market discrimination and childcare availability. It follows that the Scoreboard is likely to provide a good assessment of trends in the level and nature of poverty across the dimensions covered but may not, on its own, contribute much to understanding the effectiveness of the active inclusion policies put in place or to further developing policy.

The EU's supranational policy targets need adequately to reflect two tiers of policy logic. The first relates to the mechanisms by means of which national policies address the social problems underlying the targets. The second concerns two sets of logic: one refers to the mechanisms through which it is intended that the introduction of targets will influence the priorities and policies of Member States; the other appertains to the aggregation algorithms that ensure that the cumulative achievements of individual governments will guarantee that the EU headline targets are met.

The expectation of the European Commission is that Member States will finalise their national targets reflecting their own circumstances in just a few months. (Euro-targets were formally agreed by the European Council in June 2010 and countries are expected to submit to the Commission their draft National Reform Programmes (NRPs), which should include their national targets, in November 2010; the final NRPs are to be submitted in April 2011). Rapidity might seem counterproductive given that the many issues discussed above relating to target setting are germane to these decisions, as are additional EU-level relevancies to be discussed below. Moreover, the policy logic linking policies to the solution of social problems, as found, for example, in the European Commission's proposals for Integrated Guidelines to deliver on the Europe 2020 Strategy (European Commission, 2010), is aspirational more than technical and of limited value in setting national targets. The presumption might be that national targets will be expressed in the same metrics as EU ones but the matter of the reasonableness of targets has to be addressed by each Member State. In this regard, there may be scope for using micro-simulation models including EUROMOD to assess how readily national targets could be met through various policy strategies (Marlier *et al.*, 2007; Atkinson and Marlier, 2010). In addition, as already noted, there is also potentially much to be gained in terms of sustainability from actively engaging stakeholders in setting targets. Finally, there is considerable advantage in developing intermediate indicators that plot diagnostic steps in the implementation logic so as to help establish the effectiveness of policy, a process that needs to reflect the idiosyncrasies of national policies (Marlier *et al.*, 2007).

Moving to the policy rationale at EU level, the targets represent a strengthening of the Social OMC logic of a systematic commitment to policy improvement built upon partnership, performance measurement and peer review that is driven forward by a cyclical process of agreed objectives, plans and reports. Targets arguably make performance or lack of performance transparent and set Member States in clear competition against each other, such competition substituting for the lack of any explicit formal sanction. For targets to work, effectively on a voluntary basis, there has to be a minimum political commitment to the policy goal and target and the presumption must be that the process of agreeing the objectives through the EU Heads of State and Government will deliver at least this degree of commitment. However, Member States have, to date, shown a variable commitment to the Social OMC, policies are sometimes packaged differently for presentation to the Commission than to domestic audiences and gaming and creaming are not unknown. As previously mentioned, therefore, the championing of targets that has proved necessary to promote them domestically in France and elsewhere is likely to be needed both at the EU level and within Member States.

Whether champions – be they the EU Social Protection Committee (SPC) or a European Council/ Commission Presidential envoy – will suffice is unclear. The UK government funded civil society organisations both to champion targets and to articulate accountability while, as previously noted, the French government consulted closely with them. At EU level, anti-poverty groups have lobbied for Euro-targets and can therefore be expected to exploit them in their campaigning (Jones, 2009). However, if performance against national targets is expressed as an issue of accountability, which should be the case, there also needs to be an important role for the European Parliament and its specialist committees. There is a risk, though, that focussing on targets and performance might divert attention away the partnership in mutual learning that has helped erode a natural tendency towards defensiveness and enabled governments to admit to policy failure and to recognise scope for policy improvement.

In the UK, as discussed above, policy targets have been fuelled by financial sanctions, and conditionality is a central component in the logic underpinning the use of management targets in both the public and private sectors. There is scope, because the EU social inclusion target is included in the Europe 2020 Employment Guidelines, for it to be subject to "harder" law than the Social OMC has been hitherto with the European Commission having authority to issue recommendations to delinquent Member States (see opening chapter). There might also be potential for linking access to the EU Structural Funds to performance against targets although, since it might be counterproductive to deny resources to a Member State failing to meet a target, it would be preferable to think in terms of incentives rather than sanctions.

The aggregation logic that will generate success against EU targets based on the actions of Member States is, as yet, unclear. However, the French experience is instructive. The central government is attempting to engage lower tiers of government in targeting and monitoring poverty and social exclusion. In France, much of the responsibility for delivery of services and anti-poverty programmes lies with the *départements* and the 36,700 *communes*; 60% of the latter have less than 500 inhabitants. Nevertheless, *communes* are legally required, either singly or in concert, to establish "social action centres" that, among other responsibilities, are obliged to prepare "social needs analyses" (ABS) that include specifying goals, indicators and policy strategies to inform local policy-making and support national targets. A working party has also been established to develop indicators at *département* level and in time, to develop associated targets.

The French government therefore recognises that it is reliant on local governments but it has not always gained the local political support necessary for implementation. The European Commission is similarly dependent on the activities of Member States to deliver on Euro-targets and may, by analogy, likewise be frustrated in its dealings with Member States, especially if targets look in danger of being missed. What action it might seek to take is uncertain. It is also difficult to predict whether the EU social inclusion target will create a dynamic in which governments take seriously the interdependency which means that all Member States have to deliver on their targets if the supranational target is to be met. This is possibly unlikely, but if it occurred the Commission might find allies among Member States in its attempt to influence a recalcitrant government.

It is possible that, like France, other Member States will find the need to develop and devolve targets to local and regional governments in order to ensure that the national ones are met. This may have significant implications for the different levels of government. Lithuania, for example, although it has not to date set policy targets, has established a system analogous to the Social OMC in which a range of indicators are published for all municipalities with the intention of encouraging local politicians to compare policy outcomes with those of neighbouring municipalities (Lazutka, 2009).

While national governments may wish to impose on local authorities targets consistent with their national goals, the European Commission will presumably be keen to negotiate targets for Member States consistent with its EU ambitions. However, these ambitions are far from clear to policy-makers outside Brussels. Even if it is presumed that the EU headline targets are real, and not merely rhetorical, they could be achieved in numerous ways. For example, the target of reducing by 20 million the number of "poor or socially excluded" people according to the Euro-target definition (20 million out of the 120 million, i.e. approximately 17%) could be achieved by a 17% reduction in all countries, or by targeting countries with the highest poverty rates or the largest populations, by focussing on the countries with the smallest poverty gaps (creaming) or, most cheaply, by concentrating energies on countries with the lowest per capital GDP and, hence, the lowest poverty thresholds. It is at least arguable that this last strategy is not only economical but preferable on grounds of social justice, targeting resources to those whose poverty is most severe by EU-wide standards. However, it seems unlikely that Member States will prioritise the Euro-target above their national interests. Nevertheless, a government intent on curtailing domestic spending might seek to negotiate a less ambitious national target while arguing that other Member States could more easily contribute to the agreed EU goal. Equally, the European Commission might not favour a uniform 17% reduction since that would make the fate of the Euro-target dependent on the contribution of the lowest performing Member State unless target overshoots in some countries happened to exceed shortfalls in others.

The policy logic that the European Commission will seek to follow in its discussions on national targets with Member States has not yet found its way into the public domain. Nor is it clear what approach Member States will be taking to setting and negotiating targets. It seems unlikely, given the speed of the negotiations, that either side will make use of the EUROMOD micro-simulation although, a priori, it would seem ideally suited to generating a range of policy scenarios under different targeting assumptions. It may be that the Commission views targets as little more than a quantifiable objective and that it sees little change in the underlying logic of the Social OMC. Perhaps if the targets offered by Member States in total fall short of the 20 million EU reduction target, the European Commission will accept this as a *fait accompli* to be revisited in more auspicious times. However, it is unlikely that civil society organisations will see targets this way. Instead, it is highly probable that civil society will use the targets to ratchet up pressure on national governments and the Commission to deliver on what they will take to be "promises". If this happens, and especially if civil society succeeds in engaging the public and if the European Parliament takes a real interest, targets may usher in a new era of political accountability in EU policy-making.

9.7 Conclusions

Only with hindsight can one know whether introducing targets into the EU policy process will prove to be of lasting significance. What one does know is that if something of significance is not achieved, targets will have proved to be a failure. Policy targets are typically intended to shake up the policy-making process, to challenge ways of working and to change institutional cultures. Moreover, if they do not achieve these things, targets are unlikely to make a difference and therefore to work. It is difficult to judge the level of commitment to targets among the various stakeholders so early in the process of implementing them at EU level. If stakeholders are expecting that little will change as a result of the introduction of targets, they are being unrealistic and might well be insufficiently prepared for the consequences of working with targets. However, if they are determined that nothing will change, they may well be able to guarantee that targets prove to be ineffectual.

Targets work at national level by adding a new dynamic – measured progress – to policy-making, thereby increasing accountability and stimulating public debate and engagement that is often led by civil society organisations. Provided targets are attainable, progress is demonstrable and the system has effective political champions, policy targets can shift policy-making cultures, enhance the role of evidence and increase achievements. However, targets need accurately to reflect the causal mechanisms embodied in policy logic, that is, they must measure the right outcomes in an appropriate manner so as to avoid distortion and not to encourage gaming that means targets may be met while policy objectives are forgotten or ignored.

There are many unknowns and uncertainties as policy targets are transferred from national to EU level. These include questions about the degree of political support that exists, the nature, robustness and specificity of the policy logic at both EU and Member State levels, the attainability of the Euro-targets already set, the criteria for setting national targets and the linkages envisaged between EU, Member State and possible regional and sub-regional targets. Targets can neither capture the full complexities of the social and economic issues being tackled nor reflect all the subtle processes involved in policy delivery especially at supranational level. Hence, targets are partial and gaming is certainly possible, particularly if a culture of competition rather than collaboration is fostered between Member States; it is important that targets are used to drive policy-making rather than to replace it.

For this to happen, powerful champions must be appointed at EU and Member State level to monitor achievements and to encourage, facilitate and cajole the various stakeholders to take those actions necessary to meet the targets set. There may even be a case, based on the experience of implementing national targets, for establishing financial incentives that reward success. Furthermore, the targets provide an opportunity to enhance the legitimacy of EU's democratic institutions by foregrounding the role of the European Parliament, alongside that of civil society, in holding Member States to account as they endeavour through policy and institutional change to attain or, preferably, to exceed their targets by 2020.

Statistics on poverty, exclusion and disadvantage of all kinds demonstrate the imperative to tackle social problems across the EU and to build the political support needed to do so. Targets could fit well within the institutional structures that have been created by the Social OMC and add a new dynamism. Whether the dynamic will embrace the Eurotargets as a collective venture to be addressed through collaborative action, rather than by the simple summation of nationally focussed activities, remains to be seen.

References

Atkinson, A.B. and Marlier, E. (editors) (2010), *Income and living conditions in Europe*, Chapter 1 in Atkinson, A.B. and Marlier, E. *Income and living conditions in Europe*, Luxembourg: Office for Official Publications of the European Communities (OPOCE).

Bamfield, L. (2005), "Making the public case for tackling poverty and inequality", Poverty, 121. Available at: http://www.cpag.org.uk/info/ Povertyarticles/Poverty121/making.htm.

Carbo, S., Gardener, E. and Molyneux, P. (2007), "Financial Exclusion in Europe", *Public Money & Management*, 27(1): 21-27.

Castell, S. and Thompson, J. (2007), *Understanding Attitudes to Poverty in the UK: Getting the public's attention*, York: Joseph Rowntree Foundation.

Collard, S., Kempson, E and Whyley, C. (2001), *Tackling Financial Exclusion*, Bristol: The Policy Press.

Child Poverty Action Group (CPAG) (2008), *Child poverty: the stats: Analysis of the latest poverty statistics*, London: CPAG Policy Briefing.

European Commission (2010), *Europe 2020: A strategy for smart, sustainable and inclusive growth*, Communication COM(2010) 2020, Brussels: European Commission.

European Commission (2009), *Portfolio of indicators for the monitoring of the European Strategy for Social Protection and Social Inclusion – 2009 update*, Brussels: European Commission. Available at: http://ec.europa.eu/social/ main.jsp?catId=756&langId=en.

European Commission (2009a), *Economic crisis in Europe: Causes, Consequences and Responses*, European Economy series, No. 7/2009, Brussels: European Commission.

European Council (2010), *European Council: 17th June 2010, Conclusions*, Brussels: European Council.

French Presidency of the European Union, (2008), *High Commissioner for active Inclusion against poverty*. Available at: http://www.eu2008.fr/webdav/site/PFUE/shared/import/1015_table_ronde_pauvrete/Active_inclusion_again st_poverty.pdf.

Haut-Commissaire aux Solidarités Actives Contre la Pauvreté (HCSACP) (2009), *Suivi de l'objectif de baisse d'un tiers de la pauvreté en cinq ans*, Paris: Rapport au Parlement, Haut-Commissaire aux Solidarités Actives Contre la Pauvreté, October.

Jones, S. (2009), *Measuring the impact of active inclusion and other policies to combat poverty and social exclusion, A Contribution from the European Anti-Poverty Network*, Paper presented to the Peer Review on "Measuring the impact of active inclusion", Paris, 3-4 December.

Lazutka, R. (2009), *Active inclusion and other policies to combat poverty and social exclusion from Lithuanian perspective*, Paper presented to the Peer Review on "Measuring the impact of active inclusion", Paris, 3-4 December.

Marlier, E., Atkinson A.B., Cantillon B., Nolan, B. (2007), *The EU and Social Inclusion: Facing the Challenges*, Bristol: The Policy Press.

McKendrick, J., Sinclair, S., Irwin, A., O'Donnell, H., Scott, G. and Dobbie L. (2008), *The media, poverty and public opinion in the UK*, York: Joseph Rowntree Foundation.

O'Kelly, K. (2007), *The evaluation of mainstreaming social inclusion in Europe*, Dublin: Combat Poverty Agency.

Tomlinson, M. and Walker, R. (2009), *Coping with Complexity: Child and adult poverty*, London: CPAG.

Tomlinson, M., Walker, R. and Williams, G. (2008), "Measuring Poverty in Britain as a Multi-dimensional Concept, 1991 to 2003", *Journal of Social Policy*, 37(4): 597-620.

Walker, R. (2010), *France 2009: Measuring the impact of active inclusion and other policies to combat poverty and social exclusion: Synthesis Report*, Vienna: European Commission, Directorate-General Employment, Social affairs and Equal opportunities.

Walker, R. (2009), *Measuring the impact of active inclusion and other policies to combat poverty and social exclusion*, Discussion Paper presented to the Peer Review on "Measuring the impact of active inclusion", Paris, 3-4 December.

Walker, R., Tomlinson, M. and Williams, G. (2009), "The problem with poverty", in G. Walford and E. Tucker (editors), *The Sage Handbook of Measurement*, London: Sage, 353-376.

10. Strengthening Social Inclusion in the Europe 2020 Strategy by Learning from the Past

Hugh FRAZER and Eric MARLIER[1]

10.1 Current Approach

10.1.1 Main elements

Since 2000, the European Union (EU) and the European Commission have been cooperating in the field of social policy on the basis of the so-called Open Method of Coordination (OMC). This has provided the framework in which efforts to promote social protection and social inclusion and to tackle poverty and social exclusion in the EU have been implemented. EU cooperation and coordination in the social area have developed significantly over the last 10 years and now cover three main policy areas or "strands": social inclusion (formally launched at the March 2000 Lisbon European Council as the OMC on poverty and social exclusion), pensions (launched in 2001) and healthcare and long-term care (2004). There are also information exchanges in the field of making work pay. Since 2006, the three EU social "processes" that were progressively implemented under the OMC (one process for each main strand) have been streamlined into one integrated "Social OMC" built around 12 commonly agreed EU objectives: three for each main strand as well as three "overarching" objectives which address horizontal issues that cut across them.[2] The Social OMC is coordinated by the EU Social Protection Committee (SPC), which consists of officials from

---

[1] This chapter draws on the 10 years of experience of EU cooperation and coordination in the social area and builds on earlier work we have undertaken such as Frazer and Marlier (2008, 2010 and 2010a) and also most recently Frazer, Marlier and Nicaise (2010). Addresses for correspondence: hughfrazer@eircom.net and eric.marlier@skynet.be.

[2] The 12 EU objectives for the *streamlined* Social OMC were adopted by the EU in March 2006. See: http://ec.europa.eu/social/main.jsp?catId=755&langId=en.

The "overarching objectives" of the Social OMC provide linkage across the three social policy strands as well as between the EU social, economic and employment strategies. For instance, the third overarching objective is "to promote good governance, transparency and the involvement of stakeholders in the design, implementation and monitoring of policy".

mainly Employment and Social Affairs Ministries in each Member State as well as representatives of the European Commission. The SPC reports to the EU "Employment, Social Policy, Health and Consumer Affairs" (EPSCO) Council of Ministers.

The main elements of the OMC approach are well summarised by Marlier *et al.* (2007, pages 22-23): "The OMC is a mutual feedback process of planning, monitoring, examination, comparison and adjustment of national (and sub-national) policies, all of this on the basis of common objectives agreed for the EU as a whole. Through this *peer review exercise* (which involves the European Commission and all Member States), and thus the sharing of experience and good practices, all the countries can learn from one another and are therefore all in a position to improve their policies." As put by Vandenbroucke (2002), with this approach, the EU has found "a way that implies a credible commitment to a social Europe" which, provided certain conditions are met, "can effectively lead to social progress".[3]

Box 10.1: The three social inclusion objectives of the Social OMC

A decisive impact on the eradication of poverty and social exclusion by ensuring:

- access for all to the resources, rights and services needed for participation in society, preventing and addressing exclusion, and fighting all forms of discrimination leading to exclusion;

- the active social inclusion of all, both by promoting participation in the labour market and by fighting poverty and exclusion;

- that social inclusion policies are well-coordinated and involve all levels of government and relevant actors, including people experiencing poverty, that they are efficient and effective and mainstreamed into all relevant public policies, including economic, budgetary, education and training policies and structural fund (notably European Social Fund (ESF)) programmes.

More concretely, the social inclusion strand of the Social OMC has consisted of five main elements since 2006. As mentioned above, the first element is a set of three EU objectives for social inclusion (see

---

[3] In this chapter, we concentrate primarily on drawing out lessons from the social inclusion strand of the Social OMC. However, in doing so we set this learning in the broader context of the Social OMC as a whole (i.e. social inclusion as well as pensions and healthcare and long-term care) and we draw out lessons about the importance of social protection in building a stronger Social EU.

Box 10.1) which are part of a wider set of common objectives on social protection and social inclusion.

The second element is the National Action Plans on social inclusion (NAPs/inclusion), which are one section of the streamlined National Strategy Reports on social protection and social inclusion (NSRSPSIs). NAPs/inclusion are meant to be the means by which Member States translate the common objectives into national policies and are drawn up on the basis of a common framework. Since 2006, there have been two rounds of NSRSPSIs covering the period 2006-2008 and 2008-2010.

The third element is a set of commonly agreed indicators to enhance the analysis of poverty and social exclusion and to measure progress towards achieving the common objectives. These indicators are organised according to the structure of the common objectives for the Social OMC: one set of indicators and "context information" appropriate to the overarching objectives agreed for the Social OMC as a whole and one appropriate to each of the three social strands covered by the Social OMC (i.e., social inclusion, pensions and healthcare and long-term care). The most recent list of indicators was adopted in the second half of 2009 and provides for each indicator the agreed definition and socio-demographics breakdowns (European Commission, 2009).[4]

The fourth element is a process of regular monitoring and reporting on progress which has resulted in regular reports on social inclusion in the EU. These are the annual *Joint Reports on Social Protection and Social Inclusion.*[5]

Finally, the fifth element consists of the two Community action programmes to underpin and reinforce the process and, more particularly, to encourage mutual learning and dialogue between Member States with a view to stimulating innovation and the sharing of good practice. From 2002-2006 there was *The Community action programme to encourage cooperation between Member States to combat social exclusion* which was succeeded for the period 2007-2013 by the *Community Programme for Employment and Social Solidarity (PROGRESS)*. These programmes have promoted *inter alia*: research and policy analysis (e.g., the EU Network of Independent Experts on Social Inclusion[6]); data collection (e.g., Member States have received significant funding from these Programmes to launch the EU Statistics on Income and Living Conditions (EU-SILC) instrument, which is a major EU reference data source for the Social OMC indicators and statistics); exchange of good practice

---

[4] For more information on the EU social indicators (their construction and their use in the policy process), see for instance Atkinson *et al.* (2002) and Marlier *et al.* (2007).

[5] See: http://ec.europa.eu/social/main.jsp?catId=757&langId=en.

[6] See: http://www.peer-review-social-inclusion.eu/network-of-independent-experts.

(through transnational exchange projects, peer reviews and studies); networking across Europe of NGOs and regional and local authorities active in the fight against poverty and social exclusion; and the funding of European conferences on poverty and social exclusion.

While the above are the main elements of the social inclusion strand of the Social OMC, it is important to understand that the other two strands (i.e. pensions and healthcare and long-term care) have also played an important role in promoting greater social inclusion. This has been more evident since the three separate processes were streamlined into one overall Social OMC, though the synergies between the three strands need to be further developed (see also chapters by Daly and by Zeitlin in the present volume). The first two of the overarching objectives of the Social OMC[7] have also helped to situate the struggle against poverty and social exclusion within the broader context of developing effective and sustainable social protection systems (i.e. income support and access to services). These overarching objectives also stress the importance of social protection and social inclusion policies in reinforcing employment and economic objectives (referred to as *"feeding in"* in EU jargon) and economic and employment policies contributing to the achievement of social objectives (*"feeding out"*). Unfortunately, the mutual interaction between the employment, economic and social inclusion processes still need to be fully and systematically developed. However, at least the objectives have helped to highlight the importance of such synergies being more systematically pursued.

10.1.2 Key policy areas

From 2006, activities carried out in the context of the EU Social Inclusion Process focussed in an increasingly systematic manner around three policy themes. The first theme was *Active Inclusion*. Work on this topic led to the European Commission Recommendation on the active inclusion of people excluded from the labour market (2008b), which contains common principles and practical guidelines on a comprehensive strategy based on the integration of three policy pillars: adequate income support, inclusive labour markets and access to quality services.[8] Secondly, *child poverty and child well-being* became a key issue

---

[7] These objectives are "to promote social cohesion, equality between men and women and equal opportunities for all through adequate, accessible, financially sustainable, adaptable and efficient social protection systems and social inclusion policies" and "to promote effective and mutual interaction between the Lisbon objectives of greater economic growth, more and better jobs and greater social cohesion, and with the EU Sustainable Development Strategy".

[8] See: http://eurlex.europa.eu/LexUriServ/LexUriServ.do?uri=OJ:L:2008:307:00 11:0014:EN:PDF. See also European Commission, 2008b.

and this led to a thematic year on the topic in 2007 and the adoption of a very important report by the SPC on child poverty and well-being that can be referred to as the first EU-wide benchmarking exercise based quasi exclusively on the commonly agreed EU indicators (Social Protection Committee, 2008). Thirdly, the issue of *homelessness and housing exclusion* was the subject of a thematic year in 2009. All three issues are being given a lot of attention as key themes during the *2010 European Year for Combating Poverty and Social Exclusion* and thus also during the 2010 Spanish and Belgian Presidencies of the Council of the EU. Two other topics have come increasingly to the fore in the most recent period: the high risk of poverty and social exclusion experienced by many *migrants and ethnic minorities*, and the social impact of the *financial and economic crisis.*[9]

In the two other strands of the EU coordination and cooperation in the social field, i.e. pensions and healthcare and long-term care, there has also been a tendency to concentrate on particular areas. For instance, activities have *inter alia* covered the following topics: privately managed pensions, working longer and reducing early withdrawal from the labour market, reducing health inequalities, improving the rational use of resources in healthcare and long-term care while maintaining the quality and coordination between different healthcare sectors, effectiveness and efficiency of healthcare spending, sustainability and adequacy of EU pension systems (including long term implications of the crisis for pension systems), etc.

10.1.3 Governance and institutional arrangements

In addition to these specific policy areas, the Social OMC has also given considerable emphasis to strengthening governance and institutional arrangements in relation to tackling and preventing poverty and social exclusion (though this has been more evident in the field of social inclusion than in the pensions and healthcare and long-term care strands). As a result, seven themes in particular have emerged though progress across them has been uneven. These have been:

- first, the need to mobilise stakeholders (government agencies, social partners and non governmental organisations and the research community) in the design, implementation and monitoring of policies and programmes;

---

[9] See for instance the "Second joint assessment by the Social Protection Committee and the European Commission of the social impact of the economic crisis and of policy responses – Full Report" submitted to the EU Council of Ministers in November 2009 and available at: http://register. consilium.europa.eu/pdf/en/09/st16/st16169-ad01.en09.pdf.

- secondly, the importance of involving people directly experiencing poverty and social exclusion;
- thirdly, the fact that the social inclusion objectives have to be mainstreamed into national and sub-national policy-making;
- fourthly, the importance of improving the coordination of different departments and levels of government so that policies and programmes can better reinforce each other;
- fifthly, the need for comprehensive, multidimensional and strategic responses to poverty and social exclusion which are evidence-based and which are aimed at achieving clearly defined and quantified objectives adopted as a result of a rigorous diagnosis;
- sixthly, the necessity to coordinate and integrate the delivery of policies on the ground in a way that involves partnerships between the different agencies and that involves all; and
- seventhly, the importance of developing effective procedures for the monitoring of and reporting on the implementation of strategies and for both the ex ante and ex post assessment of the impact of policies.

10.2 Assessment of the Social OMC

Drawing on our own work on the Social OMC (e.g., Frazer and Marlier (2008, 2010 and 2010a), Marlier *et al.* (2007)) as well as on the assessment made by the European Commission (2008 and 2008a), by various commentators (e.g., Crepaldi *et al.* (2010) and Zeitlin (2007)) and by many of the Networks active in the process (e.g., European Anti-Poverty Network (2009, 2009a, 2010, 2010a and 2010b) and Platform of European Social NGOs (2009)), one can identify a fairly clear pattern of strengths and weaknesses of the EU's approach to tackling poverty and social exclusion.

10.2.1 Strengths

The first and probably the most important aspect of the Social OMC is that it has helped to put and keep social inclusion and social protection (including pensions and healthcare and long-term care) on the EU agenda (if not always as strongly as many would wish). It has created a space in which it has been possible to argue for enhanced efforts at EU, national and sub-national levels to prevent and alleviate poverty and social exclusion and promote greater social inclusion. Secondly, the Social OMC has provided an opportunity to highlight at EU level the importance of ensuring that economic, employment and social policies are made mutually reinforcing and thus also an opportunity to insist that economic and employment objectives should take more into account social outcomes. Thirdly, it has contributed to Member States, particularly through their involvement in preparing NAPs/inclusion, developing a common understanding of concepts (e.g., multidimensionality, mainstreaming, evidence-based strategies and quantified objectives, partnership between actors, participation, policy impact assessments) and to them identifying and agreeing on key policy priorities in relation to social inclusion, pensions and healthcare and long-term care at national and sub-national levels. Fourthly, it has generated a considerable body of very useful learning about how best to prevent and alleviate poverty and social exclusion and to promote stronger pension systems and enhanced healthcare and long-term care services whether from the various *Joint Reports on Social Protection and Social Inclusion*, the many studies commissioned as part of the process, the wide range of reports arising from transnational exchange projects and peer reviews, or the many reports from the different networks active in the process such as the AGE Platform Europe, the European Anti-Poverty Network (EAPN), the European Federation of National Organisations Working with the Homeless (FEANTSA), Eurochild, the European Social Network and the Confederation of Family Organisations in the EU (CO-FACE). As already mentioned, the deepening of knowledge and the exchange of learning in relation to social inclusion has been particularly evident in the areas of active inclusion, child poverty and well-being, as well as housing exclusion and homelessness.

Fifthly, as the recent evaluation of the process for the European Parliament points out (see Crepaldi *et al.*, 2010), the Social OMC has achieved significant progress in improving data, defining commonly agreed indicators and developing a stronger analytical framework so as to better understand and assess the phenomena at stake as well as better monitor and report on progress. Even though there is still a long way to walk, this has encouraged a more rigorous and evidenced-based approach to policy-making.

Sixthly, it has led to improvements in the governance of social inclusion issues in various Member States. In particular, it has encouraged mainstreaming a social inclusion concern across a broader range of policy domains, greater coordination and integration of policies to prevent and alleviate poverty and social exclusion, and improved structures to mobilise a broad range of different stakeholders, including those people experiencing poverty and social exclusion. Seventhly, in those Member States who have chosen to make full use of it, the Social OMC has proved to be a very helpful tool in strengthening their national and sub-national efforts to promote social inclusion. Eighthly, it has ensured that the need for a response to the social impact of the financial and economic crisis has been articulated in EU debates.[10] Ninthly, it has mobilised a wide range of actors and fostered EU wide networks of people involved in the struggle against poverty and social exclusion and it has given a voice to the socially excluded.[11] Tenthly, without the EU process it is unlikely that 2010 would have been designated the European Year for Combating Poverty and Social Exclusion.

10.2.2 Weaknesses

In spite of the several positive developments encouraged by the Social OMC, this process has failed in one of its main goals. There has been little progress made towards achieving the overall objective set in Lisbon ten years ago of making a decisive impact on the eradication of poverty and social exclusion by 2010, though some would argue that this was not something that such a process could achieve. The harsh reality is that the at-risk-of poverty rate for the 15 countries that were members of the EU in 2000 has remained stable: the EU-15 weighted average was 15% in 2000 and in 2008, the most recent data available, it is 16% (for the 12 newer Member States, the average poverty risk rate in 2008 is 17%; the 2008 EU-27 average is also 17%).[12] In relation to "material deprivation", the situation is however a bit more encouraging at least in the newer Member States. Indeed, if the EU-15 average has remained stable between 2005 and 2008 (12-13%), it has dropped in the 10 newer EU countries for which data are available though it still remains 2.5 times as high as in the older Member States (2005: 43%, 2006: 38%, 2007: 33% and 2008: 29%).[13]

---

[10] In this regard, it is encouraging that the 2010 *Joint Report on Social Protection and Social Inclusion* clearly recognises that "the crisis has emphasised the added value of policy coordination through the Open Method of Coordination on Social Protection and Social Inclusion (Social OMC) and provided further incentive to reinforce and exploit its potential fully" (EU Council of Ministers, 2010).

[11] See for instance European Anti-Poverty Network (2009a). For the reports summarising the main outcomes of the annual EU Meetings of People Experiencing Poverty, see: http://www.eapn.eu/index.php?option=comcontent&view=article&id=600%3A the-european-meetings-of-people-experiencing-poverty-a-process-going-forward&ca tid=16&Itemid=14&lang=en.

[12] According to the EU definition, people "at risk of poverty" are people living in a household whose total equivalised income is below 60% of the median national equivalised household income (the equivalence scale is the so-called *OECD modified* scale). All the figures presented in this paragraph are from the EU Statistics on Income and Living Conditions (EU-SILC) data source.

[13] Originally proposed by Guio (2009), this EU indicator significantly improves the multi-dimensional coverage of the EU portfolio for social inclusion. Based on the limited information available from the EU-SILC data-set, it focuses on the proportion of people living in households who cannot afford at least 3 items out of a list of 9.

Among the various explanations that have been put forward by commentators for the relatively limited impact of the Social OMC, the most important is the low political status given to the process and the lack of political leadership at EU level, particularly vis-à-vis the other strands of the Lisbon agenda (growth and jobs). In reality, the mutually reinforcing nature of economic, social and employment policy envisaged when the Lisbon process was launched has not been much in evidence. To put it in EU jargon, there has been little *feeding in* and *feeding out* between the various EU processes. In theory, it was expected that the EU's Social OMC agenda would parallel and interact closely with the Growth and Jobs agenda ("feeding in" to growth and employment objectives while growth and employment programmes would "feed out" to advance social cohesion/inclusion goals). However, as the studies by the EU Network of Social Inclusion Experts have shown (Frazer and Marlier, 2009), in practice such reinforcing interconnections have been disappointingly weak – they have existed more in theory than in practice and, more broadly, linkages with other EU policy areas (e.g. competition, agriculture, health, education, justice, migration) have been very limited.

Another reason for the relatively limited impact of the Social OMC is that up to the present it has remained a "soft" process; there have been no sanctions against Member States who fail to make progress and the European Commission has not issued recommendations to Member States on what they would need to do to strengthen their efforts (see below, Section 10.3.2). There has thus been little pressure on Member States to move forward. Furthermore, the absence of any clear EU quantified social outcome targets up until very recently (June 2010; see below) has diminished the status of the Social OMC in relation to economic and employment policies which, since 2005, have been dealt with separately at EU level in the context of the "Partnership for Growth and Jobs". All of this has meant that the Social OMC has had a very low public visibility and (until very recently) there has been a lack of public promotion of the process.

At national level, the reality has been that most Member States have failed to integrate the Social OMC process, especially the NAPs/inclusion, into national and sub-national policy-making procedures. Indeed, in many Member States NAPs/inclusion have been rather bureaucratic reporting mechanisms whereby countries inform the European Commis-

---

Figures for the newer Member States do not include Bulgaria and Romania as data for these countries are not available for all 4 years considered here. In 2008, the national rate of material deprivation (EU definition) is 51% for Bulgaria and 50% for Romania. For a characterisation of the income poor and the materially deprived in 24 EU countries and in Norway, see: Fusco, Guio and Marlier (2010).

sion and other EU Member States of what they are doing or planning to do to combat poverty and social exclusion. They have not been used, as was originally intended, as a means of reviewing policies and developing new and increased strategic efforts to prevent and reduce poverty and social exclusion. This view is borne out by the European Commission's own recent evaluation of the impact of the Lisbon process, which refers to the OMC as a method of "soft coordination" and which rightly highlights that "while the OMC can be used as a source of peer pressure and a forum for sharing good practice, evidence suggests that in fact most Member States have used OMCs as a reporting device rather than one of policy development" (European Commission, 2010a).

With a "soft" process, a key to encouraging greater effort is through effective monitoring and evaluation of the progress being made by Member States and benchmarking their performance against other Member States. In practice, there has been insufficiently rigorous monitoring, evaluation and reporting of Member States' performance in part due to weak analytical tools and resources. Furthermore, the potential of the Social OMC for putting peer pressure on Member States to do more through the use of EU benchmarking and more generally transnational comparisons has been made more difficult by the lack of timely statistical evidence.

Analyses of the NAPs/inclusion by the European Commission, the EU Network of Independent Experts on Social Inclusion and European poverty networks like EAPN, Eurochild, European Social Network and FEANSTA have highlighted that, while a few Member States have made progress, still too many have very weak governance arrangements for tackling poverty and social exclusion. Many countries lack effective mechanisms for mainstreaming social inclusion objectives in national and sub-national policies, lack effective arrangements for the horizontal and vertical coordination of policies, and/or have ineffective strategic planning and poor systems for implementing policies on the ground and for mobilising and involving all actors.

Finally, one more important factor that has undermined the impact of the Social OMC is that it has not been sufficiently backed up with resources. The potential to use the EU Structural Funds to encourage Member States in the implementation of the EU social inclusion objectives has not been sufficiently developed. EAPN among others has been critical of the limited amount of Structural Funds available to support social inclusion measures: "Overall, EAPN was disappointed that the 2007-2013 programming period was not made a more effective instrument to combat poverty and social exclusion. The European Commission's own estimates were that only 12.4% of the European Social Fund was allocated to social inclusion measures." (Harvey, 2008)

10.3 The Future

The EU process launched in Lisbon in 2000 ended in 2010. Thus there is currently much policy debate about what role efforts to prevent and reduce poverty and social exclusion will play in the EU's agenda for the next decade, *Europe 2020* (European Commission, 2010). Drawing on the experience of recent years and on important contributions from various civil society networks[14] and building on earlier work we have undertaken (e.g., Frazer (2010), Frazer and Marlier (2008, 2010 and 2010a) and also the independent report we prepared at the request of the 2010 Belgian Presidency of the EU (Frazer, Marlier and Nicaise, 2010)), the following are our suggestions as to how the process could build on past successes and address weaknesses if a more effective EU process is to develop in the future.

In making our suggestions, we would stress that the existing EU processes on social protection and social inclusion are still relatively new. As we have documented above, they are far from perfect. However, there is much that is positive and that has gradually become embedded in policy and practice. Looking to the future, it is important to build on these positives and not to throw out the baby with the bathwater by abandoning key elements of the Social OMC. So, where it is possible to strengthen the various elements of the Social OMC we should do so. Those weaknesses that we have identified that cannot be satisfactorily addressed in this way could then be pursued through the proposed EU flagship European Platform against Poverty (see Section 10.3.6 below; see also chapters by Daly and by Zeitlin in the present volume).

10.3.1 Clear EU social objectives with EU and national social outcome targets

Clear EU social objectives

If social cohesion/inclusion is to have a higher political priority at EU level, the EU's political objectives must emphasise the interdependence and mutually reinforcing nature of economic, employment, social and environmental objectives and policies. The new *Europe 2020* Strategy must be built around these four pillars and all must be developed at the same time so that they continuously interact and reinforce

---

[14] See, for example: Confederation of Family Organisations in the European Union (COFACE) (2010), Eurochild (2010), European Anti-Poverty Network (2009, 2010 and 2010b), European Anti-Poverty Network Ireland (2010), European Social Network (2010), FEANTSA (2010), Platform of European Social NGOs (2009) and Spring Alliance (2009).

each other. The objectives should also contain an explicit commitment to work both for the eradication of poverty and social exclusion and for the reduction of inequalities. An effective fight against poverty and social exclusion requires that both prevention (i.e. reducing the inflow into poverty) and alleviation (i.e. lifting those in poverty out of poverty) be addressed. This means universal policies aimed at promoting the inclusion of all and then also, when necessary, targeted policies to assist those facing particular difficulties or barriers. Comprehensive social protection systems are then also needed to ensure that all citizens have access to high quality services and to an adequate income. Finally, a prerequisite for effectively combating poverty and social exclusion (and for achieving the Europe 2020 stated goal of "inclusive and sustainable growth") is to address (excessive) inequality.

EU and national social outcome targets

In its proposals for Europe 2020, issued in March 2010, the European Commission suggested that there should be five EU headline targets to be achieved by 2020. One of these was to "reduce the number of Europeans living below national poverty lines by 25%, lifting 20 million people out of poverty" (EU definition; see above). The Commission also proposed that there should be 7 "flagship initiatives". One of these is a "European Platform Against Poverty" (EPAP), the purpose of which would be "to ensure social and territorial cohesion such that the benefits of growth and jobs are widely shared and people experiencing poverty and social exclusion are enabled to live in dignity and take an active part in society" (European Commission, 2010).

On 17th June 2010, following an extensive process of discussion and negotiation involving primarily the SPC and its Indicators Sub-Group as well as the European Commission, EU Heads of State and Government endorsed a compromise target aimed at "promoting social inclusion, in particular through the reduction of poverty" (European Council, 2010). This target is based on a combination of three indicators: the number of people at risk of poverty (EU definition; total population), the number of people materially deprived (EU definition but stricter[15]; total population), and the number of people aged 0-59 who live in "jobless" households (defined, for the purpose of the EU target, as households where none of the members aged 18-59 are working or where members aged 18-59 have, on average, very limited work attachment). The target will consist of reducing the number of people in the EU (120 million) who

---

[15] In the standard EU definition, the threshold for being considered "materially deprived" has been set as an enforced lack of at least 3 items out of 9 (see above). In the indicator used for the newly adopted EU target, it has been set as 4 items out of 9 (same list of items).

are at risk of poverty and/or materially deprived and/or living in jobless households by 20 million.[16][17]

Although the target is less ambitious than many hoped, the fact that the European Commission and all EU countries could adopt it is a major step forward in demonstrating the political social commitment of the EU. This represents a positive step towards ensuring that social cohesion/inclusion have the same status as the other political priorities outlined in the Europe 2020 agenda, all of which having linked quantified targets.

The next challenge is for each Member State to adopt one or several national and possibly sub-national (outcome) targets. Under the principle of *subsidiarity*, countries are free to set these targets on the basis of what they consider the most appropriate indicator(s) given their national circumstances and priorities. Setting targets is a difficult area for a combination of political and scientific reasons. Indeed, to be truly meaningful these targets need to be evidence-based, they should be the result of a rigorous diagnosis of the causes of poverty and social exclusion in the country and they should take into account the views of stakeholders. It is also important that Member States be asked to explain – again, on the basis of rigorous analytical evidence – how meeting their (sub-)national targets will contribute to the achievement of the EU level target. As emphasised by Marlier *et al.* (2007, page 213), "analytical tools such as tax-benefit simulation can help in projecting forward benchmark scenarios against which the level of ambition of targets can be assessed. Significant scientific work is required in this complex area, and researchers have a major contribution to make in deepening the information base for decision makers."[18]

---

[16] This is less ambitious than the original proposals which was also a reduction of 20 million but only covered 80 million people (i.e., the number of people at-risk-of-poverty).

[17] At their June 2010 meeting, EU Heads of State and Government endorsed "five EU headline targets which will constitute shared objectives guiding the action of Member States and the Union as regards promoting employment; improving the conditions for innovation, research and development; meeting our climate change and energy objectives; improving education levels; and promoting social inclusion in particular through the reduction of poverty." In the words of EU leaders, the latter will consist of "promoting social inclusion, in particular through the reduction of poverty, by aiming to lift at least 20 million people out of the risk of poverty and exclusion". EU leaders have decided that "progress towards the headline targets will be regularly reviewed" (European Council, 2010). See also Introduction and Chapter 5 in Atkinson and Marlier (2010).

[18] For a detailed discussion of targets, see: Marlier *et al.*, 2007, Sections 6.2-6.4. See also chapter by Walker in the present volume.

In order to boost political commitment and mutual learning, we believe that countries should set their (sub-)national targets in a transparent way and in a dialogue with the European Commission, and that the SPC should discuss these. Certainly, if the targets are developed on the basis we have outlined above, there is likely to be much greater public and political commitment to them. This is especially important given that the time frame is up to ten years (i.e. until 2020) and during that time governments will almost inevitably change. If the targets have been set as the result of a robust, rigorous and transparent process then there is a much greater chance that any incoming government will also be committed to achieving them.

10.3.2 Benchmarking, monitoring and evaluation

A major challenge that will need to be given particular attention in the post-2010 arrangements is to make rigorous benchmarking, monitoring and evaluation a central and visible feature of the EU process at EU, national and sub-national levels. This will require the following:

- An exploration by the European Commission and Member States of ways of making the EU social objectives more visible, measurable and tangible at EU level. Apart from the EU and (sub-)national targets discussed above, which have a key role to play in this respect, this could for instance include a more rigorous, intensive and transparent use of the full set of commonly agreed indicators underpinning EU coordination in the social field (and not just the 3 indicators on which the new EU social inclusion target is based). This could also involve the commitment of all Member States to set the goal of improving their performance on a set of commonly agreed indicators covering each relevant social protection and social inclusion policy domain (i.e. social inclusion, pensions and healthcare and long-term care).[19]

- Both a regular and thorough monitoring of and reporting on progress towards the EU and national targets and towards the improved performances on the agreed set of EU indicators, summarised in an annual report to the Spring European Council, to the European Parliament as well as to national and possible sub-national parliaments (as part of the annual *Joint*

---

[19] Marlier *et al.* (2007) identify four respects in which the commonly agreed indicators could be used more intensively in the Social OMC. They also suggest (page 155) that the EU portfolio of indicators could be complemented with a "background statistic" based on a common income threshold of 60% of the EU-wide median which could be an important way of addressing the key issue of social cohesion/ convergence across the Union.

Report on Social Protection and Social Inclusion; see also Section 10.3.7 below).

• A much more rigorous approach not only to monitoring but also to evaluation, with an increased focus on results. This should involve: more systematic use by Member States of the common indicators in their national monitoring and analytical frameworks in order to improve mutual learning (see Marlier *et al.*, 2007, Section 2.7, pages 48-53); boosting statistical and analytical capacity at EU, national and sub-national levels; promoting the use of social impact assessments in all relevant policy domains; putting in place formal arrangements in all Member States for genuinely involving civil society organisations and independent experts in monitoring and assessing social inclusion policies on an ongoing basis.

In the light of this strengthened monitoring and evaluation process, the European Commission and the SPC, as the bodies in charge of implementing the EU coordination and cooperation in the social field, should, as necessary, make clear recommendations to each Member State on actions it needs to take if it is to achieve the agreed national and EU targets. These would then be endorsed by the EU Council of Ministers.[20]

---

[20] Because of the direct link with the Employment Guidelines (through the Integrated Guideline 10), there is now a stronger legal basis for monitoring Member States' performance in relation to social protection and social inclusion issues and, when necessary, for the European Commission to issue recommendations to Member States for improvements to their policies. Independent of these new possibilities, it is important to mention that while the Treaty does not explicitly foresee the possibility of the European Commission issuing recommendations, it also does not prevent the Commission from doing so through "soft law agreements". For instance, Article 5 of the Treaty, as well as providing for the coordination of economic and employment policies, says that "The Union may take initiatives to ensure coordination of Member States' social policies". And Article 160, in outlining the role of the SPC includes among its tasks "to prepare reports, formulate opinions or undertake other work within its fields of competence, at the request of either the Council or the Commission or on its own initiative". The 2008 European Commission Communication on reinforcing the Social OMC already suggested that "The subjects that are part of the OMC could be further consolidated by formalising convergence of views whenever it arises. The Commission will contribute to this by making, where appropriate, use of Recommendations based on Article 211 of the Treaty, setting out common principles, providing a basis for monitoring and peer review." (European Commission, 2008a) In fact, a precedent for this exists within the Social OMC with the Commission's 2008 Recommendation on Active Inclusion (European Commission, 2008b).

10.3.3 Social inclusion in the Europe 2020 Integrated Guidelines for growth and jobs

The overall political decision to make social inclusion a key EU priority and, in this context, to set a quantified outcome target in relation to poverty and social exclusion at EU level is one (important) part of the jigsaw. The arrangements for implementation are also critical. On 27 April 2010, the European Commission published its proposals for *Integrated Guidelines* to deliver on the Europe 2020 Strategy (European Commission, 2010b). Ten Guidelines were proposed, under two distinct legal bases: six Economic and four Employment Guidelines. A Guideline on "Promoting social inclusion and combating poverty", which sets out policies to reach the EU headline target on social inclusion, has been included under the Employment Guidelines (Guideline No. 10). (A brief presentation of the final set of ten Guidelines as agreed later on in 2010 by the EU Council of Ministers as well as the final wording of Guideline 10 and some important accompanying "recitals" is provided in the opening chapter.)

The Guideline is drawn in a reasonably broad manner, reflecting the main strands of the existing Social OMC and, importantly, stressing the importance of access to high quality, affordable and sustainable services and the key role of social protection systems, including pensions and access to healthcare. It thus provides an important basis for building on key elements of the existing Social OMC.

Other parts of the Employment Guidelines also have a potentially important role to play in promoting greater social inclusion. In particular, Guideline No. 7 (*Increasing labour market participation of women and men, reducing structural unemployment and promoting job quality*) emphasises that flexicurity should be underpinned by an effective active inclusion approach. It stresses the important role to be played by employment services and adequate social security in supporting those at risk of unemployment. It highlights the need to fight in-work poverty and to counter labour market segmentation. The need to reach those furthest away from the labour market is also stressed.

Guideline No. 9 (*Improving the quality and performance of education and training systems at all levels and increasing participation in tertiary* or equivalent *education*) is also very relevant from a social inclusion perspective, particularly the requirement that Member States should take all necessary steps to prevent early school leaving. Tackling child poverty and exclusion and addressing the intergenerational inheritance of poverty and social exclusion will be key to making progress in this area.

In spite of the positive aspects of the Employment Guidelines, these have attracted some criticism from organisations concerned to strengthen the EU's focus on poverty and social exclusion. For instance, EAPN has stated that "poverty and social exclusion risk remaining at the margins of EU cooperation" and called for: "A better integration of inclusion and social cohesion objectives across all the Integrated Guidelines. The separation of the 'social inclusion and combating poverty Guideline' from the Employment Guidelines to guarantee that actions on social inclusion and tackling poverty are not limited to employment related measures. Explicit reference in the 'Guideline on social inclusion and combating poverty' to ensure access to rights, resources and services in line with the already-agreed common objectives of the Social OMC." (EAPN 2010a; see also EAPN 2010)

A directly related point is an "institutional" one. This is the pivotal role that the SPC should play in monitoring progress towards the EU objectives for social protection and social inclusion (including of course the new EU target on social inclusion) and in monitoring the implementation of Guideline 10 and, indeed, the social dimensions of the other Guidelines. This role would be fully in line with the spirit of Article 160 of the EU Treaty, which outlines the role of the SPC. Encouragingly, the Integrated Guidelines have moved in this direction as Recital 19 highlights that "the Employment Committee and the Social Protection Committee should monitor progress in relation to the employment and social aspects of the Employment Guidelines, in line with their respective Treaty-based mandates. This should in particular build on the activities of the open method of coordination in the fields of employment and of social protection and social inclusion. In addition the Employment Committee should maintain close contact with other relevant Council preparatory instances, including in the field of education." (EU Council of Ministers, 2010a)

10.3.4 Social protection and social inclusion strategies

To ensure that Member States develop a strategic, comprehensive and coherent approach to translating the EU's social protection and social inclusion objectives into national policies, we consider it essential that they put in place effective national action plans and that they report on these on a regular basis. Although, as we highlighted earlier, the development of NAPs/inclusion (and subsequently National Strategy Reports on Social Protection and Social Inclusion (NSRSPSIs)) has been very uneven across the EU, they have been the heart of the Social OMC and have been very important in encouraging a more strategic approach to issues of poverty and social exclusion. In particular, these national reports are essential because:

- they provide the best opportunity for ensuring the active involvement of a wide range of stakeholders in the EU coordination and cooperation in the social field, particularly those from local level. Indeed, the growing trend to develop regional and local plans to underpin national plans is the best way of addressing one of the key weaknesses in the EU process to date – i.e., the limited involvement of local and regional governments who, in many Member States, play a key role in delivering policies to promote greater inclusion;

- they are a way of ensuring that EU social objectives are not seen as just some part of a narrow and remote intergovernmental process but are a dynamic part of connecting the EU better to its citizens and building a real Social EU involving the active participation of all actors;

- they are essential to ensure that Member States do not just adopt targets to reduce poverty and social exclusion in line with the overall Europe 2020 target but that they underpin these targets with a comprehensive and strategic social inclusion approach. They are thus a means of ensuring that the necessary arrangements are in place not just to temporarily reduce poverty and social exclusion but to stop them recurring in the longer term;

- they also are a way of ensuring that national (Europe 2020) targets are not dealt with in isolation from developing a strong and comprehensive approach to achieving overall social protection and inclusion objectives;

- they provide a rich source of ideas and lessons which is essential to inform and deepen mutual learning between Member States and to promote the understanding of key concepts and key policies;

- they are an important way of identifying common issues that are present or emerging in a group of Member States and that then merit more in depth examination at EU level;

- they are an important way of ensuring a broad approach which links social protection and social inclusion issues in a mutually reinforcing way.

In our view, there are three ways that such national reports might be achieved in the context of *Europe 2020*.

Option 1

The first option is that the existing NSRSPSIs could be continued and enhanced. As regards the social inclusion strand, this will require a better integration of the NAPs/inclusion into national (and also, where relevant, into sub-national) policy-making processes and the development of closer links with national (and possible sub-national) parliaments. This might involve reassessing together with Member States and relevant stakeholders, the timing and structure of the NSRSPSIs cycle so that it becomes easier for countries to use them as strategic planning opportunities to strengthen policies and not just as a means of reporting to the EU on existing and planned policies. Moving from a three to five year cycle could help in this regard. A major advantage of this solution is that it will help to ensure that Member States adopt and report on comprehensive approaches to promoting social inclusion and tackling poverty and social exclusion that are better integrated into their national policy-making systems. A possible disadvantage of continuing with the NSRSPSIs is that unless other strong cross-cutting mechanisms are put in place, the links between the social dimension and the other strands of Europe 2020 (especially the economic and employment ones) may remain weak and lessen the chances of effective synergies ("feeding in" and "feeding out"; see above). To address this problem it would then be important to create formal mechanisms for examining and reporting on how Member States are ensuring synergies between their NSRSPSIs and National Reform Programmes (NRPs).

Option 2

The second option is for the social protection and social inclusion dimension to become a distinct chapter of Member States' NRPs. The basis for this exists with the ambitious Guideline 10, which largely encompasses the range of issues currently addressed by the NSRSPSIs, and also with the potentially very important "Horizontal Social Clause" included in the Lisbon Treaty (see below, Section 10.3.5). The advantage of this option could be to make it easier to integrate the social dimension with the employment and economic strands of the Europe 2020 process. Thus there would be the possibility of achieving stronger synergies between the processes. In addition, by being linked with the Employment Guidelines, there should be a stronger legal basis for monitoring Member States' performance in relation to social protection and social inclusion issues and, when necessary, the European Commission should be in a position to issue recommendations to Member States for improvements to their policies. However, from a social perspective there is also a serious risk with this option, which is that the social dimension could become an afterthought tagged on to the employment dimension. Furthermore, it could lead to a very narrow approach to social inclusion issues that only focuses on increasing access to employment without addressing the real problems faced by those outside the labour market or very distant from it. If, as is likely to be the case, this option is pursued it will be essential that several safeguards are put in place. In particular, as already noted above, the role of the SPC in monitoring and reporting on the social dimension should be incorporated into the Employment Guidelines. The new EPAP (see below, Section 10.3.6) should also be given a clear role in monitoring and reporting on how the social dimension, including the issue of in-work poverty and labour market segmentation[21], is being addressed in Member States' NRPs.

Option 3

The third option is a combination of option 2 (with the necessary safeguards put in place) and option 1. Here, the "social" chapter of the NRPs would be based on quality NSRSPSIs covering in a coherent way social protection and social inclusion. NRPs could then include five chapters: four "thematic" chapters addressing objectives and policies in the fields of economy, employment, social protection and social inclusion, and environment and an "overarching" chapter aimed at highlighting the interdependence and mutually reinforcing nature of the four sets of thematic objectives and policies. While we recognise that this option is more ambitious than the other two we consider that it is the one that is most likely to strengthen the EU's social dimension and lead to a really decisive reduction in poverty and social exclusion.

10.3.5 The Lisbon Treaty's "Horizontal Social Clause"

Strengthening EU cooperation and coordination in the social field is even more important and urgent because of the increased status given to social issues in the Lisbon Treaty, which came into force on 1 December 2009. Of particular significance, is Article 9 which states that "In defining and implementing its policies and activities, the Union shall take into account requirements linked to the promotion of a high level of employment, the guarantee of adequate social protection, the fight against social exclusion, and a high level of education, training and protection of human health" (European Union, 2009). A major political and legal challenge will now be to give a concrete meaning to this new social clause. In the first instance, it is to be hoped that this new clause in the EU's objectives will provide a more solid basis for requiring the EU, that is *both* the European Commission and EU Member States, to mainstream the EU's social objectives into policy-making and, for this to be effective, to systematically carry out social impact assessments of all relevant policies (see also Section 10.3.6 below). Over time, it might

---

[21]   For information on in-work poverty and labour market segmentation in the EU, see Frazer and Marlier (2010b).

also be taken into account in decisions of the EU Court of Justice leading to a stronger social dimension to the Court's decisions. This important Treaty provision is usefully referred to in the Employment Guidelines ("whereas No 2"); as it is also relevant for economic policies, this reference should also be included in the preamble of the final set of the economic policies Guidelines.

10.3.6 The European Platform Against Poverty (EPAP)

The strengthening of the social dimension of the EU, and in particular the delivery of the EU's new social inclusion target will depend significantly on how the *European Platform Against Poverty* (EPAP), one of the 7 flagship initiatives which the European Commission has proposed in the context of the implementation of Europe 2020, is developed. It is still unclear what shape this Platform will take and how it will relate to and strengthen the existing Social OMC. This may only be clarified towards the end of 2010 when the Commission is likely to publish its proposals on the EPAP.

In our view, the dual challenge to be met is to propose arrangements that can contribute not only to strengthening the future EU cooperation and coordination in the field of social protection and social inclusion but also to bringing together the patchwork of different strands that currently make up Social EU to ensure that they are better coordinated, more consistent and mutually reinforcing. For this, the EPAP must become the visible symbol of this renewed Social EU. It has to play a central role in ensuring that all other strands of EU policy-making (e.g. economic, competition, education, migration, health, innovation and environmental policies) contribute to achieving the EU's social goals, including the EU target on social inclusion.

This will require explicit arrangements to better link the future EU social process (i.e., EPAP, renewed Social OMC...) with other relevant EU processes (growth, jobs, environment, education...) so that they are mutually reinforcing. In this regard, and in line with the Lisbon Treaty's "Horizontal Social Clause", a key priority will be to mainstream issues of adequate social protection, the fight against poverty and social exclusion, and also children's rights across all relevant EU policy areas and programmes (including the Structural Funds; see Section 10.3.9 below) in particular through a more systematic application of the required social impact assessments (both *ex ante* and *ex post*) as part of the Commission's integrated impact assessment process.[22] The EPAP should play a central role in monitoring and reporting on the implemen-

---

[22] More information on the European Commission's impact assessment process can be found at http://ec.europa.eu/governance/better_regulation/impact_en. htm.

tation of the social impact assessment process and on the extent to which the other strands of Europe 2020 are contributing to the goal of reducing poverty and social exclusion. If they are not, it should have the power to make recommendations as to how they could contribute better.[23]

Whatever form the EPAP does eventually take, it will be important to ensure that sufficient resources, particularly in terms of staff, are allocated to support its implementation and the implementation of the Social OMC.

10.3.7 A thematic approach

We believe that much of the future EU coordination and cooperation in the social field should be concentrated around the key thematic issues that have emerged from the Social OMC. This is especially the case for the social inclusion strand where active inclusion, child poverty and well-being, housing exclusion and homelessness, poverty and social exclusion experienced by migrants and ethnic minorities have become key themes.[24] However, a similar approach might also be adopted in relation to pensions and healthcare and long-term care as appropriate.

Gender equality and non-discrimination should be clear cross-cutting aspects of each issue. The work on each theme should be based on clear objectives and multi-annual work programmes. Member States should be encouraged to make these themes key parts of their social protection and social inclusion strategies (see Section 10.3.4). Annual reports on

---

[23] It is important to systematically develop poverty and social exclusion impact assessments (both *ex ante* and *ex post*) for all relevant policies and not only those specifically aimed at increasing social inclusion, so that policy proposals all take into account the potential (positive or negative) impact they may have on poverty and social exclusion. Existing policies should also regularly be reviewed for their impact on poverty and social exclusion. The ultimate goal should be to systematically work at identifying possible ways (links/ synergies) of adjusting policies to strengthen their contribution to promoting social inclusion. The European Commission, in cooperation with Member States, should develop and promote the methodology for social impact assessments at (sub-) national levels. For more on social impact assessment, see chapter by Kühnemund in the present volume.

[24] In this regard, it is interesting to note that at the end of the Conference *Roadmap for a Recommendation on Child Poverty and Child Well-Being*, organised by the Belgian Presidency of the Council of the EU on 2-3 September 2010, the Trio of the European Presidency consisting of Spain, Belgium and Hungary declared itself in favour of the adoption of a European Commission Recommendation on child poverty and well-being and called for the fight against child poverty and the promotion of child well-being to be included as key priorities of the EPAP. The full declaration, including a call for the adoption of quantified sub-targets for the reduction of child poverty and social exclusion, is available on the Belgium EU Presidency web site at: http://www.eutrio.be/.

progress on each key issue should be incorporated into the Joint Report on Social Protection and Social Inclusion along the lines described in Section 4.3.2. Where appropriate data are available (e.g. child poverty and social exclusion) annual scoreboards should be considered. Building on the successful outcomes of two such experiences in recent years (Social Protection Committee, 2008 and 2009), "Task-Forces" or less structured working groups should be established as appropriate within the SPC and EPAP to carry forward work on particular issues. In progressing work on these issues, greater use could be made of existing instruments such as European Commission Recommendations and EU Framework Directives.[25]

10.3.8 Guidelines on key governance issues

The EPAP could usefully contribute to supporting Member States to strengthen their governance arrangements in relation to social protection and social inclusion issues. On key governance issues where a considerable body of knowledge and good practice has been developed, the Commission together with the SPC would agree guidelines for Member States to help them to strengthen their practice. These could then become part of the EPAP *acquis* and be used as part of the monitoring and reporting process. Four priority areas for developing such guidelines could be: mainstreaming of the social objectives and use of social impact assessments; horizontal coordination across policy areas; preparation of effective regional and local action plans on social inclusion; and minimum standards on the effective involvement of stakeholders (including people experiencing poverty) in all phases of the preparation, implementation, evaluation and monitoring of social inclusion policies.

10.3.9 Better linking EU social objectives and EU Structural Funds

There should be much closer alignment between the EU's and Member States' social objectives and the use of EU Structural Funds. In this context, the use of Structural Funds should in particular become a key part of Member States' social inclusion strategies. In order to make certain that this has a real impact it will be important to ensure that there is a link between measured performance (i.e. the impact on social inclusion) and the allocation of EU funds. This relation works in both directions. The allocation of funds may affect country performance and policy may develop towards linking allocations to measured perform-

---

[25] The European Commission Recommendation on active inclusion provides a good example of how work can be advanced with enhanced status and urgency through the use of such instruments.

ance. In relation to the use of Structural Funds for social purposes a very recent positive development is the May 2010 EU decision to extend the possibilities for the European Regional Development Fund (ERDF) to be used for supporting housing interventions in favour of marginalised communities.[26] This could play an important role in increasing resources for initiatives in this field.[27]

10.3.10 Exchange, learning and communication

Exchange and learning should be enhanced as an integral element in the EU cooperation and coordination in the social field, *inter alia* by resourcing an increased range of opportunities for exchange and learning under the 2007-2013 *Community Programme for Employment and Social Solidarity (PROGRESS)*. The process of policy learning and exchange of good practices should be strengthened with more systematic clustering of activities (e.g. studies, peer reviews, exchange projects, EU funded networks) around specific themes. Every effort should also be made to promote a wider and more systematic involvement of regional and local actors (policy-makers, stakeholders and civil society) in the process. More effective and widespread dissemination of results will be necessary. It is encouraging that the Integrated Guidelines have moved in this direction. Recital 16 highlights that when designing and implementing their NRPs "Member States should ensure effective governance of employment policy. While these Guidelines are addressed to Member States, the Europe 2020 Strategy should, as appropriate, be implemented, monitored and evaluated in partnership with all national, regional and local authorities, closely associating parliaments, as well as social partners and representatives of civil society, who shall contribute to the elaboration of NRPs, to their implementation and to the overall communication on the strategy." (EU Council of Ministers, 2010a)

10.4 Conclusions

In this chapter, we have documented and analysed the EU's current approach to promoting social inclusion and combating poverty and social exclusion through cooperation and coordination on social inclu-

---

[26] For more detail see the European Commission's proposals for an amending regulation (European Commission, 2009a) and Regulation (EU) No. 437/2010 of the European Parliament and of the Council which was adopted on 19 May 2010.

[27] Barca (2009) argues for a reformed cohesion policy for the EU and that therefore a new combination of the social and territorial agendas is required. He suggests that "The social agenda needs to be 'territorialised', the territorial agenda 'socialised'. The place-based approach to social inclusion should be the result of these two shifts." (page 36). See also chapter by Jouen in the present volume.

sion and social protection (including pensions and healthcare and long-term care). Our purpose has been three-fold. First, to describe briefly the functioning of the Social OMC as it has developed since it was launched (back in 2000): its main elements, the key policy areas it has focused on and its governance and institutional arrangements. Secondly, to carry out a systematic analysis of the Social OMC experience, high-lighting its strengths and weaknesses, with a particular emphasis on the period since 2006. Thirdly, on the basis of this critical assessment, to suggest concrete proposals for building a stronger EU social process in the future and for bringing together the patchwork of different strands that currently makes up Social EU so as to ensure that they are better coordinated, more consistent and mutually reinforcing. We hope that these proposals will contribute to the complex challenge of developing a truly social Europe 2020 and thereby to a more effective approach to combating poverty and social exclusion.

References

Atkinson, A.B. and Marlier, E. (editors) (2010), *Income and living conditions in Europe*, Luxembourg: Office for Official Publications of the European Communities (OPOCE).

Atkinson, T., Cantillon, B., Marlier, E. and Nolan, B. (2002), *Social Indicators: The EU and Social Inclusion*, Oxford: Oxford University Press.

Barca, F. (2009), *An agenda for a reformed cohesion policy: A place-based approach to meeting European Union challenges and expectations*, Independent Report prepared at the request of Danuta Hübner, Commissioner for Regional Policy, Brussels: European Commission. Available at: http://ec.europa.eu/regional_policy/policy/future/pdf/report_barca_v0306.pdf.

Confederation of Family Organisations in the European Union (COFACE) (2010), *COFACE Responses to the European Commission public consultation on the future EU 2020 Strategy*, Brussels: COFACE. Available at: http://coface-eu.org/en/upload/consultations/COFACEresponse-EU2020 en.pdf.

Crepaldi, C., Barbieri, D., Boccagni, P., Naaf, S. and Pesce, F. (2010), *EU Cooperation in the Field of Social Inclusion: Final Report*, Brussels: European Parliament. Available at: http://www.europarl.it/ressource/static/ files/EU_cooperation_social_exclusion.pdf.

EU Council of Ministers (2010), *2010 Joint Report on Social Protection and Social Inclusion*, Brussels: EU Council of Ministers.

EU Council of Ministers (2010a), *Council Decision on guidelines for the employment policies of the Member States*, Document 14338/10 dated 12 October 2010, Brussels: EU Council of Ministers.

Eurochild (2010), *Eurochild response to the European Commission Consultation on the future "EU2020" Strategy*, Brussels: Eurochild. Available at: http://www.eurochild.org/fileadmin/user_upload/Info%20Flash/

2010/02.2010/Eurochild_response_to_EC_consultation_on_future_EU2020_s trategy_Final_Jan10.pdf.

European Anti-Poverty Network (EAPN) (2010), *EAPN proposals for New Integrated Guidelines for Europe 2020*, Brussels: EAPN.

European Anti-Poverty Network (EAPN) (2010a), *Actions to combat Poverty and to foster Social Inclusion risk remaining at the margins of EU Cooperation*, Press Release, 30th April 2010, Brussels: EAPN.

European Anti-Poverty Network (EAPN) (2010b), *EAPN Proposals on the 'European Platform against Poverty'*, Brussels: EAPN. Available at: http://www.eapn.org/images/stories/docs/EAPN-position-papers-and-reports/ eapn-flagship-platform-against-poverty-proposals-en.pdf.

European Anti-Poverty Network (EAPN) (2009), *A Europe we can trust: Proposals on a new EU post-2010 strategy*, Brussels: EAPN.

European Anti-Poverty Network (EAPN) (2009a), *Small Steps – Big Changes*, Brussels: EAPN.

European Anti-Poverty Network Ireland and European Anti-Poverty Network (EAPN) (2010), *Building Social Europe*, Dublin: EAPN Ireland. Available at: http://www.eapn.ie/eapn/wp-content/uploads/2010/06/EAPN-Ireland-Feb ruary-Conference-Report.pdf.

European Commission (2010), *Europe 2020: A strategy for smart, sustainable and inclusive growth*, Communication COM(2010) 2020, Brussels: European Commission. Available at: http://ec.europa.eu/eu2020/pdf/COMPLET %20EN%20BARROSO%20%20%20007%20-%20Europe%202020%20- %20EN%20version.pdf.

European Commission (2010a), *Lisbon Strategy: Evaluation Document*, Commission Staff Working Document SEC(2010) 114 final, Brussels: European Commission. Available at: http://register.consilium.europa.eu/pdf/ en/10/st06/st06037.en10.pdf.

European Commission (2010b), *Proposal for a Council Decision on guidelines for the employment policies of the Member States Part II of the Europe 2020 Integrated Guidelines*, Communication COM(2010) 193/3, European Commission, Brussels: European Commission. Available at: http://ec.europa. eu/eu2020/pdf/proposition_en.pdf.

European Commission (2009), *Portfolio of indicators for the monitoring of the European strategy for social protection and social inclusion – 2009 update*, Brussels: European Commission. Available at: http://ec.europa.eu/social/ main.jsp?catId=756&langId=en.

European Commission (2009a), *Proposal for a Regulation (EC) No. .../2009 of the European Parliament and of the Council amending Regulation (EC) No. 1080/2006 on the European Regional Development Fund as regards the eligibility of housing interventions in favour of marginalised communities*, Communication COM(2009) 382 final, Brussels: European Commission.

European Commission (2008), *A renewed commitment to social Europe: Reinforcing the Open Method of Coordination for Social Protection and*

Social Inclusion, Communication COM(2008) 418 final, Brussels: European Commission.

European Commission (2008a), *A renewed commitment to social Europe: Reinforcing the Open Method of Coordination for Social Protection and Social Inclusion: Impact assessment*, Staff Working Document SEC(2008) 2169, Brussels: European Commission.

European Commission (2008b), *Commission Recommendation on the active inclusion of people excluded from the labour market*, Communication COM(2008) 639 final, Brussels: European Commission.

European Council (2010), *European Council 17 June 2010: Conclusions*, Brussels: European Council.

European Social Network (2010), *EU2020: Building a more Caring and Inclusive Europe. A contribution to the debate on the future of the social OMC beyond 2010*, Brighton: European Social Network. Available at: http://www.esn-eu.org/publications-and-statements/index.htm.

European Union (2009), *Consolidated Version of the Treaty of Lisbon*, Brussels: European Union. Available at: http://www.consilium.europa.eu /showPage. aspx?id=1296&lang=en.

FEANTSA (2010), *Europe 2020: Time for an EU Homelessness Strategy. FEANTSA response to the Europe 2020 Strategy*, Brussels: FEANTSA. Available at: http://feantsa.horus.be/files/freshstart/EUDocs/Social_ Inclusion/2010/23062010_feantsa_europe2020_en.pdf.

Frazer, H. (2010), "Social inclusion and poverty policies in the EU", *Spanish Review of the Third Sector*, No. 15, Madrid: Luis Vives Foundation.

Frazer, H. and Marlier, E. (2010), "Social inclusion in the European Union: Where are we and where are we going?", in *Development and Transition 15*, March 2010, Bratislava: United Nations Development Programme, Slovakia. Available at: http://www.developmentandtransition.net/.

Frazer, H. and Marlier, E. (2010a), "The EU's approach to combating poverty and social exclusion: Ensuring a stronger approach in the future by learning from the strengths and weaknesses of the current approach", *Kurswechsel*, 3: 34-51.

Frazer, H. and Marlier, E. (2010b), *In-work poverty and labour market segmentation in the EU: Key lessons*, EU Network of Independent Experts on Social Inclusion, Brussels: European Commission.

Frazer, H. and Marlier, E. (2009), Assessment of the extent of synergies between growth and jobs policies and social inclusion policies across the EU as evidenced by the 2008-2010 National Reform Programmes: Key lessons, EU Network of Independent Experts on Social Inclusion, Brussels: European Commission. Available at: http://www.peer-review-social-inclusion.eu/ network-of-independent-experts/2008/second-semester-2008.

Frazer, H. and Marlier, E. (2008), *Building a stronger EU Social Inclusion Process: Analysis and recommendations of the EU Network of independent national experts on social inclusion*, Brussels: European Commission.

Available at: http://www.peer-review-social-inclusion.eu/network-of-independent-experts/2008/first-semester-2008.

Frazer, H., Marlier E. and Nicaise, I. (2010), *A social inclusion roadmap for Europe 2020*, Antwerp/Apeldoorn: Garant.

Fusco, A., Guio, A.-C. and Marlier, E. (2010), "Characterising the income poor and the materially deprived in European countries", in A.B. Atkinson and E. Marlier (editors) *Income and Living Conditions in Europe*, Luxembourg: OPOCE.

Guio, A.-C. (2009), *What can be learned from deprivation indicators in Europe?*, Luxembourg: OPOCE. Available at: http://epp.eurostat.ec.europa.eu/cache/ITY_OFFPUB/KS-RA-09-007/EN/KS-RA-09-007-EN.PDF.

Harvey, B. (2008), *EAPN Structural Funds Manual 2009-2011*, Brussels: EAPN. Available at: http://www.eapncr.org/napsi/strukturalni_fondy/Manual%20PDF_en.pdf.

Marlier, E., Atkinson, A.B., Cantillon, B. and Nolan, B. (2007), *The EU and Social Inclusion: Facing the challenges*, Bristol: The Policy Press.

Platform of European Social NGOs (2009), *5 recommendations for an effective Open Method of Coordination on social protection and social inclusion*, Brussels: Social Platform. Available at: http://cms.horus.be/files/99907/MediaArchive/Policies/Social_Inclusion/20090929_SP%20Social%20OMC_final.pdf.

Social Protection Committee (2009), *Growth, Jobs and Social Progress in the EU: A contribution to the evaluation of the social dimension of the Lisbon Strategy*, Brussels: European Commission. Available at: http://ec.europa.eu/social/BlobServlet?docId=3898&langId=en.

Social Protection Committee (2008), *Child Poverty and Well-Being in the EU: Current status and way forward*, Luxembourg: OPOCE. Available at: http://ec.europa.eu/social/main.jsp?catId=751&langId=en&pubId=74&type=2&furtherPubs=yes.

Spring Alliance (2009), *Manifesto*, Brussels: Spring Alliance. Available at: http://www.springalliance.eu/manifesto.

Vandenbroucke, F. (2002), *The EU and Social Protection: What should the European Convention propose?*, Paper presented at the Max Planck Institute for the Study of Societies, Cologne, 17 June.

Zeitlin, J. (2007), *The Open Method of Coordination and the Governance of the Lisbon Strategy*, University of Wisconsin-Madison EUSA conference. Available at: http://aei.pitt.edu/8032/01/zeitlin-j-06e.pdf.

11. Towards a Stronger OMC in a More Social Europe 2020:

A New Governance Architecture for EU Policy Coordination

Jonathan ZEITLIN[1]

11.1 Introduction

The Lisbon Strategy, which was launched by the European Council in March 2000 as a medium-term framework for EU socio-economic policy coordination, formally elapsed in June 2010 with the adoption by the European Council of the new Europe 2020 Strategy. Almost from the outset, the Lisbon Strategy was the subject of sharply contrasting interpretations, while its governance architecture was formally or informally revised several times. This chapter examines and contributes to the ongoing debate about the future of the Europe 2020 Strategy and the appropriate governance architecture for EU policy coordination.

The chapter is divided into two main parts. The first part looks backward at the governance of the Lisbon Strategy since March 2000, providing a critical overview of the three principal phases of its development. The second part looks forward, examining the emerging governance architecture for EU policy coordination after 2010. The argument proceeds in three main steps. The first analyses the reformed governance architecture of Europe 2020, drawing attention to its reinforced social dimension as well as to serious risks to the broader EU social policy coordination and monitoring capacities developed over the past decade arising from ambiguities in the institutional design of the new Strategy. The second step advances a series of proposals to counteract these risks by incorporating into the governance architecture of Europe 2020 key components of the Social Open Method of Coordination (OMC), notably the common objectives, commonly agreed EU indicators, EU monitoring, peer review, and evaluation of national

---

[1] Earlier versions of the first part of this chapter were published in Committee of the Regions (2009) and *La Rivista delle Politiche Sociali/ Italian Journal of Social Policy* (2009). Address for correspondence: j.h.zeitlin@uva.nl.

social protection and social inclusion strategies. The final step in the argument proposes a series of reflexive reforms aimed at overcoming weaknesses identified within the OMC on Social Protection and Social Inclusion (Social OMC) itself, with a particular focus on reinforcing mutual learning and enhancing stakeholder participation.

11.2. The Governance of the Lisbon Strategy (2000-2010): A Critical Overview[2]

11.2.1 Lisbon I (2000-2005)

As is well known, the original Lisbon Strategy laid out a broad, ambitious agenda aimed at making the EU by 2010 "the most dynamic and competitive knowledge-based economy in the world, capable of sustainable economic growth with more and better jobs and greater social cohesion". This inclusive agenda was based on the concept of a "socio-economic policy triangle", with equal weight for more and better jobs and social cohesion alongside economic growth and competitiveness as EU objectives. In 2001, under the Swedish Presidency, environmental sustainability was added as a fourth "pillar" or core strategic objective.

To advance this ambitious agenda, the Lisbon Strategy inaugurated a new approach to EU governance, the OMC, based on iterative benchmarking of national progress towards common EU objectives and organised mutual learning. Extended across an ever broader set of policy fields in the wake of the Lisbon Summit, the OMC appeared for a time to have become the EU governance instrument of choice in complex, domestically sensitive areas where Member State diversity precludes harmonisation and where strategic uncertainty encourages mutual learning at the national as well as EU level (Zeitlin, 2005). But the OMC was never intended to serve as the sole governance instrument for the Lisbon Strategy: it was always supposed to be combined with other EU policy tools, including legislation, social dialogue, Community Action Programmes, and the structural funds.

Lisbon I (2000-2005) was widely criticised by the 2004-2005 midterm review for its lack of strategic focus and multiplication of objectives, targets and coordination processes. The OMC in particular was harshly criticised by the Kok Report and the incoming Barroso Commission for failing to deliver Member State commitment to the implementation of agreed reforms needed to reach the Lisbon targets (Kok, 2004; European Commission, 2005). Some of these criticisms of Lisbon I were arguably justified, notably the weakness of the overarching

---

[2] For fuller analysis and documentation, see Zeitlin (2007, 2008).

governance architecture for integrating and reconciling overlapping sectoral policy coordination processes (coordination of coordination). But other criticisms were much less justified, since the review process ignored much of the available evaluation evidence, both official and academic, which suggested that the OMC should be considered a qualified success in some key policy fields, while in others no definitive assessment was possible since the method had not yet been systematically implemented.

The national influence and effectiveness of OMC processes is notoriously difficult to assess, not only because of their variety, complexity, and relative newness, but also because of the methodological problems involved in disentangling the independent causal impact of an iterative policy-making process based on collaboration between EU institutions and Member State governments without legally binding sanctions.[3] Yet there is now a substantial body of empirical research on the operations of the OMC at national and sub-national levels, drawing on a wide range of official and unofficial sources. Most of this research focuses on employment, social inclusion, and social protection as the oldest, most fully developed, and best institutionalised OMC processes.[4]

Although the findings of this research remain controversial and subject to multiple interpretations, my reading of the available evidence supports the view that the OMC in these policy fields should be considered a qualified success in a number of important respects.[5] The first of these concerns substantive policy change. Thus, these OMC processes have helped to raise the salience and ambition of national employment and social inclusion policies in many Member States. They have contributed to changes in national policy thinking (cognitive shifts) by incorporating EU concepts and categories (such as activation, prevention, lifelong learning, gender mainstreaming, social impact assessment, and social inclusion) into domestic debates, exposing policy-makers to new approaches, and pressing them to reconsider long-established but increasingly counterproductive policies (such as early retirement). These OMC processes have likewise contributed to changes in national policy agendas (political shifts) by putting new issues on the domestic agenda and/or raising their relative salience (such as activation, pension reform, childcare provision, gender equality, child poverty and well-being, and integration of immigrants). There is also evidence from both

---

[3] For a fuller discussion of these methodological problems, see Zeitlin (2005a, pages 26-27; 2009, pages 214-217).

[4] For synthetic overviews, see Zeitlin and Pochet (2005); Heidenreich and Zeitlin (2009).

[5] For a fuller assessment, see Zeitlin (2005b, 2009) and chapter by Vanhercke in this volume.

official reports and interviews that OMC objectives, guidelines, targets, and recommendations have contributed to changes in specific national policies (programmatic shifts), in areas such as activation/ prevention, tax-benefit reforms, active ageing/lifelong learning, gender equality, child care, social assistance, and pension reform. Yet given the active role of Member States in shaping the development of OMC processes, their relationship to national policy-making should be understood as a two-way interaction rather than a one-way causal impact.

A second form of positive influence on the part of the OMC concerns procedural shifts in governance and policy-making arrangements. Here there is abundant evidence that the European Employment Strategy (EES) and the Social OMC have contributed in most Member States to better horizontal coordination and cross-sectoral integration of interdependent policy areas; enhanced vertical coordination between levels of governance; improved policy steering and statistical capacity; increased consultation and involvement of non-state actors (especially in social inclusion, but also to a significant extent in employment); and the development of transnational networks for participation of non-state and sub-national actors in EU policy-making. Here too, however, OMC processes are not the only cause of these shifts in governance arrangements, and the degree of involvement of non-state/ sub-national actors in particular also depends both on domestic institutional configurations and the actors' own strategies.

A third form of positive influence exerted by the OMC concerns mutual learning. Here we see a prevalence of indirect or higher-order over direct or first-order effects. Thus, for instance, there are relatively few examples of direct policy transfer, as national reforms typically draw analogic inspiration rather than detailed policy blueprints from other Member States. Even here, however, we find some surprising examples of more direct borrowing, such as the influence attributed by the UK to learning from Ireland and several northern European countries on its childcare, lone parents, indebtedness, and social inclusion policies.[6] More prominent instead has been the influence of OMC processes on the identification of common challenges and promising policy approaches at EU level (heuristic effects); statistical harmonisation and capacity building (at both EU and national levels); and their stimulus to Member States to rethink established approaches and practices, as a result of the obligation to compare national performance to that of other countries on the one hand, and the obligation to re-examine and re-evaluate national policies against their relative progress in meeting common EU objectives on the other (maieutic or reflexive effects).

---

[6] For these examples, see European Commission (2006, page 6).

Yet as empirical research shows, these OMC processes in employment and social protection/inclusion also suffered from significant weaknesses, which are discussed in more detail in the chapter by Frazer and Marlier in this volume.[7] Chief among these were a lack of openness and transparency, with bureaucratic actors playing a dominant role at both EU and national levels; weak integration into national policy-making, with National Action Plans (NAPs) serving more as reports to the EU than as operational policy steering documents; and limited bottom-up or horizontal policy learning, with few examples of upwards knowledge transfer and cross-national diffusion of innovative local practices. Yet most of these observed shortcomings arguably stemmed not from any intrinsic weaknesses of the OMC *per se*, but rather from procedural limitations of specific OMC processes. Hence a potentially fruitful strategy for improving the effectiveness of existing OMC processes would be to apply to their own procedures the key elements of the method itself: benchmarking, peer review, monitoring, evaluation, and iterative redesign. Ongoing initiatives within the EES and Social OMC over the past few years provide evidence of the practical viability of this reflexive reform strategy, such as the strengthening of mutual learning and peer review programmes on the one hand, and proposals by EU institutions and NGOs for greater openness, stakeholder participation, and "mainstreaming" of OMCs into domestic policy-making on the other.[8]

If the OMCs in employment and social protection/ inclusion may be judged a qualified success, the same cannot be said of their counterparts in fields such as innovation, enterprise promotion and information society. There the OMC has been widely blamed for Member States' lack of progress towards the R&D investment target of 3% of GDP set by the 2002 Barcelona European Council, and for the limited impact and visibility of eEurope policies. Yet OMC processes in these areas are characterised by "lite" recipes and fragmentary architectures, with no agreed NAPs, limited monitoring and reporting, little peer review, and weak mutual learning mechanisms. Hence according to an independent evaluation prepared for the European Commission by the Tavistock Institute (2005), OMC in these areas "cannot yet be said to be a success or failure", because it "simply has not been fully implemented".[9]

---

[7] See also Kröger (2009).

[8] For a fuller discussion of this reflexive reform strategy, see Zeitlin (2005b, pages 483-93). For recent policy proposals along these lines, see European Commission (2008a) and Platform of European Social NGOs (2009).

[9] For an unfavourable contrast of the institutionalisation of the OMC in R&D with that in education and training, see also Gornitzka (2006). For a more positive assessment

11.2.2 Lisbon II (2005-2008)

The Lisbon Strategy was formally relaunched in 2005, with a sharper focus on growth and jobs. The architectural core of Lisbon II was the fusion of the European Employment Guidelines (EEGs) and the Broad Economic Policy Guidelines (BEPGs) into a single set of 24 Integrated Guidelines (IGs) for Growth and Jobs, divided into separate macroeconomic, microeconomic, and employment chapters. In line with this architectural shift, the National Action Plans for Employment (NAPs/ employment) were replaced by sections within Member States' National Reform Programmes (NRPs). This relaunched, refocused Strategy was to be implemented through a new set of reform partnerships between the Commission and Member States on the one hand, and between national governments and domestic stakeholders on the other. These new reform partnerships were explicitly designed to shift the focus of the Lisbon Strategy away from "coordination through multilateral discussions between 25 Member States and the Commission, on individual policy themes (the OMC)" towards "a bilateral in depth dialogue between the Commission and Member States on a commitment based national action programme" (European Commission, 2005).

On the social side, the three "strands" of the Social OMCs (inclusion, pensions, healthcare and long-term care) were "streamlined" as from 2006 into a single overarching Social OMC, with both common ("overarching") and sector-specific objectives. According to successive European Council conclusions, the relaunched Lisbon Strategy was designed to provide "a framework where economic, employment and social policy mutually reinforce each other, ensuring that parallel progress is made on employment creation, competitiveness, and social cohesion in compliance with European values". This mutually reinforcing dynamic within the revised Lisbon Strategy was supposed to be achieved by a reciprocal relationship between the streamlined Social OMC and the IGs for Growth and Jobs at both national and EU levels, whereby the former "feeds in" to growth and employment objectives, while the latter "feed out" to advance social cohesion goals.

A central objective of the relaunched Lisbon Strategy was to close the implementation gap through better governance. But the experience of recent years (2005-2010) suggests that the revised governance architecture introduced under Lisbon II proved problematic in a number of major respects.

---

of the contribution of the OMC in R&D to mutual learning, and recommendations for improving its effectiveness in policy coordination, see European Commission (2009).

First, the integration of the EEGs with the BEPGs, the enhanced freedom for Member States to set their own priorities within the NRPs, and the concomitant disappearance of the NAPs/employment reduced the visibility of employment policy coordination at both EU and national levels. No less significantly, the revised arrangements led to greater unevenness in national employment policy reporting and a loss of EU level monitoring capacity.[10]

Second, in the absence of any specific institutional mechanisms to ensure a mutually reinforcing feedback between the social, economic and employment dimensions of the relaunched Lisbon Strategy, the practical effectiveness of such feedback remained decidedly limited, with wide variations across Member States. Only a minority of Member States included social cohesion objectives in their NRPs, most of which made relatively limited cross-reference to the Social OMC. Nor was there much evidence under Lisbon II of explicit "feeding out" from the Integrated Guidelines and NRPs to the Social OMC, for example through systematic impact assessments of the actual or prospective effects of Member States' economic and employment policies on social cohesion/inclusion outcomes (Begg and Marlier, 2007).

Third, according to a variety of independent sources, the NRP implementation process continued to lack public visibility in most Member States, while involvement of non-state and sub-national actors was often confined to formal consultation and/or information exercises, with limited opportunity to influence substantive policy direction or content. By all accounts, civil society actors, such as NGOs and voluntary associations, were much less involved in most Member States, often because of difficulties in obtaining access to consultation and coordination processes dominated by Finance or Economics ministries with whom they had little previous contact (Begg and Marlier, 2007; European Anti-Poverty Network, 2007; Begg, 2007; Committee of the Regions, 2008, 2009a).

Fourth, it proved extremely difficult to sustain the simplified focus of the revised Lisbon Strategy and the shift from multilateral policy coordination to bilateral reform dialogue between the Commission and Member States. Unsurprisingly, the European Council was unable to

---

[10] To compensate for this, the Lisbon Methodology (LIME) Working Group of the EU Economic Policy Committee (EPC) developed a Lisbon Assessment Framework (LAF) comprising a national implementation grid, labour reform database, impact assessment of key reform drivers, and macroeconomic modelling exercise. The EU Employment Committee (EMCO) has sharply criticised the capacity of this centralised growth accounting approach to capture accurately the relationship between the EES, national reforms, and employment outcomes, and is working to develop alternative methodologies. See EPC (2008); EMCO (2008).

resist adding new priorities to the 24 Integrated Guidelines as circumstances change, such as the four cross-cutting priority areas for more growth and jobs agreed at the 2006 Spring European Council.[11] Unsurprisingly, too, the European Council and the Commission have also launched new coordination processes and reporting obligations for Member States in response to these and other emergent priorities such as the integration of immigrants or the reduction of administrative burdens. Finally, the Commission itself appeared to have recognised the limits of bilateral dialogue with Member States on their NRPs, as can be seen, for example, from its efforts to organise mutual learning workshops within the Network of National Lisbon Coordinators on issues such as one-stop shops for setting up new enterprises, business-university cooperation, and extending working lives of older workers – albeit at some risk of duplicating the work of the sectoral OMCs.

Nor does it appear to be the case, finally, that the revised governance arrangements of Lisbon II significantly helped to unblock reforms at the national level. Thus an official evaluation of the IGs for Growth and Jobs conducted on behalf of the Commission's Directorate-General Economic and Financial Affairs (DG ECFIN) concluded that they had induced an "incremental impact" on national reform processes, not through peer or public pressure, but "mainly through framing policy issues, mutual learning, legitimising reform promoters, and enlarging stakeholders' consensus" (Euréval/Rambøll Management, 2008).

11.2.3 Lisbon III (2008-2010)

In response to persistent complaints about the weakness of the mutually reinforcing dynamic between economic, employment, and social policies within the revised governance architecture of Lisbon II, the Spring 2007 European Council resolved that the "common social objectives of Member States should be better taken into account within the Lisbon Agenda...in order to ensure the continuing support for European integration by the Union's citizens." The result was a year-long public debate under the German and Portuguese Presidencies of the EU (during the first and second half of 2007, respectively) about how best to strengthen the social dimension of the Lisbon Strategy. Two countervailing positions emerged within this debate: one advocated incorporating the EU's common social objectives into the Integrated Guidelines and linking the Social OMC more closely to the Lisbon Strategy; the other favoured maintaining the stability of the Guidelines while focus-

---

[11] These four cross-cutting priority areas were: investing more in knowledge and innovation; unlocking the business potential, especially of SMEs; greater adaptability of labour markets based on flexicurity; and energy and climate change.

ing on better implementation of national reforms. The solution adopted split the difference: at the Commission's insistence, the IGs were retained unchanged for 2008-2011, but their social dimension was strengthened by revision of the accompanying explanatory text, which called for closer interaction with the Social OMC and more systematic monitoring of "feeding in/feeding out". The Commission's Renewed Social Agenda for 2010-2015 took this approach a step further, proposing to reinforce the Social OMC by bringing it closer to the Lisbon Strategy through the use of targets, common principles, enhanced monitoring, and recommendations (European Commission, 2008).

It is hard to consider the governance architecture of Lisbon III as anything other than a flawed compromise. The disconnection between the old guidelines and the new explanatory text did not improve European citizens' understanding of EU policies, nor did it enhance ownership of the Lisbon Strategy by national actors. Neither was the institutional divide between economic and employment policies on the one hand and social policies on the other, conducive to the joined-up governance and stakeholder participation needed for innovative structural reforms. Nor was there much tangible progress in promoting greater synergy between the IGs/NRPs and the Social OMC.[12] At a deeper level, moreover, this governance architecture left the EU with multiple, overlapping, and potentially inconsistent "mega-strategies", including not only Lisbon and the Social OMC, but also the Sustainable Development Strategy and the Energy Policy for Europe (Larsson and Begg, 2007).

11.3 An Inclusive Governance Architecture for the Post-Lisbon Era? Ambiguities of Europe 2020

11.3.1 Europe 2020 as a reformed governance architecture

The relaunched Lisbon Strategy, as the preceding section shows, was widely criticised for its weak social dimension and unbalanced governance architecture. These concerns figured prominently in the EU debate about what should succeed the Lisbon Strategy after 2010, with EU civil society networks spearheading a campaign for a more balanced and socially inclusive governance architecture. This campaign, which resonated with concurrent proposals from some Member States, EU

---

[12] The SPC established a Task-Force for the analysis of the interaction between social cohesion and growth and jobs, which produced an important report on *Growth, Jobs and Social Progress in the EU*, as a contribution to the Lisbon post-2010 debate (Social Protection Committee, 2009). On the assessment of feeding in/out in the context of Lisbon III, see Frazer and Marlier (2009).

institutions, local and regional authorities, and academic commentators,[13] focused around four core demands, aimed at redressing key perceived defects of the Lisbon Strategy, especially in its relaunched version (Frazer and Marlier, 2008; Spring Alliance, 2009; European Anti-Poverty Network, 2009 and 2009a; Platform of European Social NGOs, 2009; Armstrong, 2010, chapter 8; Frazer, Marlier and Nicaise, 2010). The first of these was parity: social and environmental objectives should be given equal status with economic and employment goals as mutually reinforcing pillars of the EU's post-2010 strategy. A second demand, reflecting longstanding aspirations of social NGOs and other advocates of a stronger Social EU, was enhanced political commitment, to be embodied in specific commitments to quantified EU and national social inclusion/ poverty reduction targets, backed up by effective policy measures and financial support. A third demand was for more effective mainstreaming of social cohesion and inclusion objectives into EU and Member State policy-making, accompanied by better horizontal coordination between social and other interdependent policies at both levels. A final demand was for greater stakeholder participation: non-state and sub-national actors (civil society organisations, social partners, local/ regional authorities), along with the European and national parliaments, should be fully involved in the design and implementation of the new strategy at all levels.

Against the backdrop of mounting unease about the social impact of the global financial crisis, this campaign met with a sympathetic response from the European Commission. President Barroso himself, who was running for re-election, acknowledged in his Political Guidelines for the Next Commission the "need to revise the current Lisbon Strategy" by bringing "different strategies and instruments together", thereby "turning it into a strategy for an integrated vision of 'EU 2020'", while also calling for "a new, much stronger focus on the social dimension in Europe, at all levels of government" (Barroso 2009: 2, 15).[14]

The design of Europe 2020, as proposed by the Commission in March 2010 and approved in amended form by the June 2010 European Council, represents a more radical overhaul of the governance architecture of the relaunched Lisbon Strategy, including a reinforcement of its social dimension, than many observers (including myself) had expected. Five major developments stand out (see opening chapter). First is the broadening of the objectives of the new Strategy beyond those of Lis-

---

[13] See, for example, Committee of the Regions (2009b); Spanish-Belgian-Hungarian Team Presidency (2009); Social Protection Committee (2009, 2009a); Zeitlin (2008a, 2009a).

[14] For a fuller analysis of the political context of the Europe 2020 debate, see Armstrong (2010, pages 265-72).

bon II/III. Thus "inclusive growth", aimed at "fostering a high-employment economy delivering economic, social and territorial cohesion" figures as one of three overarching, mutually reinforcing priorities for Europe 2020, alongside "smart" (knowledge and innovation-based) and "sustainable" (greener, more resource efficient, more competitive) growth (European Commission, 2010). A second is the adoption of an EU-wide target, aimed at lifting "at least 20 million people out of the risk of poverty and exclusion" as one of five "headline targets" for the new Strategy. Following a compromise agreed by the European Council, Member States are required to set their own national targets for how they will contribute to this overall goal, based on three alternative indicators, in line with their domestic priorities and circumstances (European Council, 2010, Annex 1)[15]. A third innovation is the creation of a "European Platform against Poverty" (EPAP) as one of seven "flagship initiatives" orchestrated by the Commission to support the delivery of Europe 2020. A fourth is the incorporation of a Guideline on "Promoting social inclusion and combating poverty" as one of the ten new Integrated Guidelines for Growth and Jobs, which also underlines the role of pensions, healthcare, and public services in maintaining social cohesion. Finally, Recital 16 of the Integrated Guidelines explicitly states that the new Strategy "should, as appropriate, be implemented, monitored and evaluated in partnership with all national, regional and local authorities, closely associating parliaments, as well as social partners and representatives of civil society"; Member States are expected to involve all relevant stakeholders in the preparation, implementation and communication of their NRPs.

11.3.2 Be careful what you wish for: Ambiguities of Europe 2020

Despite these undeniable advances towards a stronger social dimension, it is nonetheless important to underline the problematic fit between the governance architecture of Europe 2020 and EU social policy coordination as it has developed over the past decade through the Social OMC. One key source of concern is the ambiguous status of the EU's common social objectives, adopted in 2000 and revised in 2006. The headline target of Europe 2020, as already noted, is focused on reducing poverty and social exclusion, while the other common social objectives for pensions and health care enter into the new social inclusion guideline primarily insofar as they contribute to these goals, even if the latter also refers to the need for modernisation of social protection systems so

---

[15] For a fuller discussion, see chapters by Frazer and Marlier and by Walker in this volume.

that they can provide adequate income support and access to health care while remaining financially sustainable. Another related issue is that the social inclusion guideline is inserted within the Employment Guidelines, thereby creating further ambiguities about the appropriate institutional arrangements for monitoring, reviewing, evaluating, and following up its implementation.

Member States' NRPs will be closely linked to the preparation of national Stability and Convergence Programmes (SCPs), and are expected to focus on macro-economic stability and "growth-enhancing reforms", as well as on meeting the headline targets, while concentrating on a limited set of priority measures. Fiscal and macroeconomic surveillance will be conducted by the EU "Economic and Financial Affairs" (ECOFIN) Council, while "thematic coordination" by the sectoral Council formations (including the EU "Employment, Social Policy, Health and Consumer Affairs" (EPSCO) Council) will focus on progress towards the headline targets and flagship initiatives, together with Member States' actions to tackle obstacles to achieving these objectives. Country-specific recommendations will be based on the Treaty articles governing the Stability and Growth Pact, the Broad Economic Policy Guidelines and the Employment Guidelines, thus leaving it uncertain whether and how they will address the implementation of the social inclusion guideline, which also fits uneasily with the predominant emphasis on breaking growth bottlenecks (European Commission, 2010a; 2010b).

It thus remains unclear how the EU's common social objectives – beyond combating poverty and social exclusion – will be monitored, reviewed, evaluated, and followed up within the governance architecture of Europe 2020, and what will happen to national reporting of performance against the common indicators developed within the Social OMC. It is likewise unclear how mutual interactions between policy fields and the social dimensions of other guidelines will be monitored, notably Guideline 1 on the sustainability of the public finances, which emphasises the need for reform of Member State pension and health care systems; and Guideline 7 on increasing labour market participation and reducing structural unemployment, in which active inclusion policies play a crucial part.[16]

These concerns about the governance architecture of Europe 2020 are compounded by the unclear relationship between the Social OMC

---

[16] It is noteworthy in this regard that the Lisbon Assessment Framework developed by the EPC did not monitor the social dimension of national reforms addressing these policy fields under the 2005-2010 Guidelines, whose provisions are largely reprised in Europe 2020.

and the EPAP, whose institutional contours have not yet been defined in any specific detail. The key question here is what will happen to the broader role of the Social OMC and the Social Protection Committee within it in coordinating, monitoring, and (peer) reviewing the full range of Member State social policies across all three strands of the current process (Social Protection Committee, 2010).[17]

Despite the stronger and more explicit social dimension of Europe 2020, these ambiguities and limitations of its governance architecture thus present a serious risk to the broader EU social policy coordination and monitoring capacities developed through the Social OMC over the past decade, at the same time as the common social objectives may be very incompletely and selectively integrated into NRPs and EU monitoring and policy guidance.

11.4 Towards a Stronger OMC in a More Social Europe 2020

11.4.1 Building blocks for a more social Europe 2020

So what should be done to counteract these risks? This section advances four proposals for building a more social Europe 2020 by incorporating into its governance architecture key components of EU social policy coordination developed over the past decade.

1) Anchor the commonly agreed EU social objectives in Europe 2020:

   The common objectives have played a central role in social policy coordination at EU level over the past decade, defining the Union's core commitments to social protection and social inclusion, delineating agreed priorities for the reform of national systems, and providing a framework for policy experimentation and mutual learning. It is therefore critical to anchor the common social objectives in Europe 2020, where they could give more specific definition to the new Strategy's overarching commitment to "inclusive and sustainable growth". At the same time, however, the common objectives themselves should also be updated to take account of the transition from Lisbon to Europe 2020 and incorporate more recent developments such as the Recommendation on Active Inclusion (European Commission, 2008b).

---

[17] A potentially significant development in this regard may be the recent creation of an Ad Hoc Commissioner's Group on Pensions, initiated by President Barroso and steered by the Secretariat-General (Barroso, 2010).

2) Link the EPAP to the Social OMC, and use both to monitor the social dimension of Europe 2020:

The new EPAP should become the visible "face of Social Europe", as the European Anti-Poverty Network (2010) has suggested. But it should also be linked organically to the Social OMC, which has become the body and the brain of Social EU over the past decade. EPAP and the Social OMC should be jointly responsible for monitoring, reviewing, and assessing not just progress towards the headline social inclusion/ poverty reduction target and the social inclusion guideline, but also the social dimension of the other Integrated Guidelines and of Europe 2020 more generally. Together, EPAP and the Social OMC should also be responsible for monitoring, reviewing, and assessing how other EU policies (including the structural funds) are contributing to achieving the Union's common social objectives, in line with the new "Horizontal Social Clause" of the Lisbon Treaty.[18] These assessments in turn should be incorporated into the Commission's Annual Growth Survey and EU policy guidance to Member States on their NRPs, including country-specific recommendations.

3) Benchmark national performance against the common social indicators:

To assess progress towards the common social objectives, stimulate improvement, and support mutual learning, Member States should be required to monitor and report national performance against the full set of common social indicators, not just those for social inclusion and poverty reduction. At the same time, however, continuing work remains necessary to complete the portfolio of common indicators, especially for pensions and healthcare, as well as to develop indicators and methods for monitoring interactions between social, economic, employment, and environmental policies.

4) Sustain national social protection and inclusion strategies:

National Reform Programmes for the implementation of Europe 2020, as we have seen, will be narrowly focused on the achievement of headline targets and "growth-enhancing reforms". Hence regular National Strategic Reports (NSRs) and/or National Action Plans (NAPs) will remain a vital component of EU social policy coordination in order to promote the development of coherent, comprehensive national strategies for social protection and inclusion, taking account of mutual interactions across policy fields;

---

[18] For a fuller discussion of the "Horizontal Social Clause", see chapters by Ferrera and by Frazer and Marlier in the present volume.

to sustain balanced monitoring, review, and assessment of Member State policies and performance across the full range of common social objectives and indicators; and to support mutual learning and exchange of good practices. These NSRs/NAPs should feed into Member States' NRPs, be anchored in national policy-making processes (including parliamentary debates), and be based on broad participation by civil society and sub-national stakeholders. (For a discussion of the various options that could be followed to implement this concretely, see chapter by Frazer and Marlier in the present volume.)

11.4.2 Reflexive reforms for a stronger OMC

Many of the main past weaknesses of the Social OMC, such as parity with other EU policy objectives, political commitment, mainstreaming, and horizontal coordination, may be remedied by the revised governance architecture of Europe 2020, especially if augmented by the additional measures proposed above. But overcoming others would require revisions to the Social OMC itself, building on the reflexive reform strategy discussed earlier. This section focuses on two main areas for improvement: reinforcing mutual learning and enhancing stakeholder participation. In each of these areas, I suggest four key measures for strengthening the Social OMC, drawing on recent proposals by NGOs and independent experts, as well as on ongoing debates and initiatives within the Social Protection Committee (SPC) itself.

1) Reinforcing mutual learning:

There is wide agreement among academic commentators, NGOs, and the SPC itself that despite the Social OMC's undeniable contributions to promoting mutual learning among EU Member States (see Section 11.2.1 above), its full potential in this area has not yet been fully exploited (Social Protection Committee, 2007; FEANTSA, 2007; Armstrong 2010). Among the many proposed measures for reinforcing the mutual learning capacity of the Social OMC, four seem especially promising.

a) *Adopt a more deliberative approach to peer review of national policies and performance:* if National Strategy Reports on Social Protection and Social Inclusion are to be continued within Europe 2020, as I believe they should, then it is important that peer review of them become more deliberative, focusing on identifying the comparative strengths and weaknesses of particular policies, and drawing out potential lessons for other Member States.

b) *Develop a stronger thematic focus:* building on recent initiatives by the SPC, as well as on proposals by NGOs and independent experts, peer review, exchange of good practices, and policy coordination should concentrate on specific issues where opportunities for cross-national learning from comparative analysis of national and local experience are greatest, such as child poverty, homelessness, active inclusion, and health inequalities (see SPC 2007; FEANTSA 2007; Frazer and Marlier, this volume).

c) *Use the common indicators more diagnostically:* benchmarking of Member State performance against the common indicators should serve as a diagnostic tool for assisting national and local actors in identifying and correcting relative weaknesses in current policies, rather than as soft sanctions or shaming devices to secure domestic compliance with EU targets. Ensuring the availability of timely, comparable, and disaggregated data to support the common indicators is likewise essential for this purpose. (See Marlier *et al.*, 2007; Social Protection Committee, 2008.)

d) *Institutionalise arrangements for involving civil society organisations, local and regional authorities, and independent experts:* this is a vital step towards enhancing the OMC's capacity to promote horizontal and bottom-up forms of learning by incorporating a wider set of perspectives and information sources.

2) Enhancing stakeholder participation:

Of all OMC processes, the Social OMC has the best record of stakeholder involvement, especially its social inclusion strand. Yet there is significant scope for enhancing the participation of civil society and sub-national actors, drawing on the new opportunities opened up by the creation of the EPAP. Here too, four key measures can be recommended, building on proposals advanced by European social NGOs (European Anti-Poverty Network, 2010; Platform of European Social NGOs, 2010).

a) Establish stakeholder fora attached to EPAP and the Social OMC at both EU and national levels, with representation of civil society organisations, social partners, local and regional authorities, and independent experts, as proposed by EU social NGOs.

b) Use these fora to ensure stakeholder participation in the preparation, implementation, and assessment of NRPs and NSRs/NAPs at both Member State and EU levels.

c) Use these fora as mechanisms for drawing on bottom-up expertise about policy effectiveness and good (and bad) practices, as well as for wider dissemination and follow-up of results from OMC mutual learning activities.

d) Develop participatory governance guidelines and indicators for monitoring, benchmarking, and assessing national practice and performance within both the OMC and Europe 2020.

11.5 Conclusion

This chapter has suggested four "building blocks" for a more social Europe 2020, namely: a) to anchor the commonly agreed EU social objectives in Europe 2020; b) to link the EPAP to the Social OMC (and use both to monitor the social dimension of Europe 2020); c) to benchmark national performance against the common social indicators; and d) to sustain national social protection and inclusion strategies through the continuation of NSRs/NAPs that should feed into Member States' NRPs, be anchored in national policy-making processes (including parliamentary debates), and be based on broad participation. The chapter has also proposed two areas where the Social OMC would need to be improved (reinforcing mutual learning and enhancing stakeholder participation) together with concrete measures for reaching these objectives.

With these proposed reforms in place, EU social, economic, employment, and environmental policies could begin to work together in a mutually reinforcing way to deliver smarter, more sustainable, and more inclusive growth, as envisaged by the architects of Europe 2020.

References

Armstrong, K.A. (2010), *Governing Social Inclusion: Europeanization through Policy Coordination*, Oxford: Oxford University Press.

Atkinson, T., Cantillon, B., Marlier, E., and Nolan, B. (2002), *Social Indicators: The EU and Social Inclusion*, Oxford: Oxford University Press.

Barroso, J.M. (2010), *Mandate of the Commissioner's Group on the Pensions*, Brussels: European Commission, D (2010)/1164. Available at: http://www. euractiv.com/sites/all/euractiv/files/PEnsions%20mandate.PDF.

Barroso, J.M. (2009), *Political Guidelines for the Next Commission*, Brussels: European Commission.

Begg, I. (2007), *Lisbon II, Two Years On: An Assessment of the Partnership for Growth and Jobs*, Brussels: Centre for European Policy Studies.

Begg, I., and Marlier, E. (2007), *"Feeding in" and "Feeding out", and Integrating Immigrants and Ethnic Minorities – Key lessons*, Independent overview based on the 2006 second semester national reports of national independent experts on social inclusion, Brussels: European Commission.

Committee of the Regions (2009), *Contributions to the 2008 Ateliers (Proceedings of the multilevel governance workshops)*, Brussels: Committee of the Regions.

Committee of the Regions (2009a), *Consultation of European Regions and Cities on a New Strategy for Sustainable Growth: A New Lisbon Strategy after 2010*, Brussels: Committee of the Regions.

Committee of the Regions (2008), *Achieving the Lisbon Goals through Coordinated and Integrated Territorial Policy-making: The LMP 2008-2009 Monitoring Report*, Brussels: Committee of the Regions.

Economic Policy Committee (2008), *Progress Report of the Lisbon Methodology Working Group*, ECFIN/EPC(2008)REP/53233_rev1, Brussels.

Employment Committee (2008), *Chair's Summary: Meeting of the Employment Committee, 27 November.*

Euréval/Rambøll Management (2008), *Evaluation of the Integrated Guideline Package (IGP) for Growth and Jobs*, final report to the European Commission, ECFIN/R/3/2007/004-IGP. Available at: http://ec.europa.eu/economy_finance/evaluation/pdf/final_report_ipg_en.pdf.

European Anti-Poverty Network (2010), *EAPN proposals on the 'European Platform against Poverty'*, Brussels: EAPN. Available at: http://www.eapn.org/images/stories/docs/EAPN-position-papers-and-reports/eapn-flagship-platform-against-poverty-proposals-en.pdf.

European Anti-Poverty Network (2009), *A Europe we can trust: Proposals on a new EU post-2010 strategy*, Brussels: EAPN.

European Anti-Poverty Network (2009a), *EAPN in dialogue with Barroso – Spring Alliance conference, EAPN Flash 225.*

European Anti-Poverty Network (2007), *Making Lisbon Deliver for People Experiencing Poverty: EAPN Response to 2006 Implementation Reports on the National Reform Programs*, Brussels: EAPN.

European Commission (2010), *Europe 2020: A strategy for smart, sustainable and inclusive growth*, Communication COM(2010) 2020, Brussels: European Commission. Available at: http://ec.europa.eu/eu2020/pdf/COMPLET%20EN%20BARROSO%20%20%20007%20-%20Europe%202020%20-%20EN%20version.pdf.

European Commission (2010a), *Enhancing economic policy coordination for stability, growth, and jobs – Tools for stronger EU economic governance*, Communication COM(2010) 367/2, Brussels: European Commission.

European Commission (2010b), *Governance, Tools and Policy Cycle of Europe 2020*, Brussels: European Commission Secretariat-General, 13 June.

European Commission (2009), *The Open Method of Coordination in Research Policy: Assessment and Recommendations, A Report from the Expert Group for the Follow-up of the Research Aspects of the Revised Lisbon Strategy*, DG Research, January.

European Commission (2008), *Renewed Social Agenda: Opportunities, Access and Solidarity in 21st Century Europe*, Communication COM(2008)412 final, Brussels.

European Commission (2008a), *A Renewed Commitment to Social Europe: Reinforcing the Open Method of Coordination for Social Protection and Social Inclusion*, Communication COM(2008)418 final, Brussels.

European Commission (2008b), *Commission Recommendation on the active inclusion of people excluded from the labour market*, Communication COM(2008) 639 final, Brussels: European Commission.

European Commission (2006), *Evaluation of the Open Method of Coordination for Social Protection and Social Inclusion*, SEC(2006) 345, Brussels.

European Commission (2005), *Working Together for Growth and Jobs: A New Start for the Lisbon Strategy. Communication to the Spring European Council from President Barroso in agreement with Vice-President Verheugen*, Communication COM(2005) 24, Brussels.

European Council (2010), *European Council 17 June 2010: Conclusions*, Brussels: European Council.

FEANTSA (2007) *Untapped Potential: Using the Full Potential of the OMC to Address Poverty in Europe*, Brussels: FEANTSA.

Frazer, H. and Marlier, E. (2009), *Assessment of the extent of synergies between growth and jobs policies and social inclusion policies across the EU as evidenced by the 2008-2010 National Reform Programmes: Key lessons, EU Network of Independent Experts on Social Inclusion*, Brussels: European Commission. Available at: http://www.peer-review-social-inclusion.eu/ network-of-independent-experts/2008/second-semester-2008.

Frazer, H. and Marlier, E. (2008), *Building a stronger EU Social Inclusion Process: Analysis and recommendations of the EU Network of independent national experts on social inclusion*, Brussels: European Commission. Available at: http://www.peer-review-social-inclusion.eu/network-of-independent-experts/2008/first-semester-2008.

Frazer, H., Marlier E. and Nicaise, I. (2010), *A social inclusion roadmap for Europe 2020*, Antwerp/Apeldoorn: Garant.

Gornitzka, A. (2006), *The Open Method of Coordination in European Education and Research Policy: Animating a Label*, Unpublished paper presented to the European Union Centre of Excellence, University of Wisconsin-Madison, 13 October. Available at: http://eucenter.wisc.edu/OMC/ New%20OMC%20links/Gornitzka%20Madison.doc.

Heidenreich, M., and Zeitlin. J. (editors) (2009), *Changing European Employment and Welfare Regimes: The Influence of the Open Method of Coordination on National Reforms*, London: Routledge.

Kok, W. (2004), *Facing the Challenge: The Lisbon Strategy for Growth and Employment. Report from the High Level Group Chaired by Wim Kok*, Brussels: European Commission.

Kröger, S. (editor) (2009), *What we have learnt: Advances, pitfalls and remaining questions in OMC research*, European Integration online Papers (EIoP), Special Issue 1, Vol. 13.

La Rivista delle Politiche Sociali/ Italian Journal of Social Policy (2009), *Special issue on the Lisbon Strategy*, Vol. 2, 4.

Larsson, A., and I. Begg (2007), *Time for Better Governance of EU "Mega-Strategies"?*, Paper prepared for the European Panel for Sustainable Development (EPSD), Gothenburg, Sweden.

Marlier, E., Atkinson, A.B., Cantillon, B. and Nolan, B. (2007), *The EU and Social Inclusion: Facing the Challenges*, Bristol: Policy Press.

Platform of European Social NGOs (2010), *Five recommendations to ensure that the "European Platform against Poverty" delivers concrete actions reducing poverty and promoting social cohesion*, open letter to José Manuel Barroso, President of the European Commission, and to the Commissioners, Brussels: Social Platform.

Platform of European Social NGOs (2009), *5 recommendations for an effective Open Method of Coordination on social protection and social inclusion*, Brussels: Social Platform. Available at: http://cms.horus.be/files/99907/ MediaArchive/Policies/Social_Inclusion/20090929_SP%20Social%20OMC_f inal.pdf.

Social Protection Committee (2010), *Social Dimension in the Europe 2020 Strategy and Its Governance*, Discussion Paper, SPC/1009/1.

Social Protection Committee (2009), *Growth, Jobs and Social Progress in the EU: A contribution to the evaluation of the social dimension of the Lisbon Strategy*, Brussels: European Commission. Available at: http://ec.europa.eu/ social/BlobServlet?docId=3898&langId=en.

Social Protection Committee (2009a), *Post-2010 Lisbon Strategy: SPC preliminary conclusion*, SPC/2009/05/8-final.

Social Protection Committee (2008), *Child Poverty and Well-Being in the EU: Current status and way forward*, Luxembourg: OPOCE. Available at: http://ec.europa.eu/social/main.jsp?catId=751&langId=en&pubId=74&type=2 &furtherPubs=yes.

Social Protection Committee (2007), *Proposals generated from the summary of Member States' replies to the follow-up questions on how to enhance mutual learning with the OMC Social Protection and Social Inclusion*, Brussels: SPC.

Spanish-Belgian-Hungarian Team Presidency (2009), *ES-BE-HU Trio Program: Draft of the Team Presidency of the Strategic Framework*, compiled version, 22 June. Available at: 20090622_cadre_strategique_ madrid.pdf (application/pdf Object).

Spring Alliance (2009), *Manifesto*, Brussels: Spring Alliance. Available at: http://www.springalliance.eu/manifesto.

Tavistock Institute *et al.* (2005), *The Analysis of Impacts of Benchmarking and the eEurope Actions in the Open Method of Coordination. How the eEurope*

OMC worked: Implications for the Coordination of Policy under i2010, Final report prepared for Directorate-General Information Society by the Tavistock Institute, London, Net Effect Ltd., Helsinki, and Istituto per la Ricerca Sociale, Milan.

Zeitlin, J. (2009), *The Open Method of Coordination and Reform of National Social and Employment Policies: Influences, Mechanisms, and Effects*, in M. Heidenreich and J. Zeitlin (2009), 214-245.

Zeitlin, J. (2009a), *Il coordinamento delle politiche nell'Unione europea dopo il 2010: idee per un'architettura di governance inclusiva*, in *La Rivista delle Politiche Sociali/Italian Journal of Social Policy* 2(4), 33-55.

Zeitlin, J. (2008), *The Open Method of Coordination and the Governance of the Lisbon Strategy*, Journal of Common Market Studies 46(2), 437-446.

Zeitlin, J. (2008a), *EU Policy Coordination Beyond 2010: Towards an Inclusive Governance Architecture*, in Committee of the Regions (2009), 213-25.

Zeitlin, J. (2007), *A Decade of Innovation in EU Governance: The European Employment Strategy, the Open Method of Coordination, and the Lisbon Strategy*, in *Perspectives on Employment and Social Policy Coordination in the European Union*, Portuguese Ministry of Labour and Social Solidarity, Lisbon, 129-144.

Zeitlin, J. (2005), *Social Europe and Experimental Governance: Towards a New Constitutional Compromise?*, in G. de Búrca (editor), EU Law and the Welfare State: In Search of Solidarity. Oxford: Oxford University Press, 213-241.

Zeitlin, J. (2005a). *Introduction: The Open Method of Coordination in Question*, in J. Zeitlin and P. Pochet (2005), 19-33.

Zeitlin, J. (2005b), *Conclusion: The Open Method of Coordination in Action: Theoretical Promise, Empirical Realities, Reform Strategy*, in J. Zeitlin and P. Pochet (2005), 447-503.

Zeitlin, J., and Pochet, P., with Magnusson, L. (editors) (2005), *The Open Method of Coordination in Action: The European Employment and Social Inclusion Strategies.* Brussels: P.I.E.-Peter Lang.

Short Presentation of the Authors

Tom Brodie is a policy officer at the international progressive think tank "Policy Network".

Mary Daly is Professor of Sociology at the School of Sociology, Social Policy and Social Work at Queen's University Belfast (Ireland). Among the fields on which she has published are poverty, welfare, gender, family and labour market. Much of her work is comparative, in a European and international context and she is especially interested in matters to do with how policies in different European countries relate to families.

Patrick Diamond is a Senior Research Fellow of the international progressive think tank "Policy Network", a Visiting Fellow of Nuffield College Oxford, and the former Head of Policy Planning in the UK Prime Minister's Office.

Maurizio Ferrera is Professor of Political Science and President of the Graduate School in Social, Economic and Political Studies of the State University of Milan (Italy). He is currently a member of the European Commission's Group of Societal Policy Advisers, of the Scientific Committee of Confindustria (in Rome), of the Board of Directors of the Collegio Carlo Alberto and the Centro Einaudi (in Turin). He has written extensively on comparative and EU social policies.

Hugh Frazer is Adjunct Professor at the National University of Ireland (Maynooth) and, together with Eric Marlier, he coordinates the EU Network of Independent Experts on Social Inclusion. From 2001 to 2006, he worked in the European Commission as an expert advising and assisting in the development of the Social Inclusion Open Method of Coordination (OMC). Prior to that, he was *inter alia* Director of the Irish Government's Combat Poverty Agency (1987-2001). He has written extensively on the issues of poverty, social exclusion, community development and community relations.

Marjorie Jouen is Special Adviser at *Notre Europe*, where she has worked since 1999 on EU policies related to regional development, rural development, territorial cohesion and local employment. She graduated in political science and is a former student of the *Ecole Nationale d'Administration* (ENA). She has held several posts as a high-level official in the French Department of Economy and EU institutions. She has written many articles and reports on social, economic and territorial cohesion in Europe.

Martin Kühnemund is Principal Consultant for European Evaluation at The Evaluation Partnership (TEP), a London-based consultancy. He specialises in the evaluation of public policies, programmes, and other legislative and non-legislative measures, and also heads up TEP's activities in the area of regulatory impact assessment.

Simon Latham is a senior researcher at the international progressive think tank "Policy Network".

Roger Liddle is Chair of the international progressive think tank "Policy Network" and a Labour member of the UK House of Lords. From 1997 to 2004, he served as Tony Blair's political adviser on Europe and was closely involved in developing the EU's Lisbon Agenda. From 2004 to 2007, he was an adviser in the European Commission, first in the cabinet of Peter Mandelson and then to the President, Jose Manuel Barroso. With Frédéric Lerais, he authored an EU consultative paper on *Europe's Social Reality* published in 2006. Since leaving the Commission, he has written widely on Social Europe, the future of Europe and the future of social democracy.

Eric Marlier is the International Scientific Coordinator of the CEPS/INSTEAD Research Institute (Luxembourg) and, together with Hugh Frazer, he manages the EU Network of Independent Experts on Social Inclusion. His main research activities include comparative social indicators, social monitoring, international socio-economic analysis (esp. on income, poverty and social exclusion) and the Social OMC. He has written widely on these issues and has also organised several international conferences on behalf of the European Commission and various EU Presidencies.

David Natali is Associate Professor at the R. Ruffilli Faculty of Political Science in Forli (Italy) and Co-Director of the European Social Observatory (OSE, Belgium). He is currently a member of the board of the European Network of Social Policy Analysis (ESPANET), and a member of the OECD working party on pension markets. He is also a member of Reconciling Work and Welfare (RECWOWE), a Sixth Framework Programme (FP6) Network of Excellence.

Rudi Van Dam is Coordinator Social Indicators at the Belgian Federal Public Service Social Security (FPSSS). He is country delegate to the Indicators Sub-Group of the Social Protection Committee. He was also coordinator of the Belgian EU Presidency Conference "EU Coordination in the Social Field in the Context of Europe 2020: Looking Back and Building the Future" (September 2010, La Hulpe, Belgium). Before joining the FPSSS he worked as senior researcher at the Centre for Social Policy at the University of Antwerp (Belgium).

Bart Vanhercke is Co-Director at the European Social Observatory (OSE, Belgium). He is finalising his PhD on "The hard politics of soft policy coordination". His current research activity focuses on the Europeanisation of social inclusion, healthcare and pensions policies through different EU policy instruments, a topic on which he also works as associate academic staff at the CESO Research Centre of the University of Leuven. He previously worked as European advisor to the Belgian Minister for Social Affairs (1999-2004), and was an assistant in the European Parliament (2004-2006).

Robert Walker is Professor of Social Policy and a Fellow of Green Templeton College, Oxford University (United Kingdom). He was formerly Professor of Social Policy at the University of Nottingham and before that Director of the Centre for Research in Social Policy, Loughborough University. He is a member of the statutory UK Social Security Advisory Committee and an expert advisor to the European Social Fund Evaluation Partnership.

Jonathan Zeitlin is Professor of Public Policy and Governance at the University of Amsterdam (Netherlands). He has published extensively on the OMC and EU governance, including "The Open Method of Coordination in Action" (2005), "Changing European Employment and Welfare Regimes" (2009), and "Experimentalist Governance in the European Union" (2010). He is currently serving as chief scientific adviser for an external evaluation of the Social OMC.

"Work & Society"

The series "Work & Society" analyses the development of employment and social policies, as well as the strategies of the different social actors, both at national and European levels. It puts forward a multidisciplinary approach – political, sociological, economic, legal and historical – in a bid for dialogue and complementarity.

The series is not confined to the social field *stricto sensu*, but also aims to illustrate the indirect social impacts of economic and monetary policies. It endeavours to clarify social developments, from a comparative and a historical perspective, thus portraying the process of convergence and divergence in the diverse national societal contexts. The manner in which European integration impacts on employment and social policies constitutes the backbone of the analyses.

Series Editor: Philippe Pochet, General Director ETUI-REHS (Brussels) and Digest Editor of the Journal of European Social Policy

Recent Titles

No.69 – *Europe 2020: Towards a More Social EU?*, Eric MARLIER and David NATALI (eds.), with Rudi VAN DAM, 2010, ISBN 978-90-5201-688-7.

No.68 – *Generations at Work and Social Cohesion in Europe*, Patricia VENDRAMIN (ed.), 2009, ISBN 978-90-5201-647-4.

No.67 – *Quality of Work in the European Union. Concept, Data and Debates from a Transnational Perspective*, Ana M. GUILLÉN and Svenn-Åge DAHL (eds.), 2009, ISBN 978-90-5201-577-4

No.66 – *Emerging Systems of Work and Welfare*, Pertti KOISTINEN, Lilja MÓSESDÓTTIR & Amparo SERRANO PASCUAL (eds.), 2009, ISBN 978-90-5201-549-1

No.65 – *Building Anticipation of Restructuring in Europe*, Marie-Ange MOREAU (ed.), in collaboration with Serafino NEGRELLI & Philippe POCHET, 2009, ISBN 978-90-5201-486-9

No.64 – *Pensions in Europe, European Pensions. The Evolution of Pension Policy at National and Supranational Level*, David NATALI, 2008, ISBN 978-90-5201-460-9

No.63 – *Restructuring in the New EU Member States. Social Dialogue, Firms Relocation and Social Treatment of Restructuring*, Marie-Ange MOREAU & María Esther BLAS LÓPEZ (eds.), 2009, ISBN 978-90-5201-456-2

No.62 – *Jobs on the Move. An Analytical Approach to "Relocation" and its Impact on Employment*, Béla GALGÓCZI, Maarten KEUNE & Andrew WATT (eds.), 2008, ISBN 978-90-5201-448-7

No.61 – *Les nouveaux cadres du dialogue social, Europe et territoires*, Annette JOBERT (dir.), 2008, ISBN 978-90-5201-444-9

No.60 – *Transnational Labour Regulation. A Case Study of Temporary Agency Work*, Kerstin AHLBERG, Brian BERCUSSON, Niklas BRUUN, Haris KOUNTOUROS, Christophe VIGNEAU & Loredana ZAPPALÀ, 2008, 376 p., ISBN 978-90-5201-417-3

No.59 – *Changing Liaisons. The Dynamics of Social Partnership in Twentieth Century West-European Democracies*, Karel DAVIDS, Greta DEVOS & Patrick PASTURE (eds.), 2007, 268 p., ISBN 978-90-5201-365-7.

No.58 – *Work and Social Inequalities in Health in Europe*, Ingvar LUNDBERG, Tomas HEMMINGSSON & Christer HOGSTEDT (eds.), SALTSA, 2007, 538 p., ISBN 978-90-5201-372-5.

No. 57 – *European Solidarities. Tensions and Contentions of a Concept*, Lars MAGNUSSON & Bo STRÅTH (eds.), 2007, 355 p., ISBN 978-90-5201-363-3.

No. 56 – *Industrial Relations in Small Companies. A Comparison: France, Sweden and Germany*, Christian DUFOUR, Adelheid HEGE, Sofia MURHEM, Wolfgang RUDOLPH & Wolfram WASSERMANN (eds.), SALTSA, 2007, ISBN 978-90-5201-360-2.

No. 55 – *The European Sectoral Social Dialogue. Actors, Developments and Challenges*, Anne DUFRESNE, Christophe DEGRYSE & Philippe POCHET (eds.), SALTSA/Observatoire social européen, 2006, 342 p., ISBN 978-90-5201-052-6.

No. 54 – *Reshaping Welfare States and Activation Regimes in Europe*, Amparo SERRANO PASCUAL & Lars MAGNUSSON (eds.), SALTSA, 2007, 319 p., ISBN 978-90-5201-048-9.

No. 53 – *Shaping Pay in Europe. A Stakeholder Approach*, Conny Herbert ANTONI, Xavier BAETEN, Ben J.M. EMANS & Mari KIRA (eds.), SALTSA, 2006, 287 p., ISBN 978-90-5201-037-3.

No. 52 – *Les relations sociales dans les petites entreprises. Une comparaison France, Suède, Allemagne*, Christian DUFOUR, Adelheid HEGE, Sofia MURHEM, Wolfgang RUDOLPH & Wolfram WASSERMANN, 2006, 243 p., ISBN 978-90-5201-323-7.

No. 51 – *Politiques sociales. Enjeux méthodologiques et épistémologiques des comparaisons internationales/Social Policies. Epistemological and Methodological Issues in Cross-National Comparison*, Jean-Claude BARBIER & Marie-Thérèse LETABLIER (dir./eds.), 2005, 4th printing 2008, 295 p., ISBN 978-90-5201-294-0.

Peter Lang—The website

Discover the general website of the Peter Lang publishing group:

www.peterlang.com